Poetics and Precarity

THE UNIVERSITY AT BUFFALO
ROBERT CREELEY LECTURES IN POETRY AND POETICS

Cristanne Miller, editor

Poetics and Precarity

Edited by **Myung Mi Kim**
and **Cristanne Miller**

Cover art: Susan Rankaitis © CT #2 2011. Courtesy Robert Mann Gallery, New York.

Published by State University of New York Press, Albany

For information, contact State University of New York Press, Albany, NY
www.sunypress.edu

Book design, Aimee Harrison

Library of Congress Cataloging-in-Publication Data

Names: Kim, Myung Mi, 1957- editor. | Miller, Cristanne, editor.
Title: Poetics and precarity / edited, Myung Mi Kim and Cristanne Miller.
Description: Albany, NY : State University of New York Press, 2018. | Series: The
    university at buffalo robert creeley lectures in poetry and poetics | Includes bibli-
    ographical references and index.
Identifiers: LCCN 2017032624| ISBN 9781438469997 (hardcover : alk. paper) |
    ISBN 9781438470009 (e-book) | ISBN 9781438469980 (paperback : alk. paper)
Subjects: LCSH: Poetics. | Experimental poetry. | Poetry--Social aspects.
Classification: LCC PN1042.P568 2018 | DDC 808.1--dc23 LC record available at
    https://lccn.loc.gov/2017032624

10 9 8 7 6 5 4 3 2 1

CONTENTS

FIGURES

ACKNOWLEDGMENTS

WE WOULD LIKE TO THANK Judith Goldman for her key role in organizing the 2016 Creeley Lecture and Poetics anniversary conference and all participants in the conference for the exciting work they brought to bear on "the (next) twenty-five years" of Poetics. We would also like to thank English Department staff, Buffalo and UB sponsors of the conference, and the many graduate students who worked long hours before and during the conference to make it possible —especially Allison Cardon. Additional thanks go to George Life, for his assistance with the final stages of manuscript proofing.

❧

James Maynard's bibliography previously appeared with the title *Poetry in the Making: A Bibliography of Publications by Graduate Students in the Poetics Program, University at Buffalo, 1991–2016*, as the inaugural chapbook in the series *Among the Neighbors* (The Poetry Collection of the University Libraries, 2016).

Introduction

Myung Mi Kim and Cristanne Miller

POETICS AND PRECARITY IS THE FIRST VOLUME of a series that we anticipate providing reflections and explorations on the work of poetry today, in the past, and as we see it extending into a spectrum of possible futures. Every volume will center around one or two lectures from the University at Buffalo SUNY (UB) series of Robert Creeley Lectures on Poetry and Poetics. This series was inaugurated in April of 2016 with Nathaniel Mackey's lecture "Breath and Precarity," and in this inaugural year the lecture was followed by a conference marking the twenty-fifth anniversary of the UB Poetics Program.

The SUNY Press series of Robert Creeley Lectures in Poetry and Poetics is intended to disperse and encourage conversation around the annual Creeley lectures and around the continuing reconception of poetry and the poetic. It takes as a given that poetics is as much a process of generating conceptual modes as it is a practice resulting in poetry. As the series' first editors, we anticipate that the UB Creeley Lectures and the ensuing SUNY Press series will feature contributions that shift the ground we think we know to enable new ways of bringing language to bear and of hearing the language of earlier and contemporary poetries.

As a lecture and publication series that seeks to situate poetry and the field of poetics as a perpetually open question in the context of heterogeneous affiliations or communities, the Creeley Lectures appropriately bear the name of Robert Creeley. Creeley taught at the University at Buffalo from 1966 to 2003. During these years and throughout his life, Creeley's work pointed toward the larger matrix of poetry, poetics, cultural work, and affective and intellectual inquiry. As many have testified, he cared about poetry in the world and he carried poetry into various contexts outside of the academy. In the city of Buffalo, it is hard to overestimate the breadth of Creeley's influence. Everyone seems to have a story about him, as a poet or a neighbor, from construction workers to community poets. Deborah Ott has written that her founding of Just Buffalo Literary Center began, in essence, with her hearing Creeley read "Love Comes Quietly" on television when she was a teenager—an event that inspired her to move to Buffalo to study with Creeley, who then inspired her dream of centering poetry in the heart of an urban community.[1] Jonathan Skinner remembers "Creeley in the doorway of Village Voice Books in Paris, sticking his phone number in my shirt pocket, saying come to Buffalo."[2]

Many students, fellow poets, and scholars came to work with Creeley. One of them, Peter Middleton, asks, "What I learned? That the indirections of anecdote could be more precise than focused analysis. That answers might not be what were needed." Creeley's colleague for decades and the maker (with Diane Christian) of two films on the poet, Bruce Jackson, writes that Creeley "was the most collaborative artist I've known: writing poetry is solitary stuff, but he also did important projects with painters, sculptors, and musicians: Georg Baselitz, Francesco Clemente, Jim Dine, Robert Indiana, Marisol, Steve Swallow, and others." Charles Bernstein, another of his colleagues at UB, writes that "For Creeley, the ordinary is not something represented but rather something enacted word by word in each poem. . . . Creeley was exemplary in his support of younger poets . . . [And] he was necessary company to those of his own generation who risked the most in their successful transformation of postwar poetic thinking." Susan Howe, also at UB in these years, remembers Bob and Pen Creeley's "Firehouse" home as "a domestic but rebellious force field inside frame fields. It was good to come in. To *return* in Robert Duncan's sense of poetry as a common property open to experiment and risk at the same time teaching." We like to think of

Creeley as being, in spirit, part of the "company" (to use one of his favored words) that these pages host and that this series will continue to gather. While at UB, in 1991, Robert Creeley participated with Charles Bernstein, Susan Howe, and Dennis Tedlock from the English Department and Ray Federman from Romance Languages and Literature in founding the Poetics Program. Former English Department chair Albert Cook and Robert Bertholf, director of the UB Poetry Collection, were important fellow travelers. The program's initial brochure describes it as "composed of five literary artists" with "an interdisciplinary approach to literary, cultural, and textual studies." Its programs would include, the brochure states, "Visiting Writer Residencies"; "Common Place" (a monthly informal meeting for discussion and "exchanges on range, qualification, definition, and bibliographies" of poetics); a series of lectures called "State of the Art" "by prominent UB faculty in all fields," including the sciences, law, and medicine—"on the poetics of each discipline as it relates to questions of human knowledge and action"; graduate seminars; affiliation with the Poetry/Rare Books Collection; a series of Nonfiction Writing workshops and consultations designed to develop and investigate "new approaches to critical writing"; translation; an emphasis on teaching innovative works of literary arts to undergraduates; and fellowships. Susan Howe remembers these early years of the program's planning and initiation, during the late 1980s and '90s, as a time of "ambitions, furies, hilarities, criticisms, enthusiasms, and disjunctive leaps."[3]

The students and faculty already involved in Poetics at UB soon attracted others interested in "poetry as process." As the program's statement of "Philosophies" in this same initial brochure continued, "Every doing carries the potential of something new, emergent, something not already predicated by poetics. Practice overtakes theory, practice changes theory . . . To write is to produce meaning and reproduce a pre-existing meaning. . . . Fiction or poetry is never about something, it is something." Calling poetics an "unruly, multisubjective activity," the program itself acquired a reputation for unruliness, variously understood.

Nathaniel Mackey is mentioned in these early documents—a fact we did not know when inviting him to be the 2016 inaugural lecturer, although one that makes his prominence at that occasion even more appropriate. In a June 18, 1991 letter regarding Poetics fellowships, English Department chair Bill Fischer wrote to Robert Rossberg, dean of the Faculty of Arts and Letters, that "The Poetics Program of the English Graduate Program gives institutional definition to [the] stature [of current faculty Creeley, Federman, Tedlock, and new faculty Bernstein and Howe] and organizes our artistic and intellectual possibilities into a productive process. The English Department intends to nurture and support it in every possible way—indeed expand it, if possible, with the appointment of African-American poet-scholar Nathaniel Mackey." [4] Writing from Waldoboro, Maine, Creeley rejoices in the administrative support given the new program: "Dear Bill, Forgive the casual note, like they say, but I wanted to keep even in passing touch about the whole Poetics Program Fellowships proposal. . . . Happily it seems to be moving along with amazing grace." [5]

From its inception the Poetics Program was definitively interdisciplinary and collaborative. Its own legacy of innovative writing contributed to and was generated by the larger legacy of innovative work in the Department of English and in the other arts at UB, both before and after the 1991 founding of the program proper. In music, John Cage's visits presaged the June in Buffalo series established in 1975 and the Center for 21st-Century Music founded by David Felder in 2006. The Center for Media Studies (now a department) was founded in 1972—one of the first programs of its kind—and was home to faculty such as Hollis Frampton and Tony Conrad. It now hosts the Electronic Poetry Center, founded (1995) and directed by Loss Pequeño Glazier. The Albright-Knox Art Gallery recently hosted an exhibit titled *Wish you Were Here: The Buffalo Avant-garde in the 1970s*, which included poetry readings, media and film art, and Buffalo-affiliated artists such as Charles Clough, Robert Longo, Roberto Mufaletto, Cindy Sherman, and Helene Winer. The English Department itself included at various times Charles Olson, John Wieners, John Barth, Donald Barthelme, Samuel Delaney, John Logan, and

J. M. Coetzee. In short, to study in Buffalo has long meant to have the opportunity to engage in a range of making in a community of innovative makers. The Poetics Program was designed to be future-focused, looking toward the incipient and "unruly." This SUNY Press Creeley Lecture series will, we hope, broaden that legacy. "Poetics: (The Next) 25 Years" was imagined as an occasion for intensive reflection on the possibilities and agencies poetry and poetics bring to bear on trajectories of the now and histories-to-be. Over three hundred people attended the conference and its related events: a "Creeley and France" symposium organized and sponsored by Jean-Jacques Thomas, the Melodia Jones chair in Romance Languages and Literature; and the Creeley Lecture and Celebration of Poetry as well as the conference itself—both coorganized by Judith Goldman, Myung Mi Kim, and Cristanne Miller.‡ Poets and critics from Australia, Canada, France, Korea, Mexico, and the United States engaged in panels and workshop seminars, organized to maximize discussion and minimize formal presentation. Appendices 2 and 3 document the range of conference participants and concerns.

Poetics and Precarity both anticipated, in its 2015–2016 inception, and marks, in its late 2017 completion, a cultural period of profound precarity. In the first decades of the twenty-first century, wars, acts of terrorism, ecological degradation, and climate change have intensified. Isolationism, misogyny, and ethnic divisiveness have been given distinctively more powerful voice in public discourse than in the late twentieth century. At times, language seems to fail, to have failed. And yet, the thinkers and writers gathered in this volume grapple with the continuing potential of language to address discord and precarity. They negotiate ways to understand poetics, or the role of the poetic, in relation to language, the body politic, the human body, breath, the bodies of the natural environment, and the body of form. Such negotiation seems daily of greater significance in a world where ideological extremity and deafness to both fact and nuance seem to reign. While these concerns were in the air as we planned the first Robert Creeley Lecture and Celebration of Poetry

---

‡   https://poeticsthenext25years.wordpress.com/

and the "Poetics: (The Next) 25 Years" conference, we did not raise them as a theme. The participants in that event, and the contributors to this volume, spontaneously forged the intersections represented here.

Contributors to *Poetics and Precarity* concern themselves with urgent issues that poetry makes audible and that poetics may help to theorize into critical consciousness, but also for which poetry functions as a cri de couer: late capitalist imperialism, misogyny, racism, climate change—all the debilitating conditions of everyday life. Hubs of concern merge and diverge; precarity takes differently gendered, historied, embodied, geopolitical manifestations. Some of the essays collected here take bold stands, with the ring of a manifesto. Most articulate a poetics that renders more generally what has not yet been crystallized as discourse into fields of force. They work with ideas in a plastic moment of conception, both cherishing the plasticity and listening for a mode that might help to frame questions that contribute to or affect change. Many of the same contributors also acknowledge beauties of sound, of poetry and music, and celebrate the power of community. They mark the surge of energy that can occur at a particular place at a particular moment and the significance of individuals who build community and keep it alive across boundaries or borders and in the face of hostilities or austerities. It is our hope that the conversation within this volume will build through its readers into a vortex for further conversation that prospectively imagines the concerns of poetics as a continuously emerging field.

As the initial contribution to this series, this volume attempts to position the conjunctions of poetry, precarity, and poetics in the most expansive sense. As its editors, we want to foreground the question of why it is urgent to keep poetics germane in a world of precarity.

For us, as for many of the contributors to this volume, poetics is a practice that faces the predicament, first, of understanding the political, cultural, and historical ways in which new knowledges have been produced and, second, of resisting the impulse to reinscribe what we already know under the banner of the new. While the conditions of precarity can be described with great distinction and factual clarity, the *figure* of precarity goes beyond cementing what we know about rootlessness or fragility and devastation. It allows us to explore how we can return to those scenes and reinitiate the force of their contact. Poetry and poetics that work the ground of precarity open themselves to thinking through categories without reifying them. Conjoining the known and the not yet imagined prompts reflection on how to experience and produce knowledges through language. How do we write the humane—or its opposite, dehumanization, the inhumane, the inhospitable?

In the context of such questions, poetry requires fluidity, the possibility to use its forms—or its resistance to form—to unveil regimental cultural norms. It allows access to the problematic—not the problem—of how certain kinds of historical matter, or registers, get articulated or excised. Language potentially corrals sense. As a social convention, language is expected to perform as perfunctory or transparently available communication, relating narrowly to meaning. Poetry, however, can create a proliferative mode of communicating. An intensive engagement with what language is and does, through poetic form and syntax, can move language away from coercive expectations of meaning. Poetics is a way of reorienting, of listening, of recalibrating conceptions or acts of belonging and kinship. It pluralizes paradigms for meaning-making, contributing to new configurations of affiliation, both local and global.

This volume begins with Nathaniel Mackey's Creeley Lecture, "Breath and Precarity." In this essay, as in his body of work, Mackey traverses the liminal. He reroutes the contours by which we might approach the interrelation of poetry, music, literary criticism, and cultural critique.[6] He unsettles disciplinary lines not simply to produce interdisciplinarity but to embolden what transdisciplinarity might initiate in critical discourse, aesthetic practice, and social othering. This inquiry undergirds Mackey's meditation on breath to register the disavowed, the unutterable, and the abrading of racially marked bodies.

"Breath and Precarity" parses the turn toward "breath" or "breathing" in American experimental poetics of the 1950s and '60s, associated with concepts such as open field composition, composition by field, and projective verse and with poets related to New American poetics, such as

Charles Olson, Robert Duncan, and Creeley. Mackey connects the acute attention to breath in New American poetics with "black music's preoccupation with breath" embodied in the work of jazz musicians such as Archie Shepp, Ornette Coleman, Roscoe Mitchell, Sonny Rollins, and Sun Ra. This interanimation, for Mackey, embeds the precarity of a post–World War II, post-traumatic historical and political landscape, which produced a cultural psychic economy driven in equal parts by "primal/ primitive doubt" and the need for "primal/ primitive assurance." Mackey suggests that when the very ordinariness of breath or breathing becomes "an object of attention, no longer unremarked on, no longer taken for granted, no longer an uninspected given, anxiety is also in the air."

By articulating an alliance between "black music" and "radically pneumatic poetics," Mackey points out that "breath, especially imperiled breath, matters," and further, that "transmutation or alchemization, the digestion and sublimation of antiblack violence, harassment, and predation, has been one of the jobs of black music, black art, black cultural and social life in general."

In the volume's next essay, "The Ga(s)p," M. NourbeSe Philip responds to Mackey's cultural and political exploration of poetics in the middle and late twentieth century by turning to feminist alternatives and grounding for the experience and perceived histories of breath and precarity. Philip asserts that "someone breathes for us" before we begin our own breathing in life, and then explores how the fact of maternal breathing affects our experiences of being, connectivity, and precarity. Reflecting on the labor of birthing in relation to writing, through the figure of breathing for others, Philip concludes by turning to her own long poem *Zong!* as she perceives its "ga(s)ps."

Jennifer Scappettone's essay, "Precarity Shared: Breathing as Tactic in Air's Uneven Common," also takes a feminist approach, using Ariana Caverero's philosophical challenge to Western metaphysical promotion of disembodied cognition (*logos*) over the "spirit"/breath of speech to argue for the recuperation of embodied breathing and spoken interchange as crucial to understanding human thought and experience. Sites of political interaction are directly related to the immediate shared "medium of vocality," or air, which has "material conditions that determine one's ability to participate in the political realm." Poetry, Scappettone proposes, takes *inspiration* literally, and thereby enables us to contend with the question of how to survive what is in our air, or "flawed commons"—a proposition she examines in the work of poets from Coleridge to Claudia Rankine.

The following two essays, by Elizabeth Willis and Vincent Broqua, echo Mackey's representation of Creeley's historic contribution to our sense of the sound and rhythm of the poetic line through focus on the UB Poetics Program, Creeley's intellectual home for so many years.

In "On Not Missing It," Willis remembers what it was like to be a student in the years preceding and following the founding of the Poetics Program, with reflections on belatedness and the serendipities of timing that could not have been planned to produce the energies of innovation they did. In "Here and Elsewhere," Broqua rehearses more formally the history of the program's importance, both in its relation to Creeley's conception of community and in poetry communities later developed in France and the UK, which were modeled on the UB Poetics Program.

Joan Retallack's essay, "Constructive Alterities & the Agonistic Feminine," continues questioning what she has pursued in earlier work on "the agonist efficacy" or "productively contentious agency" of experimental feminine dynamics in relation to alterity.[7] In particular, Retallack presents her concept of "poethics" as a feminist counter to the ethical implications of Emmanuel Levinas's "asymmetrical formulation of feminine alterity." Thinking through definitions and histories of the "Anthropocene," with reference to Sherry Ortner, Naomi Klein, and Simone de Beauvoir, among others, Retallack concludes with examples of several poets whose work arises from singular sociopolitical contexts and engages agonistically with other texts or questions in ways that (as she says of Stein) "swerve minds out of gender/genre-normative geometries of attention."

In "Precarity, Poetry, and the Practice of Countermapping," Adalaide Morris and Stephen Voyce address forms of precarity visible in the "globally constructed information and surveillance culture" of the twenty-first century, looking at maps, countermaps, and ways that poetry might participate in the discussion of disparities of resources and surveillance vulnerabilities, while maintaining the kind of "pulse and urgency" Mackey calls attention to in figuring precarity through the practice and concept of breath. Critical cartography's representations of direction, process, method, and place can, they argue, also be used to describe "multimedia poetry and poetics that troubles the distinction between close and distant readings" through modes of attention that zoom out and in.

Sarah Dowling's essay, "Supine, Prone, Precarious," focuses on a different kind of geography or mapping in an extended reading of Bhanu Kapil's *Ban en Banlieue* to query ways that the "I" of poetry resonates with theories of precarity. By focusing more on bodies—especially supine or prone bodies—than on the "I" of abstract, legal, or lyric personhood, Dowling speculates that bodies on the ground may "serve as representative figures for our time."

Heriberto Yépez, in "The Opening of the (Transnational Battle) Field," takes on a different element of embodiment, calling attention to the "Mexican episodes" of writers like Charles Olson, Jack Kerouac, William Burroughs, and Kenneth Goldsmith, to point toward the colonial appropriation of collections of Latin American documents and source texts by North American writers and universities. In contrast to such "Eurocentric" or neoliberal transnationalism, he identifies a somatic or "*melantropic*" field of transnational writing that "force[s] the 'experiment' / To become a program of world revolution / Without world coloniality."

The volume concludes with three appendices. Appendix 1 reprints James Maynard's "Poetry in the Making" bibliography of publications and presentation series organized by graduate students in Poetics from 1991 to 2016, together with what Maynard calls a "personal introduction to a public history." In this introduction, he traces his own understanding of what Poetics has been and is, given his experience in Buffalo from when he entered the English PhD program in 2001 up to the present, in his role as curator of the Poetry Collection. Appendix 2 provides the schedule of events for the long weekend of the 2016 inaugural Robert Creeley Lecture and Celebration of Poetry and Poetics. Appendix 3 gives titles of papers presented and discussed at the twenty-fifth anniversary Poetics conference, either in panels or in seminar workshops. All three appendixes will, we hope, contribute to mapping the richness of exchange in which the essays here participated and from which they have developed.

The conjunction of precarity and poetics, as we see it in this first SUNY Press Robert Creeley Lecture volume, foregrounds nonreductive, nonessentializing modes of conceptualizing difference and alterity. It imagines (and attempts to model) the bringing of poets and critics (and poet-critics) engaged in such thinking together in ways that support multiple fragilities as building toward an always shifting conception of the poetic. This conjunction lives on the boundaries of linguistic, ecological, formal, and political change—born of distress and of hope, of profound listening and of practice, of precarity and of breath.

NOTES

1. Deborah Ott has related versions of this story several times in public, and a part of it appears on the Just Buffalo Literary Center website, http://www.justbuffalo.org/about-just-buffalo/.

2. This and other recollections cited on this page are taken from a pamphlet titled "Remembering Creeley," prepared for the inaugural April 2015 Creeley Lecture and Celebration of Poetry. It is available through the UB English Department website, https://www.buffalo.edu/cas/english/news-events/alumni-news.html.

3. Ibid.

4. Correspondence in the UB English Department Office Poetics file.

5. Letter from Robert Creeley to Bill Fischer, 14 June, 1991, on UB English Department stationery, return address PO Box 384 Waldoboro, ME 04572. Taken from the UB English Department file on "Poetics."

6. Mackey has long worked at the intersections of language and music, citing both jazz musicians such as John Coltrane and Don Cherry and poets as early influences on his exploration of how language can engage with tonal and rhythmic structures as a form of improvisation. His books of poetry include (among others) *Outer Pradesh* (2014), *Nod House* (2011); *Splay Anthem* (2006); *Song of the*

Andoumboulou: 18–20 (1994)—which was also recorded with musicians; *School of Udhra* (1993); *Eroding Witness* (1985); *Septet for the End of Time* (1983); and *Four for Trane* (1978). His prose work (to date) consists of a series of four novels collected as *From a Broken Bottle Traces of Perfume Still Emanate.* Also a critic and literary theorist, Mackey is the author of *Paracritical Hinge: Essays, Talks, Notes, Interviews* (2004) and *Discrepant Engagement: Dissonance, Cross-Culturality, and Experimental Writing* (1993). He has coedited *Moment's Notice: Jazz in Poetry and Prose* (1993), *American Poetry: The Twentieth Century* (2000), and the journal *Hambone.*

7. For example, Retallack's *The Poethical Wager* (University of California Press, 2004).

Breath and Precarity

The Inaugural Robert Creeley Lecture in Poetry and Poetics

Nathaniel Mackey

> And I walked naked
> from the beginning,
>
> breathing in
> my life,
> breathing out
> poems
>
> —Denise Levertov, "A Cloak"

> live, remote, preoccupied
> with breathing and black
>
> —Fred Moten, "fortrd.fortrn"

> . . . the tenor's voice . . . an asthmatic ambush of
> itself . . .
>
> —Nathaniel Mackey, *Bedouin Hornbook*

I.

WHEN I RECEIVED THE INVITATION to deliver the inaugural Robert Creeley Lecture in Poetry and Poetics, I had already received an invitation to deliver the keynote address at a conference at Columbia University titled "Improvising Agency for Change: Celebrating Twenty Years of the Vision Festival." Organized by Arts for Art and Columbia's Center for

1

Jazz Studies, the conference was convened to honor the twentieth presentation of the Vision Festival, a week-long festival of experimental jazz, art, film, poetry, and dance held annually in New York City. I recalled reading a short piece by Creeley in the 1966 anthology *Naked Poetry: Recent American Poetry in Open Forms*, entitled "Notes Apropos 'Free Verse,' " in which he spoke of Charlie Parker and Dizzy Gillespie and of bebop's influence on his work: "I have, at times, made reference to my own interest when younger (and continually) in the music of Charlie Parker—an intensive variation on 'foursquare' patterns such as 'I've Got Rhythm.' Listening to him play, I found he lengthened the experience of time, or shortened it, gained a very subtle experience of 'weight,' all some decision made within the context of what was called 'improvisation.' " [1] Given the jazz connection, it occurred to me to put together a lecture that would speak to both occasions—the Vision Festival conference and the Creeley celebration—which is what I've done.

In recalling Creeley's "Notes," I was at the beginning of a process of thought that continued to be, in many ways, retrospective, harking back to other mid-twentieth-century developments in poetry and music that impacted me during the 1960s and after. This gives something of a retrospective cast to the remarks I'd like to offer, a harking back that ranges, I hasten to add, from a span of decades to a much smaller span, one of months or weeks. I had recently, when I began writing this lecture, that is, written a poem that touches on many of the lecture's concerns—this to such an extent that the lecture amounts to an unpacking or a repacking of a great deal that went into the poem, something of a retrospective on the poem. The poem is one in which I write, as I often do, of an invented band, a make-believe band of musicians, what might be called an air band, in this case the Overghost Ourkestra. The poem, "The Overghost Ourkestra's Next," is so integral to the matrix and the process out of which my remarks grew that I will let it conclude the lecture, comprising a second, verse part of the lecture, following this the lecture's first, prose part.

In this prose part, then, I'd like to talk about a confluence of black music and experimental poetics, a confluence about which my thinking goes back many years, back to my formative years. One way to put it would be this: as I was coming of age aesthetically, breath was in the air. What I'm referring to is an emphasis or an accent on breath and breathing that came into experimental poetics in the United States during the 1950s and the 1960s, particularly that of what came to be known as the New American Poetry via Donald M. Allen's anthology of that name. Charles Olson, the lead-off poet in the anthology, began his essay "Projective Verse" in a 1950 issue of *Poetry New York* by saying: "Verse now, 1950, if it is to go ahead, if it is to be of *essential* use, must, I take it, catch up and put into itself certain laws and possibilities of the breath, of the breathing of the man who writes as well as of his listenings." This he repeated a number of ways.

> I take it that PROJECTIVE VERSE teaches, is, this lesson, that that verse will only do in which a poet manages to register both the acquisitions of his ear *and* the pressures of his breath.

> And the line comes (I swear it) from the breath, from the breathing of the man who writes, at the moment that he writes . . .

> Let me put it baldly. The two halves are:
> the HEAD, by way of the EAR, to the SYLLABLE
> the HEART, by way of the BREATH, to the LINE

He concluded the essay this way: "a projective poet will [go] down through the workings of his own throat to that place where breath comes from, where breath has its beginnings, where drama has to come from, where, the coincidence is, all act springs." [2]

Allen Ginsberg, the most famous poet in the anthology, then and now, wrote the following in his notes for the 1959 Fantasy recording of his reading of *Howl* and other poems:

> By 1955 I wrote poetry adapted from prose seeds, journals, scratch-ings, arranged by phrasing or breath groups into little short-line patterns according to ideas of measure of American speech I'd picked

up from W. C. Williams' imagist preoccupations. I suddenly turned
aside in San Francisco, unemployment compensation leisure, to
follow my romantic inspiration—Hebraic-Melvillian bardic breath.

He went on to explain that "each line of *Howl* is a single breath unit. . . .
My breath is long—that's the Measure, one physical-mental inspiration
of thought contained in the elastic of a breath."[3] Amiri Baraka, the sole
African American included in the anthology, a fact he protested years
later, is the quintessential embodiment of the confluence I'm addressing
here. In "Charles Olson and Sun Ra: A Note on Being Out," delivered in
Gloucester, Massachusetts, as the Fourth Annual Charles Olson Memorial
Lecture in October 2013, only months before his death, he mentioned
his Totem Press having published the "Projective Verse" essay as a pam-
phlet in 1959. The essay, he said, "changed the direction of poetry in
the U.S. for many poets writing in the fifties and sixties." He quoted
from the essay and rehearsed the Olson-Ginsberg-Williams nexus that
I just sketched out.

> The lines are how you hear them, according to your breath, which
> Ginsberg set me on to when I first came to New York—that is, the
> breath phrase. That was William Carlos Williams talking, the breath
> phrase. What is your natural breath phrase? When you talk, where
> do you stop to breathe? What is your line going to be as a reflection
> of yourself, your poetic line? It's no arbitrary line. . . . You write until
> you stop, naturally, where you have to breathe.[4]

In the poem "Numbers, Letters," he calls himself a "long breath singer."[5]
    I was reading these and related poets in my late teens and early
twenties. I was listening to a good deal of relevant music as well, hearing
the relevance of the music, so that when Ginsberg spoke of the "long
saxophone-like chorus lines"[6] of *Howl* I heard something very specific,
as specific as Baraka naming Sonny Rollins's "Oleo" and Cecil Taylor's
"Of What" as the music informing his novel *The System of Dante's Hell*.[7]
I likewise heard something very specific, Olson's open field composition or

composition by field and Robert Duncan's *The Opening of the Field*, at the outset of Taylor's liner notes to his album *Unit Structures*: "The first level or statement of three an opening field of question, how large it ought or ought not to be." [8] I heard something very specific, the poetics of breath, in the title of those notes, "Sound Structure of Subculture Becoming Major Breath/Naked Fire Gesture." As I've already said, breath was in the air, a pneumatic turn that was diagnostic and symptomatic both. When breath becomes an object of attention, no longer unremarked on, no longer taken for granted, no longer an uninspected given, anxiety is also in the air. As a calming or quieting technique in yoga, various forms of meditation and everyday life or as a function thought or feared to be under siege or in danger of arrest, breathing attends anxiety, decreasing it in the first case, increasing it in the latter.

Olson's emphasis on breath reflects his interest in the performing arts, theater and dance especially, arts whose training and practice involve the learning of breathing techniques. It also reflects the increased attention to poetry readings during the fifties and sixties, the reading's increased salience as a mode of presentation in the appreciation and reception of poetry. In that sense, poetry itself became a performing art. I'm not sure, however, that anything instructional or curricular ever came of the call for more attentiveness to breath among poets, anything more than ad hoc, individual workings out of what such attention might mean in practical terms. Olson didn't clarify or specify how exactly the line issues "from the breath, from the breathing of the man who writes, at the moment that he writes." Does this mean the line doesn't end until the poet expels all the air that was inhaled at its beginning? This isn't borne out by Olson's own practice or by that of others. Ginsberg, in his notes to the recording of *Howl*, proposes the equation of line length and breath length as an ideal, one to which his reading on the recording, he quickly points out, fails to conform: "Tho in this recording it's not pronounced so, I was exhausted at climax of 3 hour Chicago reading with Corso & Orlovsky." [9] So the breathing of the poet changes from occasion to occasion, breath length and breathing pattern change from occasion to occasion. What, then, is the value of notating, if that's in fact possible, the dictates of breath peculiar to one occasion, of appearing to fix those dictates for all time, for all future readings? Might breath have been, in such discourse, less a precisely determined prosodic factor or a rigorously applied technique than a metaphor or a metonym for "the animal man," as Olson puts it in "The Resistance," "his own biosis, . . . his own physiology, . . . its fragile mortal force?" [10]

The "New American" poetics of breath, offering no consistent or comprehensive practicum, was primarily a figurative, theoretical discourse, a symbolically and symptomatically telling discourse. Taken literally, it merely states or restates the self-evident: verbal enunciation has to accommodate the speaker's need to breathe. Taken otherwise, it animates thought, encourages thought to unbind what's bound up in the self-evident. It was, among other things, a return to basics during a post-traumatic period, a return to primal or primitive doubts during the postwar years, with their Cold War jitters, a return to primal or primitive assurances as well. Williams wrote in 1941, referring to World War II as "the Death": "One of the purposes of the Death among us is to terrify the world, to use a destructive ideology to push our culture so far back that it will take a full generation, another crop of flesh and mind, before it can begin to regenerate." [11] Of the many forms of individual and collective anxiety and insecurity an artistic turn toward breath might signal and attend, especially during the post–World War II period, the threat of nuclear annihilation is the most obvious perhaps, as in Ginsberg's "America" ("Go fuck yourself with your atom bomb") or Charles Mingus's "Oh Lord Don't Let Them Drop That Atomic Bomb on Me" or Sun Ra's "Nuclear War." [12] On a more intimate, personal scale, Robert Creeley's emphatic, signature pause following lines as short as one or two words, one or two syllables even, his veritable pronunciation of each and every line break, conveyed a trepidatious, anxious apprehensiveness. His insistent, asthmatic employment of caesura, his halting, hesitant delivery, accorded with a radical loss of assurance regarding such basic amenities and givens as identity, relationship, knowledge, perception and language. His Library of Congress reading of "For Love," recorded on June 1, 1961, is typical:

Robert Creeley, "For Love," audio site, selection 1

The following URL will take readers to the site "'Breath and Precarity' Audio," where the five audio selections referred to in this essay will be found: https://www.youtube.com/playlist?list=PLpIn53PcIVhEQjo Gcp5kj2MeOLItgjkwJ, Section 1

Creeley's reading style is only the most extreme instance of a style that became pervasive during the fifties and sixties, one in which the reading, rather than following cuts and demarcations dictated by the putatively natural or normal regularities of breathing, constructed an alternate breathing pattern fraught with apprehension, insecurity, and duress.[13] Jittery times call for jittery measures. Creeley's work, which he repeatedly said was influenced by beboppers Charlie Parker and Dizzy Gillespie, struck me as the poetic analogue of the introvert, convolute playing of postbop saxophonist John Tchicai, who Baraka wrote of as "playing the alto like a metal poem."[14] Tchicai's slow, deliberative parsing and meting out of breath, phrase, query, and assertion on the New York Art Quartet's 1965 recording of "Everything Happens to Me" is a good example:

New York Art Quartet, "Everything Happens to Me," *Mohawk* (Cool Music 2044774), audio site, selection 2

The following URL will take readers to the site "'Breath and Precarity' Audio," where the five audio selections referred to in this essay will be found: https://www.youtube.com/playlist?list=PLpIn53PcIVhEQjo Gcp5kj2MeOLItgjkwJ, Section 2

A poetics of breath belabors the obvious: without breath we lose vitality, without breath we die. It defamiliarizes the obvious perhaps. Obvious or not, the salience of breath, had at, harped on or exulted in, remarks a return to primal conditions or an apprehension of never having left them, a return to primitive conditions or an apprehension of never having left them. As Baraka wrote of Sun Ra: "Sun Ra's consistent statement, musically and spoken, is that this is a primitive world.

Its practices, beliefs, religions, are uneducated, unenlightened, savage, destructive, already in the past." [15] A poetics of breath is all the more palpably evident in black music, particularly the music of wind instruments, a radical pneumaticism in which the involuntary is rendered deliberate, labored, in which breath is belabored, made strange. Breath becomes tactical, tactile, textile, even textual, a haptic recension whose jagged disbursements augur duress. Back in those days, my late teens and early twenties, the late sixties, I especially heard this in Sonny Rollins's version of "On Green Dolphin Street" on the *Sonny Rollins on Impulse!* album, recorded in 1965, a record I nearly wore out. Sonny's teasing out and toying with the head of the tune, his heavily marked withholdings and expenditures of wind, as though subject to spasmic or spastic dilation or detour, as though breath or the apparatus of breathing were jerked one way and then another, bespoke extremity and strain, albeit done with virtuosic mastery and command. I could never get over and I still can't get over the hectored, put-upon way he opens the piece, running the gamut between a stop-and-go, halting attack, a tossed, asthmatic shortness of breath, a catching of breath, and a relaxed assurance of breath so nonchalant as to barely evince effort, bely blowing. To echo Ezra Pound on Béla Bartók's Fifth Quartet, it has the sound of "a record of struggle," [16] a struggle prolonged in our hearing of it. Nor could I or can I get over the sotto voce accompaniment he offers Ray Bryant and Walter Booker during their piano and bass solos, the under-his-breath or just-above-his-breath comments that are a kind of growl, a kind of hover, a kind of heavy breathing even. I used to play this track for poetry classes when I began teaching in the mid-seventies. I would say, "This is projective verse."

Sonny Rollins, "On Green Dolphin Street," *Sonny Rollins on Impulse!* (Impulse! IMPD-223), audio site, selection 3
The following URL will take readers to the site " 'Breath and Precarity' Audio," where the five audio selections referred to in this essay will be found: https://www.youtube.com/playlist?list=PLpIn53PcIVhEQjo Gcp5kj2MeOLItgjkwJ, Section 3

To call it a beautiful, prolonged panic or anxiety attack is probably going too far, but I'm tempted to do that. W. Alfred Fraser, one of Washington, DC's *Dasein* poets, does, after all, refer to the members of the sixties band the "JFK" Quintet as "five bundles of controlled panic"; Rahsaan Roland Kirk did title one of his albums *Rip, Rig and Panic*; and the word *panic* does go back to the piper-god Pan.[17] Is it the precariousness of breath, its being provisional, without guarantee, or the blessing and bounty of breath that's highlighted by Rollins? Could it be both, a reveling in—while recognizing, lamenting, even protesting—the transient boon that breath is? I wondered then and I wonder now.

Music, like speech, is made of breath. Breath is music's open secret. To linger with its disclosure, insist on and belabor its indispensability, is a signal impulse found in the music we call jazz. Radical pneumaticism I call it, one of the music's defining features, I think. Roswell Rudd named a 1973 composition "Numatik Swing Band." Chris McGregor called his band Brotherhood of Breath. Henry Threadgill, Fred Hopkins, and Steve McCall named their trio Air. I heard and I hear it in Bill Dixon's recourse to untempered, raw expulsions of air on an album such as *November 1981*. I heard and I hear it in Archie Shepp's "incandescent croon," to borrow a phrase from Araya Asgedom, the raspy, gruff, blustery, spendthrift way he has with wind on a piece like "Cousin Mary," or his Websterian tack on ballads like "In a Sentimental Mood." I heard and I hear it in Ben Webster himself, the signature culling of subtones we hear on pieces like "Tenderly," where breath is made to tail or to shadow itself, a sonic shimmer seeming to bask in leakage, in air's propensity to escape or to be taken away. Each breath is exactingly meted out and drawn out, lingered with as if it were his last:

Ben Webster, "Tenderly," *King of the Tenors*
(Verve 519 806-2), audio site, selection 4

The following URL will take readers to the site "'Breath and Precarity' Audio," where the five audio selections referred to in this essay will be found: https://www.youtube.com/playlist?list=PLpIn53PcIVhEQjo Gcp5kj2MeOLItgjkwJ, Section 4

Ben's caressive, savoring way with breath celebrates the amenities of caring and warmth, proffers the amenities of caring and warmth, trafficking in drift all the while nonetheless. It advances an essay on frailty and fragility with a certain lightness of touch, a fleetingness of nuance and lightness according with diagnostic finesse. I've long wondered about that and I still wonder about it. Leakage, air's propensity to escape or to be taken away, seems both to halo and to haunt the piece, giving it a ghost escort or the intimation of ghostliness, making it also, whatever else it is, the tenderness of address it obviously is, a meditation on transience, mortality, expiration. On the other hand, such radical pneumatic practice parallels Olson's assertion that "breath allows *all* the speech-force of language back in (speech is the 'solid' of verse, is the secret of a poem's energy), . . . a poem has, by speech, solidity." [18] In Webster's "Tenderly" and other such work, breath is rendered solid, bodied forth as texture, tactility, palpability, an abrading aurality one feels one could reach out and touch. Is its implied purchase, the solidity it bestows on breath, a resilient measure making breath all the better to be held on to? Granted solidity, audiotactility, does breath become less airy and thus less fleeting, less ephemeral? Is radical pneumaticism as much a holding action as an elegiac lament?

Such a meditation as Webster's is one we often find N. and his fellow band members advancing in my serial fiction *From a Broken Bottle Traces of Perfume Still Emanate*. Here's what N. writes about a Websterian moment during the band's performance of a piece titled "Half-Staff Appetition," about tenor saxophonist Lambert's "performative discourse having to do with fugitive breath, tasted breath."

> "Half-Staff Appetition," I may not have said, is a ballad. A balladeer to the bone once he got into it, Lambert expounded its ballad marrow as he apportioned its ballad blood with a sound whose breathy/breathless caress brought Ben Webster to mind—the Webster of, say, "Prisoner of Love" or of "Tenderly." This Websterian recourse to subtones made for an accent which fell on wind as rudimentary voice, an insinuative return to basics, as it were, whose flirtatious, make-believe bite—a fugitive lover's blown breath or kiss—one could

never not woo the enjoyment of. Thus it was that ballad bone was a now asthmatic, now respirated baton which had made the rounds from time immemorial, a broken, half-staff capacity for aspirate expulsion, aspirate escape.

Lambert's Websterian celebration of breath couldn't help but be infused with a spectre of loss, an intimate acknowledgement if not embrace of expiration's most ominous undertones, in dialogue with which a consoling image of "inspired" leakage came into play. The latter made for a reading of aspirate expulsion (savored aspiration, inverse breathless ascent) as a cushion for what might otherwise have been unbearable, an inspired albeit merely implied pillow talk to soften its blow. Such implicative talk sugarcoated a pill which was hard to swallow, though Drennette [the drummer], it appeared, was by no means entirely won over. She bit or bought into it only to bargain for something more, keeping up her end of what was a bartered embrace with a not-to-be-bought barrage of post-romantic rescissions played on cymbals and high hat. The rest of us gradually pulled back. This was obviously between the two of them, an expulsive-appetitive pillow and rug rolled into one.[19]

Drennette, whose joining the band was announced by the male members dreaming of Djeannine (jinn, genie), embodies the spirit of repercussive critique, a disconsolate spirit that will know no consolation, know no solace, take no prisoners. She brings a stringent demand to bear on fugitive breath, the pneumatic beauty or pneumatic sublimation Lambert exacts from precarious premises, such premises the price, Drennette never tires of remembering or of reminding him, with which pneumatic beauty is bought. She would both have it and not have it, given what it's tied to. She would give it up, she implies, for it to be free of such premises, but short of that, she seems to go on, she'll hold on. As Baraka writes of John Coltrane's "Afro-Blue," both having beauty and not having it, "Beautiful has nothing to do with it, but it is."[20]

This not-having-to-do-with or having-nothing-to-do-with has to do with not settling. It wields a lever against present conditions, the precarity or the precarious premises Lambert sublimates or pneumaticizes, redeeming expiration or leakage as inspiration, seeming to say, alongside Wallace Stevens, "Death is the mother of beauty."[21] Drennette says whoa to that, advancing a more capacious, ensemblist truth that wishes not to foreclose a less precarious future, wishes not to invest in precarity, wants to insist on alternate prospects. During the gig at Soulstice in Seattle, when the comic-strip balloons bearing inscriptions appear for the first time, ambiguous balloons that are by turns implied to be flat, two-dimensional placards and suggested to be three-dimensional rubber sacs inflated with breath, she advances an even more radical pneumaticism. N., who at one point in his letters to Angel of Dust mentions a two-stringed Korean fiddle called the *haegeum* that is classified as a wind instrument due to its unusual timbre and range, is aware of the microbreathing of ostensibly nonwind instruments, nonhorns, the perturbations of air, which can be called a kind of breathing, produced by plucked, strummed or bowed strings, drum heads rubbed or struck by sticks, brushes or hands, and so on. He may have, as I have on occasion, heard Don Pullen or Cecil Taylor execute a run that made the piano whistle, or heard Henry Grimes or Alan Silva bow the bass in such a way as to exact a sirening cry. He describes Drennette's solo, following Penguin's, during which balloons had emerged from the oboe, as the drum set becoming a wind instrument—this to advance an unforeclosed futurity or futurism, post-expectant and postprecarious perhaps.

> Post-expectant futurity brought one abreast of the ground, Drennette announced, annulled, in doing so, any notion of ground as not annexed by an alternate ground. This was the pregnancy, the unimpatient expectancy, she explained, Penguin, albeit put upon and perplexed, had been granted rare speech, rare fluency by. Djeannine Street, alternate ground par excellence, inflected each run of heavy bass drum thumps with ventriloquial spectres, Drennette's recourse to the sock cymbal insistent that she and Djeannine, long spoken for, had spooked (her word was "inspired") wouldly ledge, atomistic ledge.

It was a wild, outrageous boast, but she had the chops, it turned out, to back it up. The drumset had become a wind instrument by the time she finished her solo. A gust of wind arose from each roll and with each roll the storm she brewed grew more ferocious. We felt it at our backs when we joined in again, pressing as it pestered us toward some occult articulation only Drennette, not looking ahead, saw deep enough to have inklings of. Not so much needling as pounding us now, the needling mist partook of that wind— mystical hammer rolled into one with atomistic pulse. Wouldly ledge, needling mist and Penguin's auto-inscriptive high would all, post-expectancy notwithstanding, turn out to have only been a beginning.[22]

Has such a beginning begun? If not, when will it begin? These are the questions radical pneumaticism, in both poetry and music, asks.

These matters resonate with the long state of siege to which black folk have been subjected, a long history crystallized most recently by Eric Garner's last words, "I can't breathe," and the rendering of a statement by Frantz Fanon in *Black Skin, White Masks* that it's been brought into alignment with in recent months, "We revolt simply because, for many reasons, we can no longer breathe."[23] *Bedouin Hornbook*, the first volume of *From a Broken Bottle*, ends with Jarred Bottle threatened by an encounter with the Los Angeles Police Department, an encounter he fears will end with his neck in a cop's chokehold. The book at that point recalls a letter in which N. writes of "alchemizing a legacy of lynchings,"[24] a history of black necks and black windpipes broken, whether by ropes or by cop strangleholds, characterizing Al Green's falsetto, his recourse to its attenuation of voice, as a way of saying, in so many words, "I can't breathe," albeit in a good way, a transmuted way. Transmutation or alchemization, the digestion and sublimation of antiblack violence, harassment, and predation, has been one of the jobs of black music, black art, black cultural and social life in general. Langston Hughes's Simple says something similar when he says that bebop came from police billy clubs, from "the police beating Negroes' heads": "Every time a cop hits

a Negro with his billy club, that old club says, 'BOP! BOP! . . . BE-BOP!
. . . MOP! . . . BOP! . . .' That's where Be-Bop came from, beaten right out
of some Negro's head into those horns and saxophones and the piano
keys that play it." [25] In remarking, famously, that playing bebop "is like
playing Scrabble with all the vowels missing," [26] Duke Ellington appears
to agree with Simple's characterization of bebop as a definitively percus-
sive—and, I would add, repercussive—turn in the history of jazz. In his
autobiography, *Music Is My Mistress*, Ellington refers to bebop as "the
Marcus Garvey extension." [27]

Simple speaks partly in jest, a serious jesting characteristic of blues
humor, Zen bluesism, a strain that gives us lines like "Life is a one-way
ticket" (which gave Hughes the title of a poem and of a book of poems)
or "Gonna lay my head on the railroad line, / Let the train come along
and pacify my mind," gives us the Zen-bluesist restitution the word *pacify*
gets. He makes light of police predation, makes light of it in more than
one sense. We can say that he speaks lightheartedly, specifically holding
in mind the nexus of heart, breath, and light found in *The Secret of the
Golden Flower*, an ancient Chinese meditation text that appears to have
influenced the "Projective Verse" essay and is explicitly referred to else-
where in Olson's work. In a section titled "Circulation of the Light and
Making the Breathing Rhythmical," we read the following:

> Breathing comes from the heart. What comes out of the heart is
> breath. As soon as the heart stirs, there develops breath-energy.
> Breath-energy is originally transformed activity of the heart. . . .
> Since heart and breath are mutually dependent, the circulation of
> the light must be united with the rhythm of breathing. For this,
> light of the ear is above all necessary. There is a light of the eye and
> a light of the ear. The light of the eye is the united light of the sun
> and moon outside. The light of the ear is the united seed of sun and
> moon within. The seed is thus the light in crystallized form. . . . If
> the heart is light, the breathing is light, for every movement of the
> heart affects breath-energy. If breathing is light, the heart is light, for
> every movement of breath-energy affects the heart. [28]

Where light is lightness and illumination, buoyancy and lucidity accrue to breath. Simple's comments both articulate and exemplify the light-bearing function of black artistic, cultural, and social life, the light heart it so often seeks to launch and to keep aloft. Black music, like other forms of black artistic and cultural expression, opens a space for reflection, a meditative space that bears critically on the precarious and predatory world in which its auditors and its producers find themselves. Simple's jest laughs not to cry and, more seriously, laughs not to go insane. "Focus on Sanity" is the title of an Ornette Coleman piece. Booker Little wrote a piece called "Strength and Sanity."

Violence, harassment, and predation form a backdrop that's never far from the music and sometimes, famously or infamously, very close, as when Miles Davis, in August 1959, was beaten and arrested by New York City police officers outside Birdland, where he had just finished playing a set. Such violence is only the most overt and sensational expression of a more wide-ranging program of policing and assault, whose quieter forms include poverty, unemployment, underfunded schools, under-funded infrastructure, and underfunded social services, all those factors that decrease the life chances of African Americans. *Precarity*, a word I've borrowed from a European discourse and social movement that emerged in the first decade of this century, a movement addressing the plight of immigrant or migrant workers, intermittent workers, female and young workers, is defined as "a condition of existence without predictability or security, affecting material and/or psychological welfare. Specifically, it is applied to the condition of intermittent or underemployment and the resultant precarious existence." [29] I carry it back and I apply it to the con-dition of black folk, marginalized or "remote," as Fred Moten puts it, and "preoccupied / with breathing." [30] The discourse and the social movement surrounding it arose from European labor discovering something eman-cipated African American slaves, for example, had previously discovered: Capitalism routinely, as it moves on to new profit-making strategies, aban-dons its workers (no forty acres, no mule). Horns are prosthetic lungs. Less obviously, strings, keyboards, and drums are prosthetic lungs, black music a prosthetic device more generally, tonally parallel, as Ellington might say, to the precarity and the damage it weathers and rebuts. Titles tell: Joe Thomas and Jay McShann, *Blowin' in from K.C.*; Clifford Jordan and John Gilmore, *Blowin' in from Chicago*; Dizzy Reece and Ted Curson, *Blowin' Away*; Jonah Jones, *Blowin' up a Storm*; Willis Jackson, *Keep on a Blowin'*; Horace Silver, *Blowin' the Blues Away*. And so on.

The exulting in breath and breathing I mentioned earlier is nowhere more evident than in the use of circular breathing in jazz, where it has a greater prominence than in any other Western musical idiom. Horn players use this technique to produce a continuous tone without interruption, a kind of hyper-pneumaticism, which they accomplish by breathing in through the nose while simultaneously expelling air stored in the cheeks through the mouth. The technique's origins are said to lie among thirteen-century Mongolian metalsmiths whose work with gold and silver required maintaining a pipe-sustained flame for an uninterrupted ten to thirty minutes. The technique was taken up by musicians, and its musical provenance down through the centuries remained decidedly Oriental, a technique used extensively in playing the Mongolian *limbe*, the Central Eurasian *zurna*, the Egyptian *arghul*, and other traditional oboes and flutes of Asia and the Middle East. In my early poem "Ohnedaruth's Day Begun," written in memory of John Coltrane, I have Trane pray, "Breath be with me / always, bend me East of / all encumbrance."[31] Circular breathing is that prayer and the aim of that prayer, an uninterrupted hyperabundance of breath whose continuous flow intimates eternal ongoingness, unending abidance, everlasting life. Its turn toward or its appeal to the East beckons deliverance from the Occidental exile spoken of in the Sufism of Suhrawardi and other schools of esoterism, as well as from the exoteric legacies of Western captivity and subjugation we're much more familiar with. Jazz recourse to circular breathing thus animates a mixed-emotional, mixed-messaging traffic, a clandestine circulation of breath rotating between utopian intimations of assured, everlasting pneumatic amenity and a sirening alarm at the precarity to which breath, especially black breath, is subject—triumphalist and agonistic both, a boastful exulting in breath and a dystopian struggle for it, not to mention the gradations and the qualifications in-between. Roscoe Mitchell's "The Flow of Things, No. 1" (another telling title) from 1986, a ten and a half minute piece on soprano saxophone, is a good example. Mitchell's pinched, high-pitched drone ups the ante on Oriental transcendence, as much a vehicle for Occidental embattlement if not more:

Roscoe Mitchell, "The Flow of Things, No. 1," *The Flow of Things* (Kepach Music 120090-OD), audio site, selection 5

The following URL will take readers to the site "'Breath and Precarity' Audio," where the five audio selections referred to in this essay will be found: https://www.youtube.com/playlist?list=PLpIn53PcIVhEQjo Gcp5kj2MeOLItgjkwJ, Section 5

Black music's preoccupation with breath and blowing is a technical matter and more. Blowing is belief, a stubborn, mind-made-up magic or mantra (e.g., Shepp, "The Magic of Ju-Ju"), the straight lick hit with a crooked stick, the way made out of no way. The more wind you use, woodwind and brass teachers like to say, the more wind you have—as though flesh were spirit, spirit flesh, flesh willing. Baraka wrote about Marion Brown and Pharoah Sanders in 1965: "Brown and Sanders, at Sanders' insistence, have been practicing Yoga breathing exercises in an attempt to bring more flesh into their sound."[32] The aim would appear to be to work breathing and breath in such a way as to highlight vulnerable and volatile flesh and blood, violable flesh and bone, to accent, in a way related to Webster's while different from it, mortal susceptibility, human exposure, respiration as what matters, even if at risk or especially if at risk. A certain universality resides in these black particulars, precarity being a widely human condition. That none of us is guaranteed our next breath is a truth that has to sit alongside another, equally obvious, which is that precarity has been and continues to be unequally distributed, some groups serving, for others, as a sacrifice to it or a shield against it. Black music, with its worrying of breath, articulates both, which probably accounts for its global reach and reception. What David Marriott recently wrote regarding black avant-garde poetry, glossing Aimé Césaire's invocation of "a universal rich with all that is particular, rich with all the particulars there are, the deepening of each particular, the coexistence of them all," pertains to the music as well.

> I can think of no better statement of why black avant-garde poetry should not be reduced to the usual modernist dilemma of aesthetics versus politics, or why its attentiveness to richly diverse modes of being should not be seen for what it is, i.e., a politics of the word defined by an incessant fidelity to creative negation. If this is a fidelity which can too easily be appropriated by the forces of cultural industrial control, that is because the value of its creation coincides with the terrible universal insecurity that is both its origin and truth, but one that also defines how each particular gives on to the world a newly embodied universal which provides for and bears along its own richness of meaning.[33]

Black music says, as does an allied, radically pneumatic poetics, that breath, especially imperiled breath, matters. It insists that we can, for a time at least, breathe, that what we do with breath, from which, to belabor the obvious, animacy, agency and all possibility of action arise, matters most. This is the innate, implicit activism of the music, cognate with Charles Mingus and Max Roach's founding of Debut Records, Max Roach's *Freedom Now Suite*, Bill Dixon's founding of the Jazz Composers Guild, Muhal Richard Abrams, Jodie Christian, Steve McCall, and Phil Cohran's founding of the Association for the Advancement of Creative Musicians, Patricia Nicholson Parker's founding of the Vision Festival and other such explicit manifestations. It says that black breath matters, black lives matter, at risk in multiple ways on a crowded, conflictual planet on which, though everyone is at risk and, yes, all lives matter, blackness is the sign and the symbol of risk, preeminently at risk in a scapegoating, sacrificial world order for which black is the color of precarity itself.

2.

THE OVERGHOST OURKESTRA'S NEXT

—"mu" one hundred fortieth part—

Nub's new facelift got old. War droned
   on, money stayed on top. The abandoned
boy and girl went by every name known...
                                                          Still,
   we bit the bullet and blew. "I will be and
I'll believe when I blow," we announced.
   "I will be and abide by sound, my slave day
                                                      done."
We were back on St. Sufferhead's porch or
   promontory, some same tune's temporizing
remit, reminiscent romance, the pharaoh's
                                                          black
   torso reached for and found, polis plied as
eros again... We were the pharaoh's black
   torso lost and found again, thick reed stuck to
a dry lower lip, chapped kiss calling itself song
                                                          all
   sibilance, some same tune's high cry. We
were the pharaoh's black torso cloaked, a call
   for cover, shot body sirening alarm we lost
and found again, pantomime's loose raiment.
                                                          So
   it was or so we said or so we played cant-
ing say-so, torn cloak's rule unrelenting, torn
   cloak routing the day... Could we but be a
                                                          band

it would all go away we thought or we played
   like we thought, could we but be a band it
   would all be okay. So it was we were in a band,

                                        so

   it was not so the same. What we cut we'd call
   a release, release what we called out for. It'd been
   going on for only a minute, it'd been going on
for as long as we knew, Nub said to be having a

                                   con-

versation, no such one were
we in

           •

Unable to breathe though we were, we blew,
   the crook of Nub's arm on our necks. We
played with our hands up, axes untouched,

                                  re-

lease it was tej's bet would be sweet...
"Nub held my neck in the crook of its arm," the
   unworded song we sang said. "Nub took me

                                down

   but I got up swinging." Could we only band
or bond we thought but it wasn't so, together
   as we were we suffered, original sufferheads
for all eternity it seemed, wise ones and wounded

                              ones

   it seemed ... The Empathetic String Ensemble
skipped out. A gig in the Czech Republic they
   said. So it was we were on our own, erstwhile

                               ac-

companiment the ground we got up from, hot

light spiraling behind. Pulling thread from string,
string from rope we'd have been had they been
                                                              there,
a fraught way to feel, a fugue for the wretched,
blows to the head as we blew... Hands up, wind-
pipes crushed, we blew, overghost embouchure's
                                                              be-
hest

•

A high falsetto wind put parts in our hair again.
    We heard bells, an avid choir breaking glass
  they hit such high notes, heads all honey house

                                                        it

    seemed. Choked, held, haloed we wanted to
  say but came up short, hot light popping sweat no
    matter the high wind, no matter where we were,

                                                    wher-

      ever it was we were, hot light a way we dwelt
    elsewhere, it was never just there we were. . .
      Wherever it was we were we were birds again,

                                                    each

  with our own song, each with a tutor song, "Teach
  me, tutor me," we sang. Notwithstanding we
  couldn't breathe we blew, a masonic windpipe we

                                                    re-

    sorted to circular breathing with we blew. L'ou-
    verture we called it, church key, millet beer wet
    what words there were . . . It was an underground
  pipeline we got our breath back thru, "Teach me, tutor

                                                    me"

    the words there were, thirst a way of knowing not
    knowing, gnostic more stoic now. Our first day in the
    land of the dead it was. Breathless though we were

                                                    we

    blew. Took a stand we were taken down we testified,
      arrest what of earth we remembered, all else taken
    away. So went the record, what we read into the record,

                                                    New

      Tears for Eric new tunes for another Eric, commis-
    erative, our posthumous release. . . *Live in the Land*

of the Dead we might've called it, notwithstanding

                                                           we

couldn't breathe we blew. No matter we couldn't
  breathe we blew we kept insisting, overghost trem-
  olo, overghost vibrato, overghost cul-de-sac come

                                                    to

  and come back from, overghost conversancy no
end. . . In the heart of New Not Yet, west of Egypt, no
  matter we couldn't breathe we blew. No pitch, no

                                                    tone,

  pulse only, a tutor song police batons taught us,

                                                hex-

ameters tapped out with a
stick

(liner note)

The idea was we were dead, already dead,
always, the saying went, already dead. The
  idea was we blew not yet knowing we were

                                        dead,
to blow was to hope against hope we had
  air, no matter we couldn't breathe breathe in,
breathe out, no matter we couldn't breathe

                                        keep
  breathing. The idea was we were a claim
the dead made, the idea we were a strain put on
  the living. The idea was time turned back,

                                        put
  its back to us, back at some serial onslaught,

                                        back
  at us again and
again

We convened around the corner from
Coltrane's house, the Toussaint L'Ouverture
Masonic Lodge. "Acknowledgement" hit,

                                                        we

bowed our heads. It was nothing if not
love's arcade and we wanted that, the idea
we'd round it off with that... *Live in Outer
Space* we might've called it. Why they send

                                                        us

off the planet so soon we wanted to know,
demanded someone say, got no answer.
Lynch law's return had it ever left, nightsticks

                                                        and

nooses, no new face-
lift now

———————————

Breath, even would-be breath, our even-
tual escort, hydraulic circles we blew.
Better born a dog in Nub we squalled,

call-
ing up "Step" even so. "Giant Steps"
no, not even "Steps," "Step." Step
said everything, all that would out...

Hit.
Hoist. Hover. Hover... High cyclonic

stair...
Step

NOTES

1. Robert Creeley, "Notes apropos 'Free Verse,'" *Naked Poetry: Recent American Poetry in Open Forms*, ed. Stephen Berg and Robert Mezey (Indianapolis and New York: Bobbs-Merrill, 1969), 186–87.

2. Charles Olson, "Projective Verse," *Selected Writings*, ed. Robert Creeley (New York: New Directions, 1966), 15, 17, 19, 26.

3. Allen Ginsberg, "Notes on *Howl* and Other Poems," *The New American Poetry*, ed. Donald M. Allen (New York: Grove Press, 1960), 414–15, 416.

4. Amiri Baraka, "Charles Olson and Sun Ra: A Note on Being Out" https://www.youtube.com/watch?v=KucCiMrCPSw.

5. LeRoi Jones/Amiri Baraka, "Numbers, Letters," *Black Magic: Collected Poetry 1961–1967* (Indianapolis and New York: Bobbs-Merrill, 1969), 47.

6. Ginsberg, op. cit., 415.

7. LeRoi Jones/Amiri Baraka, "Statement," *New American Story*, ed. Donald M. Allen and Robert Creeley (New York: Grove Press, 1965), 267–68.

8. Cecil Taylor, "Sound Structure of Subculture Becoming Major Breath/ Naked Fire Gesture," *Unit Structures* (Blue Note BST 84237), 1966.

9. Ginsberg, op. cit., 416.

10. Charles Olson, "The Resistance," *Selected Writings*, ed. Robert Creeley (New York: New Directions, 1966), 13–14

11. William Carlos Williams, "Midas: A Proposal for a Magazine," *Selected Essays* (New York: New Directions, 1969), 241.

12. Allen Ginsberg, "America," *Howl and Other Poems* (San Francisco: City Lights, 1956), 31. Charles Mingus, *Oh Yeah* (Atlantic SD 1377), 1962. Sun Ra, *Nuclear War* (Y Records RA 1), 1982.

13. During a visit to Duke University in October 2015, South African pianist/composer Abdullah Ibrahim remarked, "Our concept is a concept of breath, the importance of breath," and went on to accentuate the ability to alter the rhythm of one's breathing, to construct alternate breathing patterns, as a distinguishing feature of *homo sapiens*: "Breath is automatic. You're not even aware of it. But we have the possibility to change the rhythm of the breath. We are the only creatures who are able to do this." See "Talking

Music: Abdullah Ibrahim and Nathaniel Mackey," https://www.youtube. com/watch?v=mSZonRCZzzM.

Ginsberg gets at this alterability with his phrase "the elastic of a breath." Working not with an unusually short line, as does Creeley, but with an unusually long one, he stresses its departure from what might be thought of as natural or normal speech and breath rhythms: "my own heightened conversation, not cooler average-dailytalk short breath. I got to mouth more madly this way" (*The New American Poetry*, p. 416).

14. LeRoi Jones/Amiri Baraka, "New Tenor Archie Shepp Talking," *Black Music* (New York: William Morrow, 1967), 154. In the liner notes to Shepp's album *Four for Trane*, in the same volume, he writes, "Like Shepp, Tchicai carries the world-spirit in his playing, what is happening now, to *all of us*, whether we are sensitive enough to realize it or not" (158, emphasis in original). Tchicai, Afro-Danish, is an interesting, serendipitous embodiment of the intersection between free jazz and poetry in what has been called the Pound/Williams tradition. Valerie Wilmer points out that Tchicai's father was taken from Africa to Europe by Leo Frobenius, the German ethnographer who was very important to Ezra Pound:

> John Tchicai's father was brought to Europe as a teenager in 1906 by the German ethnologist Leo Frobenius. Joseph Lucianus Tschcaya (later spelt Tschakai) was born at Pointe Noire, a village near the Congo estuary, and met Frobenius during the latter's first African expedition. The youngster had learned French and German at a Belgian mission school and lived with Frobenius as a servant. He was a useful contact whom the ethnologist educated further, and moved with him to Berlin. He traveled to the Netherlands and Belgium in search of work, and eventually to Scandinavia, where he worked in restaurants and nightclubs as a doorman and cigarette seller. He had eight children with two partners before meeting Tchicai's mother. The eldest of them was the drummer Kaj Timmermann, who in 1940 formed the Harlem Kiddies, the first black Danish band. Tchicai's parents met at the Aarhus pleasure-gardens, where both were working

as waiters. Tchicai told me that his father's first words to his mother were: "I love you!" They were married soon afterwards.

The Guardian (October 11, 2012) https://www.theguardian.com/music/2012/oct/11/john-tchicai.

15. Back cover blurb for John F. Szwed's *Space Is the Place: The Lives and Times of Sun Ra* (New York: Pantheon, 1997).

16. Ezra Pound, *Guide to Kulchur* (New York: New Directions, 1970), 135.

17. W. Alfred Fraser, "To the 'JFK' Quintet," *Burning Spear: An Anthology of Afro-Saxon Poetry*, ed. Walter De Legall (Washington, DC: Jupiter Hammon Press, 1963), 15.

18. Olson, op. cit., 20.

19. Nathaniel Mackey, *From a Broken Bottle Traces of Perfume Still Emanate: Volumes 1–3* (New York: New Directions, 2010), 312–13.

20. LeRoi Jones/Amiri Baraka, "Coltrane Live at Birdland," *Black Music* (New York: William Morrow, 1967), 66.

21. Wallace Stevens, "Sunday Morning," *Collected Poetry and Prose* (New York: Library of America, 1997), 55.

22. Mackey, op. cit., 430.

23. Frantz Fanon, *Black Skin, White Masks*, trans. Charles Lam Markmann (New York: Grove Press, 226: "It is not because the Indo-Chinese has discovered a culture of his own that he is in revolt. It is because 'quite simply' it was, in more than one way, becoming impossible for him to breathe."

24. Mackey, op. cit., 50.

25. Langston Hughes, "Bop," *The Best of Simple* (New York: Hill and Wang, 1961), 118.

26. *Look* 18, no. 16 (August 10, 1954).

27. Duke Ellington, *Music Is My Mistress* (New York: Da Capo Press, 1976), 109.

28. *The Secret of the Golden Flower: A Chinese Book of Life*, trans. Richard Wilhelm (New York: Harcourt Brace and Company, 1962), 40–41.

29. "Precarity," Wikipedia https://en.wikipedia.org/wiki/Precarity.

30. Fred Moten, "fortrd.fortrn," *The Little Edges* (Middletown: Wesleyan University Press, 2015), 2.

31. Nathaniel Mackey, "Ohnedaruth's Day Begun," *Eroding Witness* (Urbana and Chicago: University of Illinois Press, 1985), 72.

32. LeRoi Jones/Amiri Baraka, "Apple Cores #2," *Black Music* (New York: William Morrow, 1967), 123.

33. David Marriott, "Response to Race and the Poetic Avant-Garde" (March 10, 2015) https://bostonreview.net/blog/poetry-forum-race-av ant-garde.

The Ga(s)p

M. NourbeSe Philip

> Women and slaves belonged to the same
> category and were hidden away not only
> because they were somebody else's prop-
> erty but because their life was "laborious,"
> devoted to bodily
> functions.
>
> —Hannah Arendt,
> *The Human Condition*

WE ALL BEGIN life in water
We all begin life because someone once breathed for us
Until we breathe for ourselves
Someone breathes for us
Everyone has had someone—a woman—breathe for them
Until that first ga(s)p
For air

      We begin life in a prepositional relationship with breath: someone
breathes *for* us. We continue that prepositional relationship, breathing
for ourselves until we can no longer do so, and it appears that this most
fundamental of acts is always a contingent one—breathing for, with,
instead of, and into. Survival demands that we learn to breathe for our-
selves, but the sine qua non of our existence is that first extended act
of breathing—a breathing for and being breathed for *in utero*. We can,
perhaps, call it a form of circular breathing or even circle breathing. Are
there wider theoretical and possible therapeutic implications to breathing

for someone and allowing someone to breathe for you? Further, how do the prepositional modifications change these implications—is breathing for the same as breathing with or instead of? Finally, while "I breathe" is semantically complete, its completion would not be possible without that original, prepositional act of breathing for.

These are the thoughts that surface on reflection a few months after listening to Nathaniel Mackey's inaugural Creeley lecture (SUNY Buffalo, Spring 2016). In the moment, as I listened to him, my memories ran along parallel tracks, thinking of my own very different arc of coming to voice and therefore breath.

After observing that Creeley discovered that reading poetry out loud often required a conscious manipulation of breath, Mackey takes us through the idea of precarity as it affects African Americans, referencing the now tragically iconic phrase by Eric Garner, "I can't breathe," as he explains the technique and use of circular breathing in music, all of it grounded in and illustrated by musical samples of jazz.

My memories take me back to my early years in Canada, and the beginnings of my very tentative presumption that I might have something to say that others would listen to or be interested in hearing. As I listen I am conscious of a heightened awareness of the flexing of empire both old and new and the very different trajectory of my writing life; I recall how my concerns as a "young" lawyer-poet were held fast by the residues of the British empire. I read the British poets—Andrew Motion and company (mostly male), the Caribbean poets and writers (mostly male), most, if not all, of whom were understandably oriented toward England. Brathwaite's "path- / less, harbour- / less spade," with Sahara dust on her feet, trying to find a place to land on in the shadow of empire epitomized the plight of the formerly colonized.[1] Wynter, Walcott, Lamming, Cesaire, C. L. R. James, and St. John Perse—these were the writers who engaged my imaginative and still incipient poetic life during those years. In my then still-unimagined role of writer-poet, determined by a colonial childhood where we, descendants of the enslaved, sang of Britons who "never never never" would be slaves, one aspect of the mental luggage I had brought with me to Canada was important: one had to engage with the polity and be a part of the struggle for liberation—the writer as public intellectual (long before the term became fashionable).[2] It would throw a long shadow over my writing life.

There was no one to follow, it seemed, in those early days here in Canada, the literary tradition among Black and African-descended people appearing very different from that of the United States, the United Kingdom, and even of the Caribbean.[3] I had heard of the novelist Austin Clarke, but not of Sonny Ladoo, whose brilliance was too quickly cut short. A pulse of joy at discovering the brilliant poet, Claire Harris, but what was she doing all the way out in Calgary? So locked was I in my Toronto-centric mind-set. Meantime the Jamaican oral tradition was exploding in the United Kingdom into the dub sounds of Lynton Kwesi Johnson (LKJ) and Benjamin Zephaniah, as well as in Toronto with the dub poetry collective De Dub Poets.

The tunnel of memory I enter as I listen to Mackey brings to mind the Four Horsemen, the Canadian poetry group comprised of Steve McCaffery, bpNichol, Paul Dutton, and Rafael Barreto-Rivera. They rehearsed in a building on Bloor St., Toronto, in the Annex area. How I had heard about them or why I attended their weekly practices, I have no recollection, but I must have liked their experiments with language and there was clearly something about what they did that spoke to me. I don't recall what I did apart from watching them. At the time I stopped attending, they were exploring the work of the Canadian composer and environmentalist Murray Schafer. I continued to practice law while "trying" to write poetry.

At that time Canada allowed me a certain freedom both to explore what appeared to be the negative space around me and to consolidate a commitment to the aesthetics of that aching archipelago of islands, the Greater and Lesser Antilles, better known as the Caribbean—a commit-ment that would have been more forcefully challenged in national spaces like the United States or the United Kingdom, both of which have longer and more consciously developed traditions of Black writing. Canada, its aboriginal traditions and cultures having been disrupted by European colonization, was for me an (un)settled land, which would become a frontier of sorts (with all the problematics of that term) with the hinterland behind and the promise of discovery and exploration ahead.

All of which brings me back to the idea of circular breathing and, as he calls it, the poetics of breath raised by Mackey, as well as those ruminations and questions raised at the opening of this piece. "Ongoingness, unending abidance, everlasting life" are some of the qualities Mackey ascribes to circular breath, and my thoughts turn to that first extended period of circular breathing we all experience. An experience that, more often than not, ends in the gasp heralding another stage of breathing—breathing for one's self.

"A convulsive catching of the breath from exertion ... (One's) last gasp: the last attempt to breathe before death" is how the *Oxford English Dictionary* describes the gasp, otherwise known as a form of paralinguistic respiration. The first ga(s)p of the newborn who has, until then, been breathed for, signals a beginning; it is the same act—that of forcefully attempting to draw air into the lungs that will mark the final moments of a life—"I can't breathe. . . ." The last words uttered by Eric Garner as he lay dying on a New York sidewalk.

—Trying to write poetry:

It meant that I had to find my own tradition and learn how to breathe myself. For myself. Once again.

Each of us has had someone, a woman, breathe for us. To keep us alive. Each of us has allowed someone, a woman, to breathe for us, our coming to life dependent on an Other breathing for us—a form of circular breathing this:

Circle breathing
Circle breath
Circling breaths
Breathing for the other

Could we, perhaps, describe this process as an example and expression of radical hospitality? Radical because although the fetus is genetically comprised of both the mother's and father's genes, physiologically the child is also a stranger. Ordinarily, the mother's body should generate activated T-cells, which would then attack the fetus's foreign antigens. There is, however, a complex and not-yet-entirely understood process by which the mother's body turns off the functions of her T-cells, which would normally result in the rejection of the fetus. It is a radical hospitality that entails housing the stranger, which includes breathing for the occupant until that child is able to breathe on its own.[4] The process elaborates a complex act of acceptance of alterity.

Hannah Arendt's idea of natality as a universal founding principal proves useful here, less for its focus on the idea that we are all natals who begin life as individuals who are then welcomed into a "web of human relationships which is, as it were, woven by the deeds and words of innumerable persons, by the living as well as by the dead."[5] It is an idea that the institution of slavery immediately confounds and complicates. The forced breeding of enslaved African women, not to mention the forced impregnation by white and European masters, immediately disrupts her model of us arriving into a world that welcomes us and where family and community are somewhat intact with links to the past. It is, instead, her attempt to use the idea of the universality of birth, natality, as generative of possible alternatives—symbolic, theoretical and therapeutic—to the erasure of the female body in general that interests me as a model. Not to mention her intention to offer a corrective to the patriarchal nature of philosophical studies, which emphasized individualism, alterity, the omnipresence of death and the world as an alien reality.[6] Physiologically, the enslaved mother has no choice but to breathe for the child that is forced on her body. Does that make her doubly a slave—to her body and her master? There is, however, a sense in which we are all slaves to the needs of our bodies and our biology, and Arendt's analysis of how women's labor has historically been crucial to the satisfaction of those needs is important in understanding the gendered differences between labor (the work that women and slaves do) and work that creates materiality in the shape of things.

Birth, however, does not necessarily entail survival or life; it can be harsh, difficult, brutal, or isolating. I want, instead, to focus on the period before birth and the practice of breath: breathing for or allowing someone to breathe for you. The idea of the mother breathing for the fetus is commonplace but bears repeating: oxygen from the air the mother inhales is cycled around to the fetus, and the carbon dioxide from the latter returns to her and is exhaled in a circle or circling of breath. Riffing off Arendt's theorizing of natality, this process of shared breath, strength, and dependency becomes useful as a model of community and connectedness in a more female-centered, embodied, symbolic universe. How then do we begin to think about shared breath, circular breath, or circle breath in the context of force—historical (enslavement) and contemporary.

Mackey uses the example of the horn player, primarily male, and his use of pneumatic breath, often in the form of circular breathing, in the playing of his instrument, within the contemporary context of the precarity of existence for African Americans in the United States today. However, in light of the seminal and formative role played by gay and trans women in formation of the Black Lives Matter (BLM) movement, I would argue that it becomes imperative to lodge the poetics of breath as identified by Mackey in the Black female imaginary. An imaginary that enlarges the idea of labor so that our acts are not solely directed to responding to the necessity of life, but are extended to embrace engagement in active subordination to systems of terror and oppression that attempt to suck the oxygen out of the air we breathe, literally and figuratively, so that the refrain, "I can't breathe" becomes universal.

These are my thoughts in August 2016, as I engage with the idea of circular breathing in Salvador, Brazil. Salvador, the beating heart of Africa outside of Africa. These are the un/remembered re/memberings that beat around my head and enfold me as I witness the profound power of Black women in community. As I look into the eyes of the Madres de Dios, the Mothers of Gods. In this extended minute I receive an e-mail from a friend and colleague about the anguish of parenting in an age in which we not only seem, but, indeed, are less and less able to carry out one of the most primal of acts—protection of our children.

E-MAIL EXCHANGE WITH ANDREA BRADY (AUGUST 2016)

M.N.P.: *I was thinking about when I was in labour with my last child and how I could only read poetry—that there was something about the breathing required for poetry that synched with the breath I needed to withstand the pain of contractions.*

A.B.: *I remember with my first, who was born in hospital after an induction, and it was all very traumatic and hard—that she got into distress and I was also panicked, and I could see that if I calmed down and breathed, her heart rate would slow too, we were in synch, and the recognition that our lives and bodies and breath only disentangled from each other slowly, over a period of many days, was one of the most powerful discoveries I made as a human being in the process of mothering. It's not separation as a bloody crash and severing, but a gentle unfurling, so that holding the newborn against your chest you stabilize their temperature and their breathing, and your bodily presence hour by hour calms and warms them. I've written about this in my book* Mutability*—which is about how both infant and adult are changed by each other, and about the "mute ability" of the speechless infant.[7]*

M.N.P.: *It was like no other pain I had felt before or since. I did not think one could endure such pain and live; as I clung to a newel post in my home I recall begging my mother—she who had once breathed for me—not to let me die, as I continued to breathe for the one who was coming through me.*

A.B.: *So much of my political thinking was shaped by this recognition that the elemental human being is not a monad, a liberal individual inside its domestic cell, but a dyad, the pair of mother and child, wrapped in mutuality and care, weakness and strength and dependency: this is the fundamental political unit, and the polities in which we live are distorted and wrecked because they are based on its repression. So a theory of the collective is not utopian, but a return to something we have all already known.*

The breath and breathing of poetry—the poetics of breath—and the sounds of the African American acapella group, Sweet Honey in the Rock, singing the words of the Lebanese American poet Kahlil Gibran, helped me to breathe through labor: "Your children are not your children," they sing. Yet we house them, I reply all these years later; "they come through you but not from you," and yet we breathe for them; "though they are with you, yet they belong not to you." They allow us to breathe for them, which I suggest is not as passive as it appears and is a vital part of the equation in the circle breath—the breather and the breathed-for.

Everyone has had someone breathe for them. Until the first ga(s)p. For air.

Do our cells carry this epigenetic memory of a form of sharing and exchange, a modeling of a "we" that we can take into our varied practices? Do they, our cells, remember what it was like to have someone breathe for us? And how, if at all, does the epigenetic cellular memory of the forced breeding of Black women affect this most generative and generous of acts? Are we marked by this—by having someone breathe for us? A memory that is a blueprint for community and interdependency. Despite the forced couplings.

What does it mean—breathing for an Other or Others? Or being breathed for? How is this affected by historical memory of enslavement? Do we ever re/present this act otherwise in our lives—on either side of the breath? And, more importantly, is there any significance to this act of radical hospitality within present day and historical contexts of systems of power that attempt to eradicate and erase the individual and those who are perceived as marginal, deficient, less than, and different?

Many of us through gender, choice, or life situation will never physically breathe for someone else, but we have all experienced being breathed for—here we come close to Arendt's idea of natality being common to us all, so that we begin life within the womb in this relationship of exchange within this nexus of dependency and strength—the circle of breath between mother and child, host and guest.

I think of breathing and the difficulties associated with it because breathing and the breath were built into the text of *Zong!*, beginning with the opening poem, "Zong! #1,"[8] which is in fact an extended ga(s)p, or rather a series of ga(s)ps for air with syllabic sounds attached or overlaid. The layout of the following four sections, "Sal," "Ventus," "Ratio," and "Ferrum," is determined by words or clusters of words seeking and finding a space in the line above so as to breathe—they can never come directly below another word or word cluster, and there is a constant movement upward to the surface of the previous line. For breath.

The conscious manipulation of breath that Mackey alludes to in the context of Creeley's development translates for me into learning how to breathe. Again. Mackey speaks of the poetics of breath, and I think of the poetics of the fragment, which *Zong!* illumines; fragments driven pneumatically by the energy of the breath in the spaces that enfold the fragments. Spaces that may be ga(s)ps, in-breathings or breathings-out, or a simple holding of the breath. This may be a distinction without a difference—the poetics of the breath or the poetics of the fragment—given that each breath we take is a fragment of the larger breathing and breath of the universe.

. . . each gap and gasp carrying the potential of a universe . . .

Someone, a woman, once breathed for us.

I return to the all-too-often erased presence of the Black woman, as the victimized, or as an individual with agency in the ongoing struggle against white supremacy; or in community as in the founders of BLM. I am reminded of Eric Garner who gasped his last words: "I can't breathe." I think of Sandra Bland whose breath was also forcibly stopped by hanging. I wonder what her last words were.

When I perform *Zong!*, I allow the words and word clusters to breathe for I 'n I—for the we in us that epigenetically we carry within the memory of our cells.[9] When I invite the audience to read with me, we collectively engage in breathing for the Other—for those who couldn't breathe—then

can't now

and, perhaps, won't be able to.

In doing so we give them a second life

I can't breathe;

                    I will breathe for you.

NOTES

1. E. Kamau Braithwaite. *The Arrivants: A New World Trilogy* (Oxford: Oxford University Press, 1978), 40.

2. The line "Britons never, never, never shall be slaves" comes from a version of "Rule, Britannia!"—a patriotic British song; James Thomson's poem "Rule, Britannia" was set to music by Thomas Arne in 1740.

3. In his criticism George Elliott Clarke has argued that sermons by Black Nova Scotian pastors constituted a literary tradition.

4. The present-day practice of surrogacy exemplifies this idea of housing of the stranger.

5. Hannah Arendt, "Labor, Work, Action," in *Amor Mundi: Explorations in the Faith and Thought of Hannah Arendt*, ed. James William Bernauer (Dordrecht, Martinus Nijhoff Publishers, 1987), 40.

6. In *Becoming Divine: Towards a Feminist Philosophy of Religion* (Manchester University Press, 1998), Grace Jantzen provides an in-depth analysis of Arendt's ideas on natality as they underpin a more feminist approach to religion, as well as an exploration of Arendt's many challenges to the patriarchal bias in philosophical studies.

7. Andrea Brady, *Mutability: Scripts for Infancy* (Calcutta and London: Seagull, 2012).

8. M. NourbeSe Philip, *Zong!* (Middletown, CT: Wesleyan Press, 2008).

9. "I 'n I" is a Rastafarian expression suggesting a collectivity.

Precarity Shared

Breathing as Tactic in Air's Uneven Commons

Jennifer Scappettone

> This air, which, by life's law,
> My lung must draw and draw
> —Gerard Manley Hopkins,
> "The Blessed Virgin Compared
> to the Air We Breathe"

> . . . then I go back where I came from to 6th Avenue
> and the tobacconist in the Ziegfeld Theatre and
> casually ask for a carton of Gauloises and a carton
> of Picayunes, and a NEW YORK POST with her face on it
> and I am sweating a lot by now and thinking of
> leaning on the john door in the 5 SPOT
> while she whispered a song along the keyboard
> to Mal Waldron and everyone and I stopped breathing
> —Frank O'Hara, "The Day Lady Died"

NATHANIEL MACKEY'S "BREATH AND PRECARITY" begins by invoking Charles Olson's canonical 1950 appeal for emphasis on the poetic line's origins in "the breath, from the breathing of the man who writes, at the moment that he writes," noting the ambient influence of this bid that hovered "in the air" of postwar poetry circles, yet wondering if "anything instructional or curricular ever came of the call for more attentiveness to breath among poets." Mackey's question is by no means limited to the

41

literary sphere or its curricula. A resurgence of attention to the constrict-
ing "laws and possibilities of the breath" since July 17, 2014—a necessary
consequence of the horror of Eric Garner's murder by chokehold, osten-
sibly triggered by the petty offense of selling loosies on the street—has
shown how socially instructive our scrutiny of laws of the breath can
be. It has led to a collective expansion and reframing, on social media
and beyond, of Frantz Fanon's 1952 statement that oppressed people
have revolted because "in many respects it became impossible ... to
breathe"—as if classical promises of civil justice and arbitration through
the discursive public sphere were deemed exhausted under existing polit-
ical structures, on a massive scale.[1] We have reached a historical juncture
at which, despite the promise of global networks to expose injustice and
broadcast dissent as never before, both the generic channels for discordant
voices (through the mechanisms of representative government, university
campuses and other educational forums, accreditation and support for
unembedded journalism, and even direct appeal to the workaday beat of
the police) and their medium of transmission—the air, as literal passage-
way for messages and life-supporting gases—are jeopardized.

The charge with which Garner leaves us—to reevaluate the laws and
possibilities of the breath at this moment—drives us once more to the
seemingly arcane realm of poetics, a counterdiscursive sphere of activ-
ity that takes inspiration as its founding trope. Seeking to excavate the
obscured site of breathing in intellectual culture as it exceeds the ableist
and patriarchal presumptions of Olson's "Projective Verse," I will turn
to the utopian feminist philosophy of Adriana Cavarero, and then to
lyric invocations and theorizations of breath that help ground Cavarero's
ideals in a dystopian historical moment. Mackey's lecture surrounding
the instructional utility of an emphasis on breath prepares us for this
trajectory by expanding the political horizons of Olson's "verse" through
rectifying emphasis on performing against, and as, sociopolitical duress.

In *For More Than One Voice: Toward a Philosophy of Vocal Expression*
(2003), Adriana Cavarero poses an expansive challenge to Western meta-
physics by fleshing out the lasting consequences of the fact that both
philosophy after Plato and Christian recastings of the Old Testament have

served to obscure the bare embodied act of acoustic emission accorded generative power in the Greek and Hebrew religions. A reigning commonplace of Western culture has since granted divine origins to the Word, or *logos*, *verbum*, and to speech's semantic function—thereby displacing the breath (Hebrew *ruah*; Septuagint *pneuma*; Latin *spiritus*) that blows upon the waters and into Adam's mouth in the ancient Hebrew texts of Genesis, or the thunderous, *langue*less vocality (Hebrew *qol;* Septuagint *phone*) attributed to Yahweh in the Psalms. Cavarero's study recalls that despite Plato's insistence on locating thought in the nobler brain, and speech, at lowest, in the mouth, thinking was rooted conceptually in the organs of respiration and phonation for many ancient cultures, including those of Greeks from Homer to Empedocles; thinking, now associated with disembodied rational intellection, was once "done with the lungs." [2] Cavarero goes on to trace the philosophical and social implications of this (mis)translation.

Recuperating the channels of reciprocal communication opened up between embodied voices, whether discursively laden or not, from philosophical abstractions of logos, Cavarero then moves discussions of voice from ontology into politics by tracing the resonance, music, and acoustic convocation that can happen *a più voci:* in plural—or, as her original Italian phrase suggests, *polyphonous*—voices. Against the logocentrism of an ideal Republic ruled by philosophers, dialogue rooted in vocality is oriented toward resonance between unique voices rather than comprehension of one by the other, "Like a kind of polyphonic song *[come una specie di canto a più voci]* whose melodic principle is the reciprocal distinction of the unmistakable timbre of each—or, better, as if a song of this kind were the ideal dimension, the transcendental principle, of politics." [3] Cavarero recognizes poetry as the primary medium in which the sovereignty of language yields to that of the voice.[4] Though her treatment of poetics is of necessity limited within a work of such sweeping scope, her analysis elucidates why Plato was hostile to poetic speech—both indirectly and by lingering on two poets in particular, archaic and current. The epic narrative of blind Homer threatens the classical philosopher who privileges acute vision because its tale cannot be extricated from the seductive pleasures of the oral medium, or *phone*, while Kamau Brathwaite's performed and printed contemporary verse obliges colonial English to vibrate via meters like the dactylic calypso by channeling the subversive music of nation language—vocalizing both the submerged memory of African languages and the ungovernable environmental forces of the Caribbean archipelago.[5]

Despite her critique of disembodiment, in the course of seeking to extricate political theory from the confines of nativist and patriarchal nationalism, and from the traditional exclusion of women, slaves, and noncitizens from the *polis* as state, Cavarero falls back into species of abstraction with regard to the body in space that diminish the efficacy of her analysis for our times. This is especially true of her reading of political space. In an optimistic theorization of globalization, Cavarero appeals to Hannah Arendt's idealized site of political interchange: "The *polis*, according to Arendt, is not physically situated in a territory. It is the space of interaction that is opened by the reciprocal communication of those present through actions and words. In the era of globalization ... this interactive space could therefore be called an absolute locality [*locale assoluto*], 'absolute' because 'unleashed' from the territoriality of place and from every dimension that roots it in a continuity."[6] While apparently liberating, the nomadic conception of discourse proffered by Arendt and Cavarero disavows the constrictions on spontaneous political participation that suffocate the voices of those relegated to the elsewhere of politics; it is now impossible to deny that globalization denotes not only an era, but a form of geographical colonialism and expanse. Seeking to extricate speech from a "perverse binary economy that splits the vocalic from the semantic and divides them into the two genders of the human species," thereby excluding feminized subjects from rational discourse, Cavarero calls for a strategic stripping of identity and championing of singularity that can then place itself into dialogue with other singularities, in what appears, in practical terms, to be a void: for "the deconstruction of belongings, the marginalization of qualities, and the depoliticization of the what."[7]

Brathwaite does not sideline the qualities of the speakers whose language he seeks to uphold, but instead exposes the way the very disabling conditions inflicted by imperialism bind subjugated speakers together in specific landscapes and qualify them for the subversive reoccupation of European languages through geographically inflected speech. The "total expression" Brathwaite identifies in *History of the Voice*, similar in political function to the absolute local insofar as it is predicated on an oral continuum of griot and audience that together compose a discursive community, comes about through the hardship of a collective of people unhoused, unprotected, and forced to rely on breath rather than the prostheses of writing—"because people be in the open air, because people live in conditions of poverty ('unhousellèd')[,] because they come from a historical experience where they had to rely on their very *breath* rather than on paraphernalia like books and museums and machines."[8] A confrontation with the vocalic continuum of oral culture as the consequence of collective privation is not within Cavarero's purview.

Ashon T. Crawley offers a compelling extension of and corrective to Cavarero's abstraction of breathing space in his recent *Blackpentecostal Breath: The Aesthetics of Possibility* (2016) by tracing the link between breath and racialization. Crawley argues that categorically distinct zones of thought are predicated on the ur-distinction that dualistic thinking draws between blackness and whiteness, which in addition to skin targets an ample range of cognitively charged sensual experiences—those of sound, smell, and touch. Unlike the disembodied cognition presumed to take place in a vacuum, such experiences rely on air as their medium of transmission—air that can be as stifling as that of the crawlspace to which Harriet Jacobs was relegated for seven years. Crawley points out that as Enlightenment philosophy hankers to establish immaculate, bounded zones of thought, it pursues the evacuation of air. "Air, the impure admixture, had to be let out of thought, had to be evacuated. Thought's flourishing, its leaps and bounds, must be strangled."[9] Countering this tendency, in what Crawley defines as Blackpentecostalism, the distressed occupation of air compels attention to particular conditions of restraint or, in aesthetic terms, compression, so that the rarefied notion of advocating a position becomes inextricable from the occupation of a particular space. As a touchstone for this focus on conception's material constraints, Crawley cites Nathaniel Mackey's assertion in *Bedouin Hornbook* that "any insistence on locale must have long since given way to locus, that the rainbow bridge which makes for unrest ongoingly echoes what creaking the rickety bed of conception makes."[10] In Mackey's articulation, conception writ large is perpetually exposed for its ramshackle foundations through the echoing of a bed in which it took place; the concept becomes reembedded in its particular, humbling location through acoustic resonance. We might recall here, additionally, Mackey's more pointed and parodic staging of thought's origins in breath throughout a work like *Atet A.D.*: in this dreamy epistolary fiction, literal "thought balloons" emerge at affective peaks from the musician protagonists' wind instruments upon blowing, inscribed with intimate confessions surrounding scent and the "erotic-elegaic affliction" it represents, until finally being popped, or vaporizing without explanation in the presence of overly insistent "tar pit premises." These scenes foreground not only the buoyancy of musical thought as conveyed by the breath—what Mackey calls "post-expectancy's non-attached address"—but its instability, its vulnerability.[11]

By grappling with sites of political interaction as real rather than virtual spaces, and with the medium of vocality as a substantial one— that of air, we can build on Cavarero's proposal for "thinking done with the lungs" while contending with the material conditions that determine one's ability to participate in the political realm. For no space of human interaction can ethically be theorized in isolation from environmental forces in our historical moment; no discursive site is freed of the territoriality of geography and its concomitant distribution of inequities based on race, gender, sexual orientation, ability, class. Ralph Ellison, for whom Heraclitus's axiom "Geography is fate" served as a touchstone, recalled the way Bessie Smith articulated the concept of "territory" in "Work House Blues";[12] Smith's lines "Goin' to the nation, goin' to the terr'tor, / ... / Bound for the nation, bound for the terr'tor," sing the "terror" in that delimited domain as well as its promise of freedom.

The carnal channel of poetics, when apprehended across its plurality of sensory demands, enables us to amend the utopian oversights of Cavarero's political theory. Notwithstanding its grounding in language, poetry has historically balked the abstractions of discourse, and hailed inspiration explicitly as matrix. Deriving from the Latin for "breathing in," the Western notion of inspired poetics can be traced to the Homeric epics and to Hesiod's *Theogony*, which opens with a description of the Muses who breathe the voice of divinity into the poet.[13] Passed down through the Romanticism of Coleridge and Shelley, and reemerging in Olson's "Projective Verse" as an interest in recuperating "certain laws and possibilities of the breath, of the breathing of the man who writes as well as of his listenings," this tradition rarely affirms the notion of isolated genius ascribed to it by modern and contemporary literary clichés.[14] In canonical texts, the breathing apparatus and its context dramatize lyricists' contending with pervasive forces beyond ourselves—with relentless physical, sociohistorical, and environmental conditions of alterity and subjection. The wind causing Coleridge's "Eolian Harp" to shudder provokes a reflection on "the one Life within us and abroad," binding all, such that all of nature can be seen as countless vulnerable "subject Lute[s],"

> . . . diversely framed,
> That tremble into thought, as o'er them sweeps
> Plastic and vast, one intellectual breeze,
> At once the Soul of each, and God of all?[15]

Flexible and vast, the air joins and dooms us somatically. Though each soul, or *anima* (from the Greek *anemos*, for "wind" or "breath"), may be framed in a different way and therefore vent a distinct melody, the air nevertheless constitutes "one intellectual breeze" demanding apprehension *through* the polyphony.

Seen not as an empty virtual space but as particulate, air makes for a democracy of harm that has had artists and authors strategizing for remedies for generations—remedies that are always necessarily incomplete. A focus on air demands that we visualize the content of an apparent void, and permits us to think through what we share intimately, often unawares. The flight paths of migratory birds that link the Americas recently animated by the Cornell Lab of Ornithology and the dust particles from Saharan sand storms that blanket the Caribbean, raising the heat index, incapacitating those with asthma and allergies, and weakening tropical cyclones, only render cartographically what Juliana Spahr powerfully identified from within the post-9/11 surge of U.S. nationalism as *This Connection of Everyone with Lungs*. Attempts to condition and purify a medium as pervasive as air ineluctably end up underscoring the founding exclusions of discrimination: Buckminster Fuller and Shoji Sadao's planned geodesic dome over Manhattan proposed in 1960 to regulate weather and reduce air pollution in a utopian key, but its bald selection of two miles of earth (covering only the gamut of Midtown, from the East River to the Hudson River and 21st to 64th Streets) highlighted above all the way the priorities of designers and their state or private backers determine radically divisive living conditions; Ant Farm's 1970 *Clean Air Pod* performance, using an inflatable to mock a safe space for breathing on the Berkeley campus, mocked the restrictive scope of any act of contouring a site for unimpaired breathing.

Refusal to confine our sense of the local to that of an unconditioned haven or self-sustaining organism allows us the opportunity to grasp what binds and still divides us as communities of breathers. These conditions help us to situate the poetic notion of inspiration within an expanded sensorium where breath is acknowledged not only as its literal foundation, but an agent subject to contemporary realities of contamination and chokehold. As air is life-giving in some places, but injurious in others— and as some are given the opportunity to breathe freely while others are not—this notion of inspiration highlights the uneven distribution, even the privatization, of rights and resources assumed to be shared equally by all. Air's condition as the commons we all inhabit, like it or not, makes breathing itself a survival strategy, and a political tactic.

Cavarero commences her study with Italo Calvino, an author for whom oral culture, with its implicit "vibration of a throat of flesh," were central to intellectual life and literary composition. We might take a cue from Calvino's writings on utopia in revising Cavarero's breath-based politics.[16] In a 1973 essay, Calvino argues that utopia "must be sought in the folds, in the shadowy places, in the countless involuntary effects that the most calculated system creates"—in the very air that designers of modern cities thought they would render immaculate, and its so-called externalities.[17] Both literalizing environmental damage and figuratively imagining its etherealization, Calvino describes his utopia as "less solid than gaseous: ... a utopia of fine dust [or "pulverized," *polverizzata*], corpuscular, and in suspension."[18]

Why turn to poetry, the form that "makes nothing happen," as Auden reminded us in torment, to reflect such all-encompassing damage? Poetry allows us to breathe this pulverization, for better or worse, which is fundamentally different from understanding. It samples from what can be perceived in a reciprocal exchange while admitting to being *uncomprehensive*; it inevitably falls short of, and therefore resists, the cartographic pretense of being visually intact.

The notion of poetic inspiration as the act of taking in a pulverized commons was made literal as early as Shelley's 1819 "Ode to the West Wind," in which the wind becomes a form of revolutionary Zeitgeist, with the poet's words becoming ashes and sparks.

> Drive my dead thoughts over the universe
> Like wither'd leaves to quicken a new birth!
> And, by the incantation of this verse,
> Scatter, as from an unextinguish'd hearth
> Ashes and sparks, my words among mankind![19]

And in Gerard Manley Hopkins's 1884 "The Blessed Virgin Compared to the Air We Breathe," rhythmic modulations emphasize the extended field and panting of anthropocene breath, its subjection to any number of girdles, its quandary with pentameter.

> WILD air, world-mothering air,
> Nestling me everywhere,

> That each eyelash or hair
> Girdles;...
>
> ....
>
> ... that's fairly mixed
> With, riddles, and is rife
> In every least thing's life;
> This needful, never spent,
> And nursing element;
> My more than meat and drink,
> My meal at every wink;
> This air, which, by life's law,
> My lung must draw and draw [20]

Serving as parish priest in the slums of manufacturing cities, where coal was being burned at unprecedented rates to fuel Britain's rise to power, Hopkins understood that the air was both perpetually available and perpetually endangered—through harm to the atmosphere—by the very sun: "flashing like flecks of coal," and potentially "In grimy vasty vault." His iambic tetrameter, and the alliteration that forces awareness of exhalation effects, draws you to huff and puff your way through these lines, becoming aware, in breathlessness, of air as mixed, unimmaculate nurse possessing the insidious power to sustain or damage the lyric subject.

In the seemingly unrestricted free verse of Frank O'Hara, we see the influence of Olson's renewed appeal to "catch up and put into [verse] certain laws ... of the breath" nine years out, and a simultaneous effort to mend the excisions of Olson's thinking. O'Hara's "The Day Lady Died" bases its tempo on the explicit space-time of Midtown Manhattan, July 17, 1959; capacious and breathless by turns, its lines sound the teeming of unrationalized sensations generated by a roaming fueled by quandariness and the lungs' coping absorption of nicotine. Verse's nervous forward motion comes to a halt with the mute, unnamed portrait of Lady (for which we must return to the title—since in the poem itself she is indexed only as "her") on the *Post*'s front page. Recalling a night in 1957 when Billie Holiday sent a melody across the keys of Mal Waldron's piano via a whisper conveying bodily affliction, stopping the breath of horn players and listeners alike, O'Hara stops those of readers in turn, abandoning them in the space of a voice deserted, extinguished, and unresolved by a full stop. The breathing that matters here is not simply that "of the man who writes, at the moment that he writes." It is that of the woman genius who sings, of her interlocutors in breath and the perturbed air of plucked strings, and of her listeners, as well as that of the belated reader for whom an immediate hearing has been prematurely denied. This reader and mediated listener may recall from several removes of history that due to past drug offenses, the New York Police Department had denied Holiday a cabaret license—so that the song O'Hara remembers her whispering at the Five Spot literally broke the law.[21] Given that the poetic speaker has just purchased two cartons of Gauloises and Picayunes, we assume that the immediate salve for the anguish of her death will be the nervous taking up of a cigarette: a fleeting legal fix for addiction and aspirational act of empathy through pollution of the lungs.

What form would verse need to take now to chart the fleetingly nurturing, and often sickening, unwitting kinship structures in which we participate daily—to articulate the sustained unfreedom that breath and its constriction makes palpable? Nathaniel Mackey's body of fiction, essays, and verse above all constitutes an invaluable answer to this question. As he points out in "Breath and Precarity," extending yet implicitly critiquing the masculinized presumption of stamina in Olson's breath-based poetics, the word *panic* has its etymological roots in the piper-god Pan. Pan and Dionysus, gods whose blowing of wind instruments displaces discourse, are associated with the self's dispossession. The consequences can be ecstatic—Nietzsche refers to the effect as an "unchaining" from individuality[22]—and its expression can generate the exultant music that Mackey identifies as "multiply tongued." [23] They can also be devastating. Both aspects of breathing are represented when, for example, his Djeannine in *Atet A.D.* blows across a bottle, awakening a djinn that empowers her to cover, and surpass, the Billie Holiday standard "I Cover the Waterfront" via this rudimentary instrument by lamenting the loss "not of love, but of power"—of cover itself. Djeannine's song assumes not only Holiday's accent on the first syllable of "cover" but the freighted sound of an Arabico-Berber flute suggesting leakage, the bottle's genie finally emerging as "wasted wish as well as wasted breath, an abrasive wind intent on scouring the air."[24] Mackey's representation of breath's devastation and its musical overcoming form a singular contribution to evolving understandings of the matter of breathing, and of the poetics and politics of air.

On p. 9 of his essay in this volume, Mackey calls this a "radical pneumaticism" on display in black music and especially that of wind instruments, "in which the involuntary is rendered deliberate, labored, in which breath is belabored, made strange," transmits at once the singularity of a voice and the commonality of shared suffering. Twisting a medium riddled with hazards into collaboration through labored virtuosity, the breath of these performers "becomes tactical, tactile, textile, even textual, a haptic recension whose jagged disbursements augur duress." Verse now, 2017, if it is to be of *essential* use in a historical moment in which people of color, immigrants, women, LGBTQIA folk, and the poor are under threat unbridled even in the rhetorical performances of ascendant politicians, must extract from itself certain laws that otherwise must be hauled. As Mackey further expresses on p. 20 of his essay, through lungs drawn and drawn, verse should disclose that traffic of alternating utopian mastery and disquiet being animated through circular breathing in jazz,

> a mixed-emotional, mixed-messaging traffic, a clandestine circulation
> of breath rotating between utopian intimations of assured, everlasting
> pneumatic amenity and a sirening alarm at the precarity to which
> breath, especially black breath, is subject—triumphalist and agonistic
> both, a boastful exulting in breath and a dystopian struggle for it . . .

No literary form modulates breath more self-consciously or expresses the tactics of surviving a flawed commons more clearly than poetry—poetry being the art form that takes inspiration most literally while forcing us to contend with what "sweeps / Plastic and vast," as semi-intellectual breeze, "At once the Soul of each, and God of all." Mackey's writing across poetry and poetics provides a rejoinder to ubiquitous neo-liberal fantasies that simply practicing breathing in and out, shamelessly appropriating ancient Eastern tactics in the service of capitalist production, can somehow subtract contemporary citizens of the West from the stresses, exclusions, and violent suppressions of the polis.[25]

A lyrical book that has been categorized through any number of generic terms, as it largely eschews verse, yet was composed by an author identified as a poet, provides us with a closing paradox. The original edition of Claudia Rankine's *Citizen* ended many pages with the forward slash associated with a cited line of poetry, as if every page recounting the punishing conditions of breath's precarity had been captured from a past history of lyricism. Rankine makes the fact that "subject Lute[s]," as Coleridge once put it, are diversely framed (if sharing the same rank air), a theme of her second collection, *Citizen: An American Lyric. Citizen* underscores the commonality and the division sounded and perpetuated by lyric, with its corporeal matrix in the breath. For Rankine, vocalizations like the sigh that Cavarero might have championed as expression unleashed from the discursive sphere are only partially voluntary utterances—dubious acts of *poesis* in the sense of making, or fabrication. Like the compulsory action of exhaling only to again inhale pernicious ambient forces, the sigh manifests a problem with Olson's postulation of poetic subjectivity, or "the pressure of his [that is, the poet's] breath," under conditions of subjugation.

> The sigh is the pathway to breath; it allows breathing. That's just self-preservation. No one fabricates that. You sit down, you sigh. You stand up, you sigh. The sighing is a worrying exhale of an ache. You wouldn't call it an illness; still it is not the iteration of a free being. What else to liken yourself to but an animal, the ruminant kind?[26]

The sigh does not prevail over conditions of duress but only permits breathing to occur, temporarily clearing the obstruction of a general ache in favor of self-preservation, an individual's continuing to live. *Citizen's* "just" relates flatly that this is a questionable achievement in a context in which one's fellow citizens cannot breathe, are left to die.

In "Projective Verse," Olson affirms the linear progression from "the HEART, by way of the BREATH, to the LINE," confident that "breath is man's special qualification as animal" because "[s]ound is a dimension he has extended"—presumably by succeeding in modulating the pace of breathing, and therefore breaking vocalization into precise units of sound, gradually establishing the fine motor skills needed to form language. (This qualification is not, of course, the result of man's heroic agency, as Olson intimates, but arises through the glacial and objectively determined evolution of the human species.)[27] Rankine, who in this volume largely relinquishes the line of verse and its "qualifications," goes further: to trouble the line between man and animal (and, for that matter, woman) by reminding us of the discomfitingly hybrid nature of the vocal channel. Speaking entails a primary dislocation not only of breathing but of eating, and vice versa; the Latin *rumen* signifies the throat, and in its extended form means chewing over again, thereby confusing thinking and its vocalic transmission with the cow's chewing of cud, of regurgitated matter. A continuum of racial oppression, from a host of seemingly involuntary microaggressions perpetuated against professionals in professional settings to unending dismissals of illegal chokeholds by the security state, and the chronicle of unfreedom registered in age-old lyric form, ensures that pressure is on the breathing of speakers of color rather than the other way around. Atmospheric, this pressure is, by extension, on all poets, and all speakers, to answer Rankine's piercing question: "Did that just come out of my mouth, his mouth, your mouth?" [28]

NOTES

1. See Frantz Fanon, *Black Skin, White Masks*, trans. Richard Philcox (New York: Grove Press, 2008), 201. Fanon's statement has been widely misquoted as if it were written in the first person plural through its circulation on social media, a fact fascinating in itself. By contrast, the original French reads, "Ce n'est pas parce que l'Indochinois a découvert une culture propre

qu'il s'est révolté. C'est parce que 'tout simplement' il lui devenait, à plus d'un titre, impossible de respirer."

The thinking reflected in this essay owes much to conversations over the course of 2015–16 with Caroline Bergvall and Judd Morrissey, with whom I shared a Mellon Collaborative Fellowship in Arts Practice and Scholarship at the Gray Center for Arts and Inquiry to work on a project called The Data That We Breathe. Thanks as well to our students in the Breathing Matters: Poetics and Politics of Air seminar at the University of Chicago.

2. Adriana Cavarero, *A più voci: Per una filosofia dell'espressione vocale* (Milan: Feltrinelli, 2003), available in English as *For More Than One Voice: Toward a Philosophy of Vocal Expression*, trans. and with an introduction by Paul A. Kottman (Stanford, CA: Stanford University Press, 2005).

3. Cavarero, *For More Than One Voice*, 201, but translated differently by me so as to reflect the musical implications of Cavarero's initial phrase.

4. See *For More Than One Voice*, 10.

5. Cavarero discusses Brathwaite in a brief section under the heading "The Hurricane Does Not Roar in Pentameter," while referring to Homer throughout the book. See *For More Than One Voice*, 146–51.

6. *A più voci: Filosofia dell'espressione vocale*, 222, my translation. In the English edition this quote falls on page 204.

7. *For More Than One Voice*, 207, 205.

8. Kamau Brathwaite, *History of the Voice: The Development of Nation Language in Anglophone Caribbean Poetry* (London and Port of Spain: New Beacon Books, 1984), 18–19. Cavarero discusses the vocalic continuum in Brathwaite in *For More Than One Voice*, 150.

9. Ashon T. Crawley, *Blackpentecostal Breath: The Aesthetics of Possibility* (Bronx, NY: Fordham University Press, 2016), 15.

10. Original quote is from Nathaniel Mackey, *Bedouin Hornbook* (Lexington: University of Kentucky Press, 1986), 30.

11. Nathaniel Mackey, *Atet A.D.* (San Francisco: City Lights, 2001), 56, 114.

12. See "Going to the Territory," in *The Collected Essays of Ralph Ellison*, ed. John F. Callahan (New York: Modern Library, 1995), 605: "Geography as a symbol of the unknown included not only places, but conditions relating

to their racially defined status and the complex mystery of a society from which they had been excluded."

13. For a condensed history, see "Inspiration," in *The Princeton Encyclopedia of Poetry and Poetics*, eds. Roland Greene et al. (Princeton, NJ: Princeton University Press, 2012), 709–11.

14. Charles Olson, "Projective Verse," in *Collected Prose*, ed. Donald Allen and Benjamin Friedlander (Berkeley: University of California Press, 1997), 239.

15. Samuel Taylor Coleridge, "The Eolian Harp," in William Wordsworth and Samuel Taylor Coleridge, *Lyrical Ballads and Other Poems* (Ware, Hertfordshire: Wordsworth Editions, 2003), 236.

16. Italo Calvino, "A King Listens," a libretto conceived for a work of musical theater in collaboration with Luciano Berio, qtd. in *For More Than One Voice*, 2.

17. The grid of the 1811 Commissioner's Plan for Manhattan was "to unite regularity and order with the public convenience and benefit and . . . promote the health of the City . . . [by allowing] a free and abundant circulation of air." Edwin G. Burrows and Mike Wallace, *Gotham: A History of New York City to 1898* (Oxford and New York: Oxford University Press, 1998), 420. The notion that city parks act as "the lungs of the city" has become a cliché so pervasive that its etiology is difficult to pin down.

18. The 1986 English translation reads "a utopia of fine dust," but Calvino uses the term "*polverizzata.*" Italo Calvino, *The Uses of Literature: Essays*, trans. Patrick Creagh, 1st U.S. ed. (San Diego: Harcourt Brace Jovanovich, 1986), 255. The essay was originally titled "Which Utopia?" and published in 1973.

19. Percy Bysshe Shelley, *The Poems of Shelley, Volume Three: 1819–1820*, ed. Jack Donovan, Cian Duffy, and Kelvin Everest (New York and London: Routledge, 2014), 212. James Chandler writes of Shelley's "defining poetry against the rational will, and aligning it with the spirit of the age, precisely because this alignment lifted it clear of the calculating faculty. . . . The Wind makes Shelley make the Wind make Shelley make the Wind. But perhaps better: Shelley is led by the events of post-Revolution history to construct an account whereby he and post-Revolution history make each other." James Chandler, *England in 1819: The Politics of Literary Culture and the Case of Romantic Historicism* (University of Chicago Press, 1998), 553–54.

20. Gerard Manley Hopkins, *Poems and Prose* (New York: Penguin, 1985), 54. I am also indebted to Julie Carr, "Hopkins's Wildness," a talk as yet unpublished, for drawing me to this poem.

21. See Brad Gooch, *City Poet: The Life and Times of Frank O'Hara* (New York: Harper, 2014), 328.

22. See Friedrich Nietzsche, *The Birth of Tragedy*, trans. Francis Golffing (New York: Doubleday, 1956), 82.

23. Nathaniel Mackey, with reference to the horn of Eric Dolphy, in *Paracritical Hinge: Essays, Talks, Notes, Interviews* (Madison: University of Wisconsin Press, 2005), 224.

24. *Atet A.D.*, 87, 89.

25. Examples of this tendency are abundant, but I will cite a recent audio work called "Transcenmentalism": "In some modern societies, the economy has achieved the status of a living, breathing human being. Often it is afforded greater protection and rights than the communities it is supposed to support. Although all-knowing and all-powerful, the economy still struggles, fails and sometimes, even 'hurts.' To some, these conditions make it even more holy. As our society's most powerful contemporary deity, don't we owe it to the economy to not only sacrifice our time, our loyalty and our children's future, but our very spirit? This guided economic mediation will harness your conscious experience, allowing you to finally become one with the most supreme being of our times." Jessie Borrelle, "Transcenmentalism," *Paper Radio*, Podcast audio, August 30, 2015, http://www.paperradio.net/fm/transcenmentalism, accessed January 5, 2016.

26. Claudia Rankine, *Citizen: An American Lyric* (Minneapolis: Graywolf, 2014), 60. Olson quote is from "Projective Verse," 273.

27. See, for example, Philip Lieberman, "The Evolution of Human Speech: Its Anatomical and Neural Bases," *Current Anthropology* 48, no. 1 (February 2007): 39–66.

28. *Citizen*, 9.

On Not Missing It

Elizabeth Willis

I HAVE TO START by confessing that I am something of an interloper in the Poetics Program. By the time Susan Howe and Charles Bernstein arrived in 1988 or '89, I had finished my coursework in the PhD program and was working at the Poetry Collection and Rare Books Room, reading and writing poetry and trying to appear to be making enough progress on a dissertation that nobody would ask me why I was still there. The longer I stayed, the more interesting things got. When my funding ran out, I pieced together nonacademic, secretarial, library, and community service work, so I could stay in town for the action.

When I arrived in Buffalo in 1983, in a ten-year-old Toyota Corolla that my brother helped me push through customs when it stalled on the Peace Bridge, the Poetics Program, as a concept, was still at least five years away. But nobody seemed to think I had come to Buffalo too early. Instead, I was told I had just missed it. Everything glorious inhabited a luminous past that was referred to as if it had just happened, though at that point the historical reference must have been about twenty years old.

Charles Olson still cast a long hot shadow, John Barth had left years before, Michel Foucault's presence had become the stuff of urban legend. Leslie Fiedler was about to retire. The legendary, clock-stopping readings of John Wieners were still in the air. The modal vibe was one of belatedness.

Robert Creeley was our Ishmael—survivor of the Olsonian shipwreck. The one who took responsibility not only for escaping to tell us, but for making something *of* the shipwreck. For making something new from what was left of the ship.

As many commented during the April 2016 "Poetics: (The Next) 25 Years" conference, and over the years, Bob had a genius for inclusion and for assembly. The two words he said most often were *particular* and *company*. He was full of self-ironizing wit, but it was combined with an equally genuine Romantic sincerity.

For me, there was in his work, and in his person, a sense of wonder at the genesis and location of words, the fact of writing as a physical experience, felt in the body, a passage one followed without a clear sense of where it was taking you. Here are a few stanzas from his early poem "The Door," which he dedicated to Robert Duncan.

> It is hard going to the door
> cut so small in the wall where
> the vision which echoes loneliness
> brings a scent of wild flowers in a wood.
> What I understood, I understand.
> My mind is sometime torment,
> sometimes good and filled with livelihood,
> and feels the ground.
> But I see the door,
> and knew the wall, and wanted the wood,
> and would get there if I could
> with my feet and hands and mind.
> [...]
> I will go to the garden.
> I will be a romantic. I will sell
> myself in hell
> in heaven also I will be.
> In my mind I see the door,
> I see the sunlight before me across the floor
> beckon to me, as the Lady's skirt
> moves small beyond it.[1]

This was the magical path on which I set foot when Robert Bertholf hired me to work part-time in the Poetry Collection, where the Robert Duncan papers were housed—and where I worked, with Mike Boughn and Lisa Jarnot and Marta Werner and Mike Basinski the year that Robert Duncan died and his notebooks and papers came into our lives.

In addition to taking every class I could with Robert Creeley, including what must have been one of the first courses on L=A=N=G=U=A=G=E poetry, I studied medieval literature, the eighteenth-century novel, film, autobiography, and Victorian literature. I studied documentary fieldwork with Bruce Jackson, the domestic novel with Nancy Armstrong, and Blake with Diane Christian and Jack Clarke (in a seminar whose bibliographic points of reference included early episodes of *Star Trek*). From the vantage point of my patchy education, this looked like my big break. I sat in on lectures by Rodolphe Gasché, Henry Sussman, Slavoj Žižek, Joan Copjec, Michel Serres, and J. M. Coetzee.

But much of my education in Buffalo happened outside of the classroom in places that amazingly enough mostly still exist: at Just Buffalo, at the Central Park Grill next to the Trico plant on Main Street, at Hallwalls, at Talking Leaves Bookstore, at the Tralfamador Café; and in the music halls where I discovered Sun Ra, Morton Feldman, and John Cage; at the firehouse where Bob and Pen lived; and in the low-rent apartments where I hung out with my friends, who remain some of the most intellectually generous people I know.

Hey, Sheila Boughner, Mary Cappello, Pam Beal, Jim Morrison, Paul Hogan, Gwen Ashbaugh. What's up, Harvey Brown, Lisa Jarnot, Mike Boughn, Marta Werner, Juliana Spahr? These are some of the people I stood with in my corner of the local field into which Susan Howe and Charles Bernstein arrived.

We were a motley assembly in a rich cultural landscape that was ready for the next thing to happen—an emergent context that was ready to explode into another form. The arrival of Susan and Charles, and the constellation of a program that, in addition to Robert Creeley, included Dennis Tedlock and Raymond Federman, had, for those of us who were already on the ground, a cosmic impact.

They extended what we knew, critiqued it, turned it over, made new things seem possible. Susan allowed me to audit her graduate seminar on conversion and captivity, and I demonstrated my understanding of the course materials by riding my bike across an international border in the snow to meet with her. Charles let me audit his seminar on contemporary poetry and taught me to value my own propensity for parataxis and contingency thinking, to embrace my resistance to narrative and argumentative structures, which had up until that point, made the idea of actually completing a dissertation seem unfathomable.

Charles taught me if I wasn't clear about the sequence, maybe it wasn't a narrative, just shuffle the cards.

Susan taught me not to be afraid of my own enthusiasms.

Bob taught me not only to embrace change but to look for opportunities in which to enact it.

I mention all of this because I want to speak in praise of hanging on and hanging out, of nonproductive, nonprofessional life—which has, I think, been wildly underestimated and is, to my mind, an important part of what distinguished Buffalo from other programs.

If I had completed my degree on time, if I had not believed so thoroughly that everything was secondary to the life of the poem, I would have missed the Poetics Program altogether. So my one pedagogical moment here is to say that sometimes you have to appear to do nothing in order to be a part of something larger and more meaningful. One of my favorite passages in Fred Moten and Stefano Harney's book *The Undercommons: Fugitive Planning & Black Study* and one that I often think about as I'm preparing for class is this sentence: "The only possible relationship to the university today is a criminal one."[2] And I think, why does this assessment of the transaction that is about to take place seem so true? I hear this sentence not as an interpretation of our situation but as a statement of fact and as an imperative. For the university to be a site in which we do real things, make real art, build real friendships, we have to steal its fire, exploit its available resources, use its equipment, test its limits, take the experience beyond that which can be monetized. I would even go so far as to say that we have an obligation to do so.

For many of us, the Poetics Program has been this kind of resource and refuge, a gathering place whose value lies, I believe, at least as much in the nonproductive labor of its off-hours as in its degree-granting authority. I hope we will continue to talk, beyond these events, about ways we can create common places that will make possible other kinds of consciousness, of relationships, and of circumstances. Other futures.

So hey, all you new people, you didn't miss it. Not at all. It's up ahead. It's all just coming on.

NOTES

1. Creeley, Robert. *Collected Poems*, 1945–1975. (Berkeley: University of California Press, 2006), 199–201.

2. Moten, Fred, and Stefano Harney. *The Undercommons: Fugitive Planning & Black Study*. (Brooklyn: Minor Compositions, 2013), 26.

Here and Elsewhere

Creeley's Notions of Community and Teaching as Circulation

Vincent Broqua

> Who's there,
> old
> question, who's
> here.
>
> —Robert Creeley, "Window"

IN HIS POEM "WINDOW," included in his collection *Windows*, Robert Creeley writes a section that problematizes his relation to "here" and "elsewhere" in terms of the "old" spectral question asked by Barnardo in the incipit of *Hamlet*.[1] Because "Who's there" is the first cue in Shakespeare's play, it allows the playwright to create at once both the dreaded nocturnal atmosphere in a daytime performance (Denmark fears an invasion and the sentinel is precisely "there" to watch in case of an attack), the self-referential illusion of theatricality (who's "there" and who's "here" simultaneously, being one of the most crucial questions of drama), and the disquieting sense that something is already "out of joint" in this ghostly landscape of Elsinore: presence is then to be understood in terms of a spectrality that oscillates between the here and the there.[2] Creeley's jagged four-line section in "Window," quoted as an epigraph, can thus be read in several ways: as a dismissal of the "old question," hence pitting the "here" (and the poetics of immanence) against the "there"; as a humble albeit forceful statement of the preeminence of the contemporary poet in relation to the old Bard; and, more subtly and literally, as creating a relation between the here and the there, or the here and the elsewhere. Creeley often foregrounds the here-and-now of presence in his poems and interviews while invoking a "there" of ghostly presence that is both here and there at the same time. Indeed, the articulation of "who's here" and "who's there" is densely woven into Creeley's poetry and participates in his conception of community and his sense of being in space. This tension between the here and the there also can be found in "Place," the poem just after "Window": "Patience to learn / to be *here*, to savor / whatever there is / out there, without you / *here, here* / by myself." [3]

The three notions of community, teaching, and space are related in Creeley's life to a tension between locality, displacement, and circulation. Creeley articulated his being "here" and "elsewhere" in relation to his sense of teaching. More particularly, his generative and conflicted sense of noninstitutionalized forms of teaching were related to his singular conception of community. It is, I will argue, Creeley's notions and practice of community, which were given institutional form through the founding of the Buffalo Poetics Program, that have been and still are disseminated in poetry communities in France and in the United Kingdom. [4]

IDIORRHYTHMIC COMMUNITIES

IN *Comment vivre ensemble* (*How to Live Together*), his 1976–77 seminar at the Collège de France, Roland Barthes begins by outlining his own fantasy of idiorrhythmy.

> It's not a case of Two-People-Living-Together, of a pseudo-conjugal Discourse succeeding (by some miracle) the Lovers' Discourse. [It's] a fantasy of a life, a regime, a lifestyle, *diaita*, diet. Neither dual or plural (collective). Something like solitude with regular interruptions: the paradox, the contradiction, the aporia of bringing distances together—the utopia of a socialism of distances. [5]

Barthes found the perfect historical model of this fantasy in the community of monks who live on mount Athos in Greece. Some of these monks experience what he calls *idiorrhythmy*: they live isolated, like hermits, led by their own rhythm and at the same time develop a form of community, so that they do not lead eremitic lives entirely.

Although Creeley did say, "I do live in an isolated sense," I am not proposing that Creeley was like those monks, and neither is Barthes saying that this model is widespread.[6] Barthes speaks positively of a *fantasme*, a "fantasy." What he considers, then, is the conceptual power of the term *idiorrhythmy* and how it enables one to reflect on social or individual relations, and envisage a utopian and fantasmatic way of living; how it enables one to combine ideas of escaping the alienation created by social institutions while still thinking of the necessity of looser forms of communities. It seems to me that Creeley's life and his conception of his relation to others as it emerges from his letters, interviews, and poems respond to the term *idiorrhythmy*. In fact, he comes strikingly close to Barthes's formulation in "Some Senses of the Commonplace," when speaking of the Navajo habitat; as he says,

> I've always been impressed by the Navajo habit of hogans, seemingly kept so separated from other relations. But they *aren't*, is the point. You're just talking about a spatial term. You're not talking about the experiential fact of how people come together, or what their imaginations of the place then become. The relationships in fact are as dense as they could be ... There's an insistent presence of diversity, and yet it excludes nothing, you know, because everything's related.[7]

Like Barthes, Creeley uses other forms of social organization to imagine a possibility for being together *here* and yet preserving an elsewhere where one might escape. Elsewhere thus allows one to think about *here* and togetherness reflexively.

This thinking is precisely what Creeley does in the note appended at the end of *Hello: A Journal, February 29–May 3, 1976*.[8] *Hello* is the extraordinary poetic journal he kept while touring nine countries of the Asia Pacific region for two months under the aegis of the Department of

State.[9] The one-page note is crucial. Over these two paragraphs Creeley charts notions of singularity and traveling, meeting different models of social organization, contrasting our individualistic Western societies with other ethnographic models without being too caricatural about it. He thinks about living *in* the world, saying,

> To move in such fashion through nine countries ... in a little over two months is a peculiarly American circumstance, and the record thus provoked is *personal* in a manner not only the effect of my own egocentricity, but again, a fact of American social reality. The tourist will always be singular, no matter what the occasion otherwise—and there is a sense, I think, in which Americans still presume the world as something to look at and use, rather than to live in.[10]

In this note, Creeley identifies with the tourist's egocentricity and his or her isolation, but values a different kind of tourist, a tourist who "wants, at last, to be *human*, however simplistic that wish" and who, abstaining from the strict and "alienating" models on which our Western societies are built, articulates the wish to be human, the isolation and singularity of the traveler, his or her *fantasme*, to the wish for a "company," which he said he found.[11] His conception of "living together" is further outlined in his opposition between our sense of "isolation" and the "collective" that the countries he visited seem to rely on: "Whereas our habit of social value constantly promotes an isolation—the house in the country, the children in good schools—theirs, of necessity, finds center and strength in the collective, unless it has been perverted by Western exploitation and greed." [12] If one reads superficially and merely follows the stark opposition between the two terms ("an isolation" vs. "the collective") and its seeming invalidation of the value of "isolation," this passage seems to negate Creeley's sense of idiorrhythmy.

Yet, Creeley doesn't so much disapprove of isolation, he takes issue with the kind of isolation that rhymes with domination and he proposes, instead, idiorrhythmic isolation. Indeed, the idiorrhythmy that he carefully outlines in this note is a politics of singularity that doesn't amount to the problematic and damaging conceptions of the freedom of the individual—what he calls seeing and using others without thinking about living with others. It is, rather, a politics of singularity that presents an ethics of freedom. This is also the reason why the notion of idiorrhythmy is important in the context of Creeley's sense of community. The tension between here and elsewhere, between the solitary I and the necessity for a collective organization is a constant preoccupation: "the common isn't really the collective. That's like the Lonely Crowd: you can certainly collect a lot of people, and find them adamantly—and find *oneself* among them adamantly—isolated." [13]

Creeley practiced such modes of living together with his fellow poets and friends. Although in hindsight he is constantly grouped with such important poets as Olson, Duncan, and Ginsberg, he regarded widespread notions of their community as false.

> All the persons were not ever really together with one another. I remember in Vancouver a couple of years ago, Charles [Olson] or Robert [Duncan] or somebody said, gee, this is the first time that we've all been together. It was really the first time in our lives that the three of us were present at the same time.... Olson I'd known at Black Mountain. But I mean we *weren't* a nucleus geographically ever. [14]

Creeley repeatedly argued in interviews that he didn't wish to push a global political vision in his poetry and that his poetry was not activist, however the note to *Hello* as well as his conception of idiorrhythmy in general make apparent his subtle sense of a broader political concern: his life choices, his teaching, and his thinking about and around other forms of educational institutions foster what he calls "that unimaginable *plural* of I." [15]

RETHINKING TEACHING INSTITUTIONS

CREELEY HAD AVOWED unorthodox views about teaching. Not only were they congruent with his complex and plural notion of idiorrhythmic communities but they were intrinsincally linked to his practice of here and elsewhere. Indeed, when teaching with what he called the "lovely company" of Black Mountain, he would come and go, just like Olson. Even when he started teaching in Buffalo, he would teach a semester and then leave to teach at the University of New Mexico. The British scholar Peter Middleton, who was a TA in Buffalo in 1977, recalls: "he only spent half the year [in Buffalo]. In the spring he disappeared off to Albuquerque."[16] But these constant movements were not just a means of escaping the institutional constraints of universities, it was also part and parcel of his thinking about teaching. He would make the point that the geographies of teaching are not just those of a stable here and now, that the possibility of an elsewhere was crucial to teaching: "it's ... interesting to demonstrate that ... this activity of coming and going is relevant to education."[17] Talking to John Sinclair and Robin Eichele, he refers to Alex Trocchi's project of a "spontaneous university," and discusses a new form of college.[18]

> This college that we had in mind was as viable and as momentary and as moving as the fact that people moved around in their lives. The different attentions at different moments in time. So it was a place to *go*. [He then refers to the Vancouver conference.] It really was that place we were talking about apropos this conference: a place to go sit down when you wanted to and we weren't limited: people were always drifting through, coming back, coming for the first time.[19]

These movements in an educational context are pitted against "the problem that [contemporary education] has an increasingly static or unwieldy *location*."[20] However, the fantasy of an idiorrhythmic community and Creeley's escape from static academic institutions doesn't mean that he didn't have an intrinsic sense of place or of the local. Indeed, his sense of idiorrhythmy and of other forms of higher education led to his developing a new *rapport* with the community in Buffalo, both local and distant.

In his poem "July: Fargo Street"—Fargo Street was one of his addresses in Buffalo—which he collected just after his poem "Neighbors," he writes,

> respite from work
> for all these
> surrounding neighbors.[21]

It appears that rather than keeping a tight community separated from the rest of the city, as in Black Mountain, Creeley tried to do something different with the neighborhood in Buffalo; he tried to create what one might call an "elastic community." One of his former student recalls,

> If waterfront workers once objected to academics and students disrupting their home, Creeley's reading in their bars and raising his newborn child in their neighborhood have convinced many that we too are indeed living in Buffalo and wished that "there be commerce between us."[22]

Of course, poetry in Buffalo didn't happen because of Creeley only. Charles Abbott, the founder of the Poetry Collection was key, as was Albert Cook, professor of comparative literature and poet who came to the University at Buffalo English Department in 1963 and who, according to Mac Hammond, "made it possible for professors to become poets here in Buffalo."[23] Yet, with his idiosyncratic understanding of place, Creeley established new relations with the city at large and created a reading series at the Albright Knox Art Gallery with readings on Sunday afternoons, as well as the "Walking the Dog" series on campus. He also subsidized student magazines. He thus spent his David Gray Professor endowment in order to weave poetry into the city. Robert Basil calls this "unselfconscious diplomacy."[24] Middleton goes a little further, speaking of Creeley doing much of the politicking behind the establishment and continuation of the Poetics Program.[25] Such attempts to affect events are apparent in a letter to Charles Bernstein dated March 30, 1990, a

year before the founding of the Poetics Program and while Susan Howe
was in the process of being hired. Creeley asks Bernstein to "let go a
few innuendos apropos" to their preference for Howe over another can-
didate.[26] What made the Poetics Program initially so successful was its
mix of idiosyncratic personalities and Bernstein's unflagging intellectual,
poetic, and generative energy, but the specificities of the Poetics Program
were also absolutely integral to Creeley's ethos as a poet and a teacher.[27]

In fact, Creeley taught in diverse contexts before Buffalo: first at
Black Mountain College (in 1954 and in 1955), and although recent
studies have qualified the perception of Black Mountain as a cohesive,
utopian community of teachers and students, Creeley's experience there
shaped the myth of that utopian noninstitutional place for teaching, and
the myth lasted throughout his life.[28] Creeley's movement among uni-
versities (first to New Mexico, then to Vancouver, then to New Mexico
again, and then intermittently to Buffalo and New Mexico) reflected his
need for change as well as his dissatisfaction with the traditional university
models. In a 1962 letter to Irving Layton he explains: "I suppose the one
continuing criticism I do have of the academic, is that it literally wastes
time, so much of it, day after day, with the speciousness of 'forms' always
taking precedent over what is elsewise to be said." [29] And although he saw
the university as a potential "center for energy," in another letter to his
friend dated January 23, 1963, he adds, "If you hire a plumber you DO
NOT expect him to fix the TV, and if you hire a writer, you MIGHT use
him CLEARLY in that capacity." [30]

Because he disapproved of conventional models, he also tried to
act in ways that put his ideas to the test, which led him to associate with
or create events and programs such as the Vancouver Poetry Conference
in 1963 and the Poetics Program. Middleton notes that Creeley cre-
ated "scenes of instructions," by which he means that Creeley "was an
outstanding teacher of an unusual kind, that his teaching room was
the stanza, and his discourse." [31] From his Black Mountain days (when
he was already a well-known poet and prose writer) to his Buffalo days
(when he had become "the poetic equivalent of a rock star") some stu-
dents recall being disconcerted, or dissatisfied, with Creeley's teaching

style, while others recall being enthused.[32] In keeping with his days at Black Mountain, his teaching was not didactic or academic, it was an open-ended project or, as Middleton recalls, "an endlessly deferred resolution." [33] This doesn't mean that his teaching was self-indulgently weak; the strengths of his speaking are evident from his talks on Pennsound.[34] Elizabeth Willis, who was a student at the University of Buffalo just before the Poetics Program started, puts it beautifully.

> Bob's approach was not to succumb to institutionalized thinking but to use the institution as a tool to make other things happen. Not to be changed by the institution but to change *it*. He's a perfect example of a poet who worked within the academy without being *of* it. In many ways he was the opposite of an "academic" poet—it was never the site of his authority as an artist.[35]

Teaching was a risk Creeley enjoyed taking.[36]

These unorthodox views about teaching institutions helped inspire the founding of the Poetics Program in Buffalo. As former student of the Poetics Program Peter Gizzi claims,

> On the Black Mountain model, he was more interested in bending institutions to support poetry. That was one of his labors. Teaching at Buffalo was less Romantic on the surface than driving an ambulance in the Second World War or chicken farming (Bob's first career!) or living on the cheap in Mallorca and writing fiction, as he did in the 50s, or even teaching at Black Mountain. But it was no less bold a gesture and speaks to the persistence of his self-determination. He made that inhospitable landscape thrive for nearly 40 years, eventually bringing in Susan Howe and Charles Bernstein. He and his beloved Penelope made their home a locating center for generations of poets.[37]

Creeley's teaching experiences, which took place in "diverse contexts," helped to create the enduring personal myths regarding community and teaching that paved the way for him to contribute to the invention of the model of the Poetics Program. For him teaching was not disconnected from all the other forms of intervention in the public and private spheres. In a way his project as a teacher and a poet was always about rethinking modes of living together. Or, to put it in the terms of my argument, his idiorrhythmy allowed him to create what he himself called "a terrific company."[38]

ELSEWHERE: TRANSNATIONAL GHOSTS

COMING BACK to the "old / question" of the emergence of the ghost in the here and now, phantoms can be generous and generative. Indeed, *phantom* is a cognate of *fantasme*, fantasy: literature is peopled with ghosts that we try to have conversations with. Creeley's reception in France and the UK has to do with this productive spectrality. For one thing, Creeley's reception depended on translations and appropriations, which were not as widespread as with other poets and yet he is decidedly present in the French poetic landscape. Creeley's poetry has been translated into French by poets Jean-Paul Auxeméry, Stéphane Bouquet, Martin Richet, and, most consistently, by a poet of an older generation than Bouquet and Richet: Jean Daive.[39] Daive's translations explain why, until recently, translations of Creeley's work could be understood as appropriations, in so far as Daive fantasized the correspondences between his work and that of Creeley.[40] Comprised of an essay, translations, and a poetic response to Creeley's work, Jean Daive's contributions gathered in the twelfth issue of *Formes poétiques contemporaines* show an example of such appropriation.[41] More recently, a striking example of the transnational disseminations of Creeley's work is the poetic essay in English that the California poet Robert Grenier wrote as a response to Martin Richet's French translation of Creeley's work. Grenier's publication couldn't appear as a preface to the translation for lack of space in the volume; instead it appeared subsequently in the Brazilian online journal *Sibila*.[42] Another example of such striking transnational circulations typical of Creeley's sense of community is that meeting the young Jonathan Skinner in "the doorway of the Village Voice Bookshop in Paris, [Creeley stuck] his phone number in [Skinner's] shirt pocket, saying come to Buffalo."[43] Skinner did attend the Poetics Program and then got a PhD there.

It is my contention here that Creeley's conceptions of community, idiorrhythmy, and teaching were among the elements that made transnational circulations possible, and that the dissemination of ideas of the Poetics Program is germane to the thinking that I expose above. In particular, what Creeley, among others, contributed to by campaigning for teachers and thinkers such as Howe and Bernstein was the basis for the development of links with France, which one sees in the recurring invitation of French poets to teach and read in Buffalo, starting with Christian Prigent in 1993, and Anne Portugal and Olivier Cadiot in 1994; the first Poetics Program French Poetry Festival occurred in 1995, with Hocquard, Claude Royet-Journoud, Jacqueline Risset, Jean Frémon, Michel Deguy, and many more. Most of these readings can be listened to on the Pennsound website.[44] In his introduction to the first Poetics Program French Poetry Festival, Raymond Federman argues that bringing over French poets is an attempt to "connect more closely French poetry, French poetic theory and what we are doing here in Buffalo and in America . . . to try to bridge the gap not only of poetry but of language."[45]

The bridge took many forms: material and immaterial, and the digital medium was one of these bridges. Indeed, Creeley's picking up e-mail and fax and technologies early was one of the vectors facilitating the technological dissemination of poetry via the Poetics Program, which Elizabeth Willis confirms: "He was way ahead of me in his interest in electronic media. It seems to me it was an affinity he and Charles shared (rather than something one transmitted to the other)."[46] One of the logical echoes of this interest was the founding of the the Electronic Poetry Center (EPC) in 1995, by Bernstein and librarian and UB PhD student Loss Pequeño Glazier.[47] The EPC continues to be a decisive resource for people like myself, who need to keep track of (or bridge the gap between) what was being done in the United States and our distant situations. The British poet and scholar Redell Olsen recently confirmed its ongoing importance: "I also used and still do the EPC—which really changed what it was possible for me to teach in a classroom." [48] Although Creeley didn't have anything to do with founding the EPC directly, this web platform can be seen as a continuation of his particular sense of dissemination and ideal of making things happen not just in one place or space. For many years, the connection between the EPC and France was not just the resource it provided to researchers, translators, and readers (thus extending Creeley's idea of "company"), the EPC also hosted—and still does—the website of the French nonprofit organization Un Bureau sur l'Atlantique. [49] These interrelations were prepared, announced, and made possible by the legacy of Creeley's sense of poetic communities. The Poetics Program created powerful bridges with France by hosting some of its prominent writers and by promoting the dissemination of contemporary French poetry on U.S. soil. [50] Conversely, or as a result, the ideas of the Poetics Program percolated in France either directly or in retrospect, such as with the Centre d'Etudes Poétiques (CEP) or the research program Poets and Critics. [51]

Although Creeley's translation and appropriation by French poets and the dissemination of the Poetics Program in France have generated productive fantasmatic relations, the situation is slightly different in the UK. Both Creeley and the Poetics Program have had a more tangible presence there, partly because the awareness of what went on in American Poetry from the 1950s to now is much greater and more detailed among poetry specialists and poets in the UK than in France.

Middleton went to Buffalo before the founding of the Poetics Program and returned afterward. He recalls how vital both Creeley and the Poetics Program have been to his sense of teaching. [52] Redell Olsen, a much younger scholar, poet, and performer, also speaks of how American poetry and the poetics of Buffalo poets (Howe, Bernstein, and others) were instrumental in her sense of both how she conceives her poetic work and how she built the influential MA in Poetics Practice at Royal Holloway. In an e-mail interview, she says,

It is true the poetics program at Buffalo was very important to my thinking of how to design the MA in Poetic Practice at Royal Holloway. I visited there in 1998/9 to do work for my PhD thesis: Scriptovisualities: Contemporary Women Writers and the Visual Arts. I got a travel grant to go from the University and I worked in the library on the journal 0-9 and early photocopies of How(ever) magazine. I would have liked to go there as a PhD student myself but didn't have the funds. I really wished that I could have worked with Charles Bernstein, Susan Howe and Robert Creeley and been their student. I was reading everything I could by LANGUAGE writers and I just thought Buffalo sounded like an amazing place to be.[53]

These remarks suggest that the Poetics Program is less of a fantasmatic and spectral reality in the UK than in France and more of a direct influence. Zoë Skoulding, a UK poet and critic, confirms its significant influence: "the wide-ranging theoretical enquiry of the [Buffalo] Poetics Program is an influence on many of the PhDs I have subsequently supervised and examined across the UK."[54]

In "Some Sense of Commonplace," Creeley himself wrote,[55] You're not talking about the experiential fact of how people come together, or what their imaginations of the place then become. . . . There's an insistent presence of diversity, and yet it excludes nothing, you know, because everything's related.

If studied in terms of his thinking about the potentialities of "here" and "elsewhere," Creeley's apparent ambivalence about teaching is not so much an ambivalence as a clear idea of what he wanted and what he disliked. His sense of teaching was staunchly linked to wider notions of community and dissemination. Indeed, to him teaching was a serious matter. He strove for alternative forms of educational communities, defined not just by their presence in the same locality, but by the dialectics between here and elsewhere. In a wish to further ways of living together that allowed people to keep their ethics of freedom as well as their relatedness, Creeley pushed for singular forms of community or, to quote Barthes again on the notion of idiorrhythmy, for a "socialism of distances."

The circulation of ideas of teaching and community is a fundamental part of the transatlantic exchanges in poetics, poetry, and critical thinking about poetry, and the basis for such circulation goes back to ideas and practice developed by Creeley, together with others at Buffalo, through the auspices of the Poetics Program. Of course, to some, these ideas might seem marginal, but such marginality creates the conditions for thinking alternative spaces that are both inscribed within the institution and challenge some of its reified and reifying forms. As far as teaching goes, Creeley's legacy is multifaceted. Its dissemination transnationally cannot be analyzed simplistically as direct influence or appropriation, for exchanges and cross-pollination never entirely happen that way. Cultural transfers take unexpected byroads and detours, sometimes unforeseen deferred temporalities. As has been the case with Robert Creeley's poetry and the Buffalo Poetics Program in France, they happen on the fantasmatic, even on the phantomatic level.

NOTES

1. Creeley, "Window," *Windows*, 33–38. This article is an expanded and restructured version of a talk given at the University of Buffalo and published in *Formes Poétiques Contemporaines* 12 (2016) as "Circulations in the USA, France and the UK, Notes on Robert Creeley's Teaching and the Poetics Program." I wish to thank Professor Jean-Jacques Thomas for allowing me to republish this article in a different version.

2. William Shakespeare, *Hamlet*, eds. Ann Thompson and Neil Taylor, "Bloomsbury Arden Shakespeare" (London: Bloomsbury, 2006), 147n1.1 and n1.2.

3. Creeley, "Place," *Windows*, 39. The tension between "here" and "there" is the subject of "Here, for Bob Creeley," an e-poem that Loss Pequeño Glazier wrote as a tribute to Robert Creeley, in *RIF/T* 06 (Fall 1997). http://wings. buffalo.edu/epc/rift/rift06/rift0601.html.

4. The Poetics Program in Buffalo was founded in 1991 by Robert Creeley and a younger generation of poets and scholars such as Charles Bernstein, Susan Howe, Dennis Tedlock, and Raymond Federman, with Creeley as its first director. The program has acquired an extraordinary reputation in North America as well as in Europe, where, as I shall argue, it has the status of a fantastic and fantasmatic model.

5. Roland Barthes, *How to Live Together*, trans. Kate Briggs (New York, Columbia University Press, 2012), 6.

6. Creeley, *Contexts of Poetry: Interviews 1961–1971*, ed. Donald Allen (Bolinas: Four Seasons Foundation, 1973), 119.

7. Creeley, "Some Senses of the Commonplace," in Tom Clark, *Robert Creeley and the Genius of the Commonplace* (New York: New Directions, 1993), 89.

8. Creeley, "A Note," *Hello: A Journal, February 29–May 3, 1976*, in Robert Creeley, *So There: Poems 1976–83* (New York: New Directions, 1998), 86.

9. In the order he visited them and mentions them in *Hello*: Fiji, New Zealand, Australia, Singapore, The Philippines, Malaysia, Hong Kong, Tokyo, South Korea.

10. Ibid.

11. "I found that other cultural patterns, be they Samoan, Chinese, Malaysian, or Filipino, could not easily think of one as singular, and such familiar concepts as the 'nuclear family' or 'alienation' had literally to be translated for them." All references Ibid.

12. Ibid.

13. Creeley, "Some Senses of the Commonplace," 110.

14. Creeley, "John Sinclair and Robin Eichele: An Interview with Robert Creeley," in Creeley, *Contexts of Poetry: Interviews 1961–1971*, 68.

15. Creeley presents his political stance in relation to writing, for instance, in a 1969 interview: "I don't see that art and politics, or that order of present experience involved with the post-political, should all be kept separate. I don't see how they can be. One can't, perhaps, entirely respect an art committed to propagandizing or to a use of life not clearly initiated in its own activity. But when men and women are outraged by political malfeasance, it's hardly likely that their art will not make that quite clear. As far as my own work

is concerned—I've not been able to write directly to a purpose of political involvement. It's not given to me in my own nature to be able to do so, but I hope that I've made clear where I stood nonetheless." Robert Creeley, *Collected Prose* (Berkeley: University of California Press, 1989), 517–18. See also Peter Middleton, "Scenes of Instruction: Robert Creeley's Reflexive Poetics," in Steve McCaffery and Stephen Fredman eds., *Form, Power, and Person in Robert Creeley's Life and Work* (Iowa City: Iowa University Press, 2010), 159–80.

16. Middleton, e-mail interview conducted by Vincent Broqua, February 21, 2016.

17. Creeley, "John Sinclair and Robin Eichele: An Interview with Robert Creeley," 68.

18. Ibid.

19. Ibid., 69.

20. Ibid., 68.

21. Creeley, "Neighbors" and "July: Fargo Street," *So There. Poems 1976–83*, 130 and 131, respectively.

22. Robert Basil, "Creeley Teaches in Buffalo," in ed. Carroll F. Terrel, *Robert Creeley: The Poet's Workshop* (Orono: The National Poetry Foundation/ University of Maine at Orono, 1984), 302.

23. Cynthia Kimball and Taylor Brady, "Poetry & Poetics at Buffalo: A Timeline 1960–1990," in Nick Lawrence and Alisa Messer, eds., *Chloroform: An Aesthetics of Critical Writing* (Buffalo: Chloroform, 1997), 239.

24. Basil, "Creeley Teaches in Buffalo," 302.

25. Middleton, e-mail interview conducted by Vincent Broqua, February 21, 2016.

26. Creeley, *The Selected Letters of Robert Creeley*, eds. Peter Baker, Kaplan Harris, and Rod Smith (Berkeley, Los Angeles, London: University of California Press, 2014), 383.

27. For instance, in his first days at Black Mountain College, where he taught small classes, he sent a letter to his wife Ann: "teach them writing, what is that?" (Ekbert Faas, *Robert Creeley: A Biography*, Hanover and London: University Press of New England, 2001, 154). This conception later affected the Poetics Program's emphasis on "teaching reading rather than creative

writing" (Susan M. Schultz, "Poetics at Buffalo," *Jacket* 1 (October 1997). http://jacketmagazine.com/01/schultzbuffalo.html).

28. See Martin Duberman, *Black Mountain: An Exploration in Community* (New York: Dutton, 1972); Eugen Blume and Gabriele Knapstein eds., *Black Mountain: An Interdisciplinary Experiment (1993–1957)* (Leipzig: Spector Books, 2015); or Jean-Pierre Cometti and Eric Giraud eds., *Black Mountain College: Art, démocratie, utopie* (Rennes: Presses Universitaires de Rennes/ Centre International de Poésie Marseille, 2014).

29. Irving Layton and Robert Creeley, *The Complete Correspondence, 1953–1978*, eds. Ekbert Faas and Sabrina Reed (Montreal & Kingston: McGill-Queen's University Press, 1990), 253.

30. Ibid., 255.

31. Middleton, "Scenes of Instruction: Robert Creeley's Reflexive Poetics," 159–80.

32. Smith, Baker, and Harris, "Editors' Introduction," in *The Selected Letters of Robert Creeley*, xxvii–xxxviii.

33. Middleton, "Scenes of Instruction."

34. See particularly the discussions at the 1963 Vancouver Conference: http://www.writing.upenn.edu/pennsound/x/Creeley.php.

35. Willis, e-mail interview conducted by Vincent Broqua, April 5, 2016.

36. See how Creeley speaks about experimenting in class in "Writing," an article about teaching, originally published in Jonathan Baumback's *Writers as Teachers/Teachers as Writers* (New York: Holt, Rinehart, and Winston, 1970): "First of all, begin with what's there—by which I mean, the literal fact of the people. You can ask them 'what they want to do' and may well get the answer, 'nothing'—but that's enough, i.e., push that, 'what is that state of activity,' or literally *do* nothing, if that is chosen as the state of possibility" (Creeley, *Collected Prose*, 525). His advocacy for an open-ended form of teaching is in keeping with the definition and etymology of experimentalism, both referring to open-ended forms and risk taking.

37. Peter Gizzi, "Robert Creeley, 1926–2005," *St. Mark's Poetry Project Newsletter* (August 1, 2005).

38. Kimball and Brady, "Poetry & Poetics at Buffalo: A Timeline 1960–1990," 238.

39. Creeley, *Echos*, trans. Jean-Paul Auxeméry (Bordeaux: Un bureau sur l'atlantique, 1995); *La fin: poèmes*, trans. Jean Daive (Paris: Gallimard, 1997); *Le sortilège*, trans. Stéphane Bouquet (Caen: Nous, 2006); *Là: poèmes, 1968–1975*, trans. Martin Richet (Geneva: Héros-Limite, 2010); *Dire cela*, trans. Jean Daive (Caen: Nous, 2014).

40. On Creeley's reception among French poets and translators, see Abigail Lang, "Creeley's Reception in France," *Formes poétiques contemporaines*, 12 (2015–2016): 113–30.

41. Daive, *Formes poétiques contemporaines*, 12 (2015–2016): 131–80.

42. Robert Grenier, "A TESTAMENT (Martin Richet / Robert Creeley, 'Figure of Outward')," http://sibila.com.br/english/ro bert-grenier/3842.

43. Jonathan Skinner in *Remembering Creeley*, http://www.buffalo.edu/ cas/english/graduate/poetics/PoeticsResources.html.

44. A great number of recorded readings in Buffalo are available at the following address: http://writing.upenn.edu/pennsound/x/ Buffalo.php.

45. My transcription of Raymond Federman's introduction to Olivier Cadiot and Anne Portugal's reading (November 16, 1994). http://writing. upenn.edu/pennsound/x/Buffalo.php.

46. Willis, e-mail interview conducted by Vincent Broqua, March 5, 2016.

47. Loss Glazier was a Librarian at UB and then enrolled in the PhD program in the early 1990s. His dissertation ("The Electronic Poetry Center: A Poetics of the Web"), which he defended in 1996, was supervised by Charles Bernstein. Among others, Creeley was on his committee. Around the 2000s Glazier was appointed assistant professor in Media Studies at UB. He is now a full professor there. I thank Charles Bernstein for this note.

48. Redell Olsen, e-mail interview conducted by Vincent Broqua, March 28, 2016.

49. Founded in 1989 by the French Poet Emmanuel Hocquard, Un bureau sur l'Atlantique is one of the crucial organizations in the translatlantic poetic relations of the last twenty-five years. Its founder describes the aim of the association as furthering "the knowledge of American contemporary poetry in France." (http://epc.buffalo.edu/orgs/bureau/presentation_a.html.)

50. The structure of the Poetics Program made it possible for younger generations of students on both sides of the Atlantic to further the discussion

between American and French Poetry. Poets such as Kristin Prevallet, Alan Gilbert, Peter Gizzi, Jena Osman, or Jonathan Skinner and many others are all related to French poetry in vast ways.

51. For a more detailed account of the relevance of the Poetics Program to the CEP and to "Poets and Critics," see Broqua, "Circulations in the USA, France and the UK, Notes on Robert Creeley's Teaching and the Poetics Program."

52. Middleton, e-mail interview conducted by Vincent Broqua, February 21, 2016.

53. Olsen, e-mail interview conducted by Vincent Broqua.

54. Zoë Skoulding, e-mail interview conducted by Vincent Broqua, March 27–April 3rd, 2016.

55. Creeley, "Some Senses of the Commonplace," 89.

Constructive Alterities
& the Agonistic Feminine

Joan Retallack

> Antigone: I stand convicted of impiety,
> the evidence, my pious duty done . . .
>
> Chorus: The same tempest of mind
> as ever, controls the girl.
>
> —Sophocles, *Antigone*

I

THE FIRST HALF of my title is aspirational; the second half, conjectural and conversational. Conversational with others, but also among the importantly divergent logics of poetry and discourse, discourse and essay. Decades ago, skeptical about the force of a woman-centered feminist theory whose reactive stance seemed to corroborate the secondary status of the feminine in an age-old M/F binary, I was struck—in a sense, saved—by the idea of a fluidly gendered, transgenre, transgressive *experimental* feminine principle, rooted in female experience but integral to all struggles (ethical and aesthetic) with the cultural coercions of masculine hegemony. At the time I was in the process of writing "Rethinking Literary Feminism: Three Essays onto Shaky Grounds" in response to an invitation from scholars Lynn Keller and Cristanne Miller for their collection *Feminist Measures: Soundings in Poetry and Theory*.[1] What I have particularly valued about the dialogic contexts that essay collections, conferences, and panels in poetry and poetics create is the targeted forms of experimental writing they can encourage. At their best they set scenes for seriously playful work: intellectual and imaginative thought experiments and wagers.

Thinking from the perspective of the modernist rejection of transcendental romanticism, Theodor Adorno noted that "the unresolved antagonisms of reality reappear in art in the guise of immanent problems of artistic form." [2] The major "antagonism" of interest was between ideologically based "official thought" and the freedom and independence of mind necessary for creativity. Looking for a discursive form that could, like certain poetries, resist (in my view, implicitly masculine, specifically patriarchal) "official thought," particularly in Germany, Adorno argued on behalf of the exploratory essay in the French tradition. His characterization of it could serve as a description of an agonistic poetics of the experimental feminine at odds with the patriarchal "law of the father," as Jacques Lacan and others—after Freud—have put it. The productively contentious agency of the experimental feminine gives it a dialogic expansiveness that allies it with *queer* values and interventions—along with those of any other group (Blacks in the U.S., Palestinians in Israel and the occupied territories) cast into shadow realms of alterity by a self-reinforcing status quo. Try substituting *feminine* for *essay* in the following assertion by Adorno:

> Emancipation from the compulsion of identity gives the essay something that eludes official thought ... The essay's innermost formal law is heresy. Through violations of the orthodoxy of thought, something in the object becomes visible which it is orthodoxy's secret and objective aim to keep invisible. [3]

In the midst of complex global crises, including dire threats associated with climate change; in recognition of a contingent futurity shared by all us creatures of the self-organizing genius of evolution; in grave, and necessarily humorous consideration of our anthropo*scenes*, anthropo*scenities*; carried along by historical developments that continue to be dominated by default male values—I must continue to query what has been / is / can be the agonistic efficacy of experimental feminine dynamics. This question is all the more necessary to the extent that it eludes simple answers, even as it wagers on the constructive alterity of feminine agency.

2

THE CONSCIOUSNESS that led scientists to coin the term Anthropocene is an ethically illuminated act of scientific poesis.[4] How should we construe the anthropos that is propelling earth's biosphere toward possible catastrophe? Anthropos, a male-gendered ancient Greek word now translated as "human" but originally, quite specifically, "man," is a remnant of a time when men and women were considered members of different species. Woman, lacking logos (the rational principle) could not be a citizen of the polis. Her nature, like that of animals and earth, required taming, domestication—subordination to the rationally creative forces of "masculinity." (This, of course, is not just ancient history. Think of the struggle for women's suffrage that continued into the twentieth century and is still not a global right.[5]) Alexander the Great remains the prototype of heroic masculine accomplishment—brilliant strategist of large-scale taming and domestication that may require slaughtering tens of thousands to create and sustain colonial empires. One might reasonably feel that the anthropos in "Anthropocene" is still properly "man."

Pierre Bourdieu coined the term habitus for the consciously and unconsciously supported status quo that persists in every society, often against its own best interests. He came to identify its psychological and sociopolitical intricacies with self-perpetuating masculine power.[6] In *The Logic of Practice*, Bourdieu describes in detail how beliefs connected with the dominance of male values are choreographed into the stance and movement of male and female bodies in relation to each other and to a natural world itself "naturalized" by the cultural belief system. Although his analysis is primarily focused on the Kabyle, ethnic Berbers in Northern Algeria, he finds the same phenomenon in European society, "as if the *habitus* forged coherence and necessity out of accident and contingency."[7]

> The *habitus* tends to generate all the 'reasonable,' 'commonsense' behaviours (and only these) which are possible within the limits of these regularities, and which are likely to be positively sanctioned because they are objectively adjusted to the logic characteristic of a particular field, whose objective future they anticipate. At the same time, 'without violence, art or argument,' it tends to exclude all 'extravagances' ('not for the likes of us').[8]

Might excluded "extravagances" include an excess of the feminine erupting beyond acceptable decorum, threatening the rule of masculine defined propriety? This happens frequently in Greek tragedy. In other contexts it's been associated with the devil, witchcraft, perversion, feminism. Feminism, after being reviled, went through a period of domestication—programs and departments in academic institutions where docile enough bodies could climb career ladders the better to never erupt again. Now it's gone back to being widely reviled—albeit, less vociferously— subtextually. Generic male pronouns are undergoing something like the return of the repressed in the moderately intellectual media. On the matter of grammatical habitus, Gertrude Stein is brilliant: "All these sentences are fruitful they may be included in embroidery." "A sentence is very manly they need not be nervous."[9] Noting that *alterity* and *alternative* are cognate but not identical, for alterity to become alternative it must be agonistically transvalued and embraced. An agonistic feminine is a necessary extravagance for the ethos, logos, pathos of our culture to exceed the dreary fatalism of Man and His perpetual lust for conquest, Man and His self-aggrandizing orthodoxies.[10] What violence, art, or argument can help in this global labyrinth of complicit words and dubious values? Why is it that "Father Nature" and "Mother Time" just don't sound right? Why is it that white male privilege is still the default?

Even before I mentioned "docile bodies," you may have noticed how close Bourdieu's "choreography" is to Foucault's revelatory analysis of "methods, which made possible the meticulous control of the operations of the body, which assured the constant subjection of its forces and imposed upon them a relation of docility-utility ... coercions that act upon the body, a calculated manipulation of its elements, its gestures, its behaviour. The human body was entering a machinery of power that explores it, breaks it down and rearranges it." [11] Foucault claims that this intense focus on manipulating bodies for sociopolitical purposes was an invention of seventeenth- and eighteenth-century French society in search of the "ideal figure of the soldier." Although he enlarges the scope to include authoritarian pedagogy, male micromanagement of female dress and demeanor—perhaps the most distinctive and universal signature of masculine power—goes unremarked. Not entirely surprising. Foucault's privileging of the masculine in his readings of history, consonant with ancient Greek glorification of the male body and logos can prevent him from noticing implications everywhere in his purview—in the positioning of the female on Greek vases, for instance, or the culture of Parisian couture. In fact, would the "Maid of Orleans" have been burned at the stake had she merely heard voices, not refused women's dress? But Foucault's docile body analysis is importantly instructive with respect to traditions of masculinity. Take the trajectory of "Man-the-Machine": man designs the machine, runs the machine, becomes the machine. The feminine must not interfere. [12]

Fillippo Tommaso Marinetti provides a Futurist advance release postscript underscoring the link between misogyny and violence.

> *We will glorify war*—the world's only hygiene—militarism, patriotism, the destructive gesture of freedom-bringers, beautiful ideas worth dying for, *and scorn for woman*. We will destroy the museums, libraries, academies of every kind, will fight moralism, feminism, every opportunistic or utilitarian cowardice.
>
> —Manifesto of Futurism, 1909

3
A BRIEF POST-HELLENIC, PRE-POST FUTURIST
HISTORY OF BEING SCHE

Keywords: *Alteritas, Alterity*

HERE ARE SOME "first usage" examples from the *Middle English Dictionary* (MED) and the *Oxford English Dictionary* (*OED*). Together they construct a Garden of Etymologies yielding the originary female transgression against "the law of the father": Male God, Patriarchal Man in His image. Many of us like to think *sche* revolted against enforced ignorance with her valiant act of curiosity. (Noteworthy coincidence? *Curiositas* became an official sin in the early Christian church around the time Augustine was struggling with his lust for women.)

> c.1415. *Alterity:* oþerhed(e) (n.) Old English version of "otherhood" or perhaps "otherhead." A state of being different from one another (existing between two beings who have been in harmony), a separateness; also, an otherness, a difference.
>
> —*MED*

> c. 1425. Alteritas: oþerhed. from *Speculum Sacerdotale*: When he is ded, þenne owe belles to be rongen . . . for a womman twyes. Why? For sche made an alterite and an oþerhede in that tyme that sche made alienacion and partynge bitwene God and man.
> —*MED, OED*[13]

> 1631. R. Fludd *Answer vnto M. Foster* iii. vi. 50 They are called Alteritas or Alterity, that is, composed of two. And the two are Male and Female, Adam & Eve.

Further Usage

Keyword: Wont

Women whisper among themselves as industrious insects
are *wont* to do. *Wont*—chronically conjoined to *yielding*
and *bestow.*

> *yeldyng* therof to the chief lordis dewe
> as sche was *wont* all *yeldyng* to *bestow*
> uthir service that on theyr frutys dew
> was *wont* to fal his good dame
> was *wont* to *bestow* the best roome
> in here house on him who here did lay
> his *wonts* uppon here *yeldyng* brestes[14]

The History of Being Sche   Never Uncomplicated

> Eve: beautiful woman—
> I have seen her
> when she was so handsome
> she gave me a start,
> able to write simultaneously
> in three languages—
> English, German and French—
> and talk in the meantime;
> equally positive in demanding a commotion
> and in stipulating quiet:
>
> . . .
>
> 'See her, see her in this common world,'
> the central flaw . . .
>
> —Marianne Moore, "Marriage" [15]

4

DOES FOCUS ON *anthropos, man, s(c)he, woman, female, male, feminine, masculine, nature,* and *culture* imply that this M/F business is primarily a matter of language? It does, because language is the most consequential form of human life in the biocultural world. *Female/male* and *nature/ culture* are venerable binaries daily negotiated in "metaphors we live by," and they are stunningly interrogated by Sherry Ortner in her 1972 essay "Is Female to Male as Nature Is to Culture?" [16] The relevance of Ortner's anthropological question endures globally in patriarchal societies where the female-identified, like *nature* "herself," is treated as proprietary resource to be exploited/disposed of for the benefit of largely male values embedded in material and symbolic power structures. But it's important to keep in mind that binaries defined in *oppositional* terms are themselves naturalized constructs. I'd like to suggest a rethinking of Ortner's interrogative hypothesis by shifting the focus from female versus male (F/M) to the dynamics of *feminine* and *masculine* (F-M). The latter assumes that feminine and masculine traits are available to persons (and poetics) of all biocultural gender (and genre) variations.

There is inherent *antagonism* in binary constructs, or perhaps it's the other way around—a lurking binary in antagonistic dynamics. Antagonistic conflict is intended to end when a designated victor and vanquished emerge, often just a bit before the contest begins all over again. "Truce" is only temporary cessation of the conflict, by definition nontransformative of either side. This chronically repetitive dynamic is hardly a process of development. Binary terms—us/them, friend/enemy, neighbor/stranger, female/male, feminine/masculine—appear in ancient and contemporary documents and dictionaries frighteningly unmutated by historical experience.

> Recent entry: masculine, adj. having qualities or appearance traditionally associated with men, especially strength and aggressiveness. Antonym: feminine.
>
> —*New Oxford American Dictionary*, updated 2010.
> Preinstalled in all Mac OS X operating systems.

Binaries assume the logic of *dichotomy*—rigidly static opposition that, despite cultural construction theory, casts *feminine* and *masculine* (traits in persons of every gender) into realms of would-be biological constraint. Masculine and feminine—like Molière's prose and verse—are literally defined against one another. Hence, fear of the power of the feminine to create or uncreate the masculine contributes to the enduring substrate of misogyny in male-dominated cultures. The necessity of an "extravagant" agonistic feminine seems clear.

This brings on a revision of Ortner's hypothesis. Not to replace it—she is concerned with the universality of female subordination—but to think further about a poetics of the agonistic feminine in relation to entrenched masculine dynamics. Nature and culture—equally "naturalized"—are entirely interwoven in biocultural ecologies of complex systems dynamics. With the historical "Law of the Father" sacralized in major world religions that long ago inseminated secular assumptions, male-dominated cultures have contained (or tried to) the agonistic feminine—whether practiced by Antigone or Gertrude Stein or Adorno's heretical essayist (no doubt, male)—through ridicule, exclusion, or physical violence. That Stein is prominent in the modernist canon has not extinguished the ridicule; that Adorno doesn't seem to have written in emancipatory heretical forms himself—unless one counts the aphoristic *Minima Moralia* as tending in that direction—is instructive. It's hard to do because the collective sociopolitical mind is poised to misunderstand and/or delete. Which not so simply means that heretical forms are vital poethical wagers.

An *agonistic* poetics involves not binaries but generative polarities—with "in-between" energy fields. Mid-twentieth century, a staple binary inscribed in the book of Genesis—order versus disorder—was transvalued by a new logic, that of Chaos Theory. Scientists redefined "chaos" as a dynamic exchange *between* order and disorder, generative of the constantly changing pattern-bounded indeterminacy central to every complex system—from weather and other turbulent patterns in our biosphere to history, economics, the neurophysiology of the human brain and all other sufficiently complex systems. Disorder is no longer

an unspeakable disturbance of the logos. Without it there would be no
life on our planet.

Might the fate of F&M turn out to be an agonizingly long fairy
tale in which, after enduring countless hardships, many inflicted on one
another, they manage to embrace chaotic otherness and (together) face
a gorgeously foreboding sunset?

5
WHEN THE FAIRY TALE ENDED
WHAT HAPPENED TO MOTHER EARTH?

Jimbo's *Inferno*, Canto xx

BYOB. Soon it'll feel just like home. We're a DIY
kinda place but intellectuals have nothing to fear.
Note Zeno's redline arrow whiz out of frame while
remaining smartly in place. Everything's just as it
should be. Okay, three famous abstract nouns are
decomposing in the heat. No sweat. Just keep your
distance, turn up the A/C, pinch your nose. You're
in luck. You have arrived in the knickknack of time.
All knickknacks 50% off—all applications for ex-
tended credit fast-tracked. Jimbo's *Inferno* offers
more luxury benefits—yours to peruse from our
climate-proof VIP lounge—than any VIP club that
turned you down in the wretched life you clung
to far too long. We love you. You love us.
Love us or leave us—that's the deal. If, of course,
thou canst find thy way.

Coda
What wounds I see upon their limbs

ancient and recent seared and gougèd in

if thou escape from these dark places

and come to rebehold the beauteous stars,

shall it yet pleasure thee to say "I was"

to feel thy mind incline . . .

—Dante's *Inferno*, Canto xvi[17]

6

Human rights and emancipation movements . . . [have] fought valiantly against industrial capitalism's treatment of whole categories of our species as human sacrifice zones, no more deserving of rights than raw commodities. These struggles have . . . won major victories against the dominance-based paradigm—against slavery, for universal suffrage, for equality under the law . . . Karl Marx, for instance, recognized capitalism's "irreparable rift" with "the natural laws of life itself," while feminist scholars have long recognized that patriarchy's dual war against women's bodies and against the body of the earth were connected to that essential, corrosive [philosophical] separation between mind and body— and between body and earth—from which both the Scientific Revolution and Industrial Revolution sprang.

—Naomi Klein

IN *This Changes Everything: Capitalism vs. the Climate,* Naomi Klein criticizes the mostly male geoengineers who pledge a fix for climate change that won't dislodge any of our clearly implicated, heavily invested lifestyles and habits.[18] She quotes the MIT marine microbiologist Sallie Chisholm on what continues to be (from at least archaic Greek and other ancient cultures on) our human proclivity to assume a "feminized" (passive, compliant) nature that will always be, if not easily, inevitably outwitted by the masculine genius of our technologies. It's the ancient Promethean scenario with Klein and Chisholm among the contemporary Pandoras. Chisholm puts things this way:

> Proponents of research on geoengineering simply keep ignoring the fact that the biosphere is a player (not just a responder) in whatever we do, and its trajectory cannot be predicted. It is a living breathing collection of organisms (mostly microorganisms) that are evolving every second—a 'self-organizing, complex, adaptive system' (the strict term). These types of systems have emergent properties that simply cannot be predicted. (267)

Klein comments,

> I have been repeatedly struck by how the hard-won lessons about humility before nature that have reshaped modern science, particularly the fields of chaos and complexity theory, do not appear to have penetrated this particular bubble [of geoengineers]. On the contrary, the Geoclique is crammed with overconfident men prone to complimenting each other on their fearsome brainpower. (267)

Klein's use of the word *prone* is almost amusing. She has earlier discussed Francis Bacon's "vision of the Earth as a prone woman" and James (steam engine) Watts's triumphalism at having found her "weak side." Just a few examples among countless gendered metaphors we have lived by for millennia: earth as "mother" has been both reassuring and troubling—particularly when in mythology she is being furrowed and inseminated by the man with the phallic plow, or decapitated by mountain-topping machinery. One can see how easy it is for violence to be commonplace on either side of the female-earth metaphor, as the myth of Persephone's rape and interment starkly illustrates. Page duBois's *Sowing the Body: Psychoanalysis and Ancient Representations of Women* is full of such examples.[19] Life on the body of our planet today is full of such examples: from the violence of deforestation, strip-mining, and fracking, to the drug rape equivalent of chemicals poured into streams, and of course the partly buried monuments of frenetic consumerism—enormous landfills seeping toxins.

On a global scale neither poverty nor climate change is gender-neutral. Women tend to be economically destitute in most traditional and "developing" societies—cut off from control of the vital resources they manage daily for their families' survival. Intimate experience with natural resources of their regions makes them experts on the inroads of climate change, but that knowledge remains largely untapped even as they are disproportionately vulnerable to increasing droughts, wildfires, and floods. UN Women Watch reports point out that, with the children they are trying to save, women are most likely to die in natural disasters for reasons that touch every dimension of their lives. Traditional limitations in physical training as well as dress codes imposed for the sake of modesty can fatally restrict mobility when trying to escape rising waters, raging fires. The male/female dynamic of it all is (should be) alarming as the ancient entitlements of men to rape the women of their family, or of the conquered territory, endure. This, along with genital mutilation, widow burnings, and honor killings make Western women's multi-trillion-dollar compliance with male-regulated rules of attractiveness seem almost benign. *If* one forgets that the fashion industry's profit margin depends on "third world" para-slavery of girls and women who, out of economic desperation and in perilous conditions, make the garments, the stilettos, the plastic adornments, the cosmetics and facial cleansers whose by-products come to adorn every landfill and contaminate the waters of the earth. Approximately 96 percent of Fortune 500 CEOs steering us down this absurd road to planetary ruin are men. Why does "Father Nature" not sound right? Perhaps for the same reason that "Man and Nature" has a long history of seeming just fine.

> She says, 'Men are monopolists
> of "stars, garters, buttons
> and other shining baubles"—
> unfit to be the guardians
> of another person's happiness.'
> He says, 'These mummies
> must be handled carefully—
>
>   —Marianne Moore, "Marriage" [20]

7

Comparing man and woman generally, one may say
that woman would not have the genius for adornment,
if she had not the instinct for the *secondary* role.

> —Nietzsche, "Apophthegms and Interludes"

When you stopped preparing quotes from the
ancient misogynists it was clear that you would soon
forget my street.

> —Rosmarie Waldrop, "Facts"

Man is the measure of all things, including woman.

> —Addendum to Apocrypha, Author Unknown

ANCIENT GREEK and Judeo-Christian cultures have bestowed upon us
a potent legacy of alterities. Preeminent among them, from the patriar-
chal point of view, is the indelibly stained otherness (unknowability) of
woman. Although the philologic of female alterity is dualistic and should,
therefore, be reciprocal, it has been conceived as dramatically asymmetri-
cal. "Sche," Eve, the female, the feminine, the girl, the woman carrying
both the child and the original sin *is* alterity, not only in theological con-
texts but in philosophical traditions. Not surprising in Nietzsche who
generously distributed misogyny across the sexes: "In the background
of all their personal vanity, women themselves have still their imper-
sonal scorn—for 'woman.' "[21] But it is, at least initially, surprising in the
renowned ethical philosopher Emmanuel Levinas.

For graduate students in literary and cultural criticism, Levinas is
considered a source of primary importance for ethical theory and the con-
cept of alterity. Now and then I'm asked whether *poethics* is "Levinasian."
The short answer is no. The longer version is my strong disagreement
with the ethical implications of Levinas's asymmetrical formulation of
feminine alterity. In 1946–47 lectures published as *Time and the Other*,
Levinas locates the feminine as "absolute alterity" on a remarkable, quasi-

deductive continuum. Its arc begins with the overwhelming existential presence of death for the male subject (despite his philosophical prowess) and proceeds to a recovery of "futurity" accomplished by "the father," by means of the metaphysically ordained role of "the feminine." That role is remarkably, if not entirely, passive. Levinas has a worldview whose values are, like Foucault's, sourced from idealized masculine agency. Alterity is identified doubly—as the "mystery" of the feminine and the "mystery" of death, in disconcertingly close proximity. The value of the feminine, unlike death, is that it can be plucked from the shadows of alterity in which it dwells, for the sake of an eros that enables survival of the male ego—that is, the survival of civilization itself.

Levinas terms this process, this use of the feminine, "fecundity." Although fecundity requires the sexual activation of the feminine (the embodied *female* nowhere in sight), the creative force itself is not feminine. It is not *her* fecundity, not *her* maternity that Levinas is talking about. It is instead quite explicitly *his* paternity that ensures futurity via birth of "the son." In his identification with the father, it is the son who ensures the continuation of history. This legacy of paternity, lends value to the feminine as helpmeet to the great project of Man-and-God—Time's fruition in Civilization. Needless to say, this is a messianic vision in which the feminine will always be accessory to the great event. The messiah will never be a woman. Here are samples of Levinas's argument in his own words.

> It is thus not according to the category of cause, but according to the category of the father that freedom comes about and time is accomplished . . . I began with the notions of death and the feminine, and have ended with that of the son . . . Plato did not grasp the feminine in its specifically erotic notion.[22]

Can it really be that only the threat of death (extinction of the father's ego) legitimates the value of the feminine? That the highest significance of the feminine is vehicle of potentially messianic reproduction? The feminine/female contributes nothing to futurity in her own right?

The idea that "female is to male as nature is to culture" is deeply embedded in Levinas's theologically based ontology of sexuality and gender. The Aristotelian prototype of a secular ethical domain—one that can benefit from cultural change—is missing here. The feminine remains trapped in the mind of the "ancient misogynists" rationalizing her subjugation with turbulent philosophical rhetoric. The fundamentally reductive import of passages like these are awash in phantom eloquence.

> What is the alterity that does not purely and simply enter into the opposition of two species [male and female] of the same genus? I think the absolute contrary contrary (*le contraire absolument contraire*) whose contrariety is in no way affected by the relationship that can be established between it and its correlative, the contrariety that permits its terms to remain absolutely other, is the *feminine*. (LR, 48)[23]

Is there any ethical thought at all in this characterization of the feminine, or is it purely theological? The cultural construct of the "absolute other" has always been a target of fear, rage, oppression, violence, erasure of independent recognition and agency. The "absolute other" is a problem demanding strategies of management and control which often lead to the "absolute other's" death. Docile and utilitarian bodies of women and peoples of color, a compliant natural world—these are operational goals of unreconstructed (and white supremicist) patriarchal society.

Simone de Beauvoir and other feminist theorists were outraged by Levinas's treatment of the feminine in *Time and the Other*, his frank assignment of the status of reproductive vessel to woman—ever ready to emerge from the shadows of alterity, stimulate ejaculatory mechanics (eros?), receive the sperm. Levinas himself doesn't address the bodily mechanics of his metaphysical fable—an account arrestingly similar to Apollo's in the *Eumenides* of Aeschylus.

> The mother is no parent of that which is called
> her child, but only nurse of the new-planted seed
> that grows. The parent is he who mounts. A stranger she

> preserves a stranger's seed, if no god interfere.
> I will show you proof of what I have explained. There can
> be a father without any mother.[24]

De Beauvoir pointed to the complete absence of female consciousness or ego in Levinas's prose, "which is intended to be objective, [but] is in fact an assertion of masculine privilege."[25] She and many other feminists derived energy from this and put it to use in revolutionary feminist analysis. De Beauvoir's *The Second Sex* is the pathbreaking example. Here is Levinas's response to his feminist critics.

> I do not want to ignore the legitimate claims of the feminism that
> presupposes all the acquired attainments of civilization ... In the
> most brutal materiality, in the most shameless or the most prosaic
> appearance of the feminine, neither her mystery nor her modesty
> is abolished ... [The feminine] is not merely the unknowable, but
> a mode of being that consists in slipping away from the light ...
> Hiding is the way of existing in the feminine, and this fact of hiding
> is precisely modesty. (LR, 49)

Levinas, to my knowledge, never disavowed this view of the feminine function consonant with most orthodox religious beliefs originating in ancient and medieval world cultures. There is always a primal asymmetry —only one "other," which is woman. For Levinas alterity is never reciprocal. He did, in a puzzlingly abstracted manner, address "maternity" in later work—without mentioning "woman," the "feminine," or the "maternal." In *Otherwise Than Being or Beyond Essence*, maternity is "the complete being 'for the other' ... the very signifyingness of signification" (LR, 98). In "Revelation in the Jewish Tradition," there is a corporeal evocation of maternity once again with no woman on site: "But man is also the irruption of God with Being ... Man is questioned at his judgment by a justice which recognizes this responsibility; mercy—the *rahamim*— the trembling of the uterus in which the Other (*L'Autre*) gestates with the Same, God's maternity, if we can call it that ..." (LR, 202).

Some feminist scholars have attempted to defend Levinas against accusations of sexism by pointing to this odd "revelation" of maternity as active metaphysical principle. Derrida, echoing De Beauvoir, intentionally or not, responds by noting the masculine nature of philosophical metaphysics. In "Violence and Metaphysics, An Essay on the Thought of Emmanuel Levinas" he writes that Levinas, abjuring the Greek and Joycean "feminine logic"/ "woman's reason" of *Ulysses*, is essentially a philosopher of the masculine mind. The Levinas text he mentions is entirely coherent with *Time and the Other* in that respect.

> On this subject, let us note in passing that [Levinas's] *Totality and Infinity* pushes the respect for dissymmetry so far that it seems to us impossible, essentially impossible, that it could have been written by a woman. Its philosophical subject is man (*vir*) ... Is not this principled impossibility for a book to have been written by a woman unique in the history of metaphysical writing? Levinas acknowledges elsewhere that femininity is an "ontological category." Should this remark be placed in relation to the essential virility of metaphysical language? But perhaps metaphysical desire is essentially virile, even in what is called woman. It appears that this is what Freud (who would have misconstrued sexuality as the "relationship with what is absolutely other," *TI*), thought, not of desire, certainly, but of libido.[26]

Derrida, whose playful feints at philosophical orthodoxy I see as enactments of an agonistic feminine poetics of the philo-literary essay, says on the last page of "Violence and Metaphysics" that "alterity had to circulate at the origin of meaning, in welcoming alterity in general into the heart of the logos" (153). He clearly sympathizes with Levinas's view (borne of self-knowledge?) that hypocrisy is "not only a base contingent defect of man, but the underlying rending of a world attached to both the philosophers and the prophets"(153). There are of course many more in the room. Add poets, women, native peoples, people of color, lesbians, drag queens, the entire queer spectrum, and other biocultural barbarians to the cohort rending Western historical orthodoxies. If alterity is at the heart of logos—the multifaceted abundance of language as form of life—it must implicate all gender variants as primary subjects. This in turn should be reflected in a necessary mutability of the rules of discourse and genre, should it not? The putative, tacitly assumed or strenuously theorized, equilibrium of masculine hegemony and feminine alterity—well-oiled mechanism of everyday life in most contemporary cultures—must be strenuously challenged in the academy no less than in the marketplace of images supporting the habitus. Even as students of philosophy, literature, and cultural criticism (docile or done for in pursuit of graduate degrees) are sent to insufficiently challenged canonical figures for guidance, and the stock of legitimating quotations studding every thesis.

For the moment, however, I want to take up Levinas's interesting assertion of the feminine *as* contrariety: "the contrariety that permits its terms to remain absolutely other, is the *feminine*." In the thicket of that very odd grammar lies a wormhole boring straight through to the mind-set of misogyny. The actor is the philosopher's abstract noun *contrariety*, which (spawning a verb) "permits" *feminine* slippage into cultural darkness (alterity), which just happens to be the philosopher's a priori characterization of the *feminine*. The sleight of syntax may momentarily disguise the fact that *feminine* "contrariety" is what consigns "contrariety" to the *feminine*. This seems to me a bit of metaphysical violence toward lived experience: categories like "absolute alterity/other" invade reality as noir fairytale jargon custom-made by conscientious patriarchs for their little girls—shaping and supporting real-world misogyny. Of course feminine contrariety exists. The feminine is contrary to masculine hegemony. Feminine contrariety is transvalued when it becomes an agonistic feminine, an active principle of ethical responsibility, biocultural agency with real-world responsibilities: to counter misogyny, racism, xenophobia of every sort, the pillaging of the planet. That is the kind of ethical imperative missing in *Time and the Other*—and in the chronic docility that keeps destructive machinations of the habitus humming. The agonistic feminine, as I'm suggesting it, is a fully embodied dynamic whose agency operates in a continually developing complex relation (creative, intellectual, imaginative) to the hegemonic masculine and well beyond that socio-political template. A dynamic of gender and genre order-disorder, in its conversational agon, has been reconfiguring choreographies in the charged field *between* F-M polarities for millennia—but without sufficient notice in cultures at large.

8
AGON IN STRANGE PARTS

ASSERTIONS AND ENACTMENTS of gender fluidity are one form of serious play in a biocultural agon whose M-F polarities/alterities—construed as unassailable binary—have been the ancient pillars of patriarchy. Neither the agon nor the fluidity is entirely new. Apollonian-Dionysian and yin-yang dynamics have stirred crosscurrents in traditional societies for millennia. Meanwhile the agonistic feminine thrives in multiple guises. The most culturally acclaimed occurs in male embodiments: Plato's philosophical alter ego—the coy and playful Socrates who introduces his female mentor Diotima in the *Symposium*; sixth-century philosopher-poet Boethius in *The Consolation of Philosophy* bringing philosophy and poetry beyond a Platonic 'logos versus irrational quarrel' into conversation with one another as "Lady Philosophy" and the Muses; Dadaists and progeny interrupting logical constructions of "official thought" with cutups and other disarming forms; James Joyce's *Ulysses* further feminizing the *Odyssey* in which heroes frequently dissolve into (*feminine*) tears.

> Throwing his arms around his marvel of a father, Telémakhos began
> to weep. Salt tears rose from the wells of longing in both men ...
> So helplessly they cried, pouring out tears, and might have gone on
> weeping so till sundown ...[27]

The sea level of the Aegean is rising with the emotional outpouring but Ulysses and Telémakhos also have manly work to do. The narrative of the return must continue; suitors must be massacred—brutality and emotional vulnerability are linked in the Ancient Greek "nature of man."

In subsequent eras, tragedians will explore this in the nature of woman. What is perhaps most interesting about the internalization of the M-F agon in Homeric males is how puzzling it's been to scholars. Meanwhile, Joyce's narrative ends with Molly Bloom's soliloquy, in which a male author ventriloquizes (expresses?) the (his?) agonistic feminine.

The greatest example of the agonistic feminine embodied as female author/persona may be that of the thoroughly disembodied Sappho. While we postmoderns have come to think that texts are the embodiments that make the difference, Sappho's have been disintegrating from one cultural and personal context to another in an irresolvable ordeal of transmission. An agon of neglect and censorship countervailed by curiosity, happenstance and, over time, the growing need for an ancient gender-fluid heroine. As embodiments of contingency and accident—not to say chronically inter-rupted intentionality—the fragment resurrected from ancient tatters, or created anew, is now revered (though not always acknowledged) as a poetics of the feminine. "Sappho" is the canonical urtext of silences that under-score alterity while rendering it benign. Are silences—rather than innate modesty, as Levinas would have it—the safest hiding places from misog-yny? Would fragmented Sappho now be so beloved (even sacred) had she remained whole—as text and as female persona?

It's an excellent irony that composition by and despite assaultive and entropic contingencies transformed Sappho's lyrics into a poetics that eludes official grammars—an agon of reciprocal alterity between a kind of prototypical feminine and the brutal exclusions of history. Gertrude Stein, agonist in her own right, has much to say about that sort of thing in her prose-poem "History or Messages from History": "Now think how is a history of think with them think with him think for him think for them think they were with him they thank and they thank him with them for him ... What is history? They make history." [28] Sappho's gravely beautiful indeterminacy, Stein's beautifully humorous play agonistically swerve minds out of gender/genre-normative geometries of attention.

Fast forwarding for more examples, past a no doubt enormous number of works refused recognition and therefore lost, there is, of course, Marianne Moore; Mina Loy—interestingly ambiguous figure in this inquiry, one whose

sadly submissive (to Marinetti) "Feminist Manifesto" belied her own inno-
vative capacities; Dorothy Richardson, perpetually in the shadow of Joyce;
Beckett creating his own shadows, his self-interruptions; Virginia Woolf's
The Waves, with the deconstructive "Bernard" addressing the ruse of the
narrative plenum.

> "How tired I am of stories, how tired I am of phrases that come down
> so beautifully with all their feet on the ground! ... How I distrust
> neat designs of life." [29]

Bernard the character, Virginia the author complicate gender paths like a
tandem *Orlando*. More recent examples of agonistic poetics in dynamic
fields between polar alterities include the work of Mahmoud Darwish col-
lected in *The Butterfly's Burden*; the experimental poetic essays of Édouard
Glissant in *Poetic Intention*; Muriel Rukeyser's *Breaking Open*; Etel Adnan's
The Arab Apocalypse; John Ashbery's *Girls on the Run*; Peter Inman's *Written
1976–2013*; Tina Darragh's *Striking Resemblance*; Leslie Scalapino's *How
Phenomena Appear to Unfold*; Jena Osman's *The Network*; Evelyn Reilly's
Styrofoam; Amy King's *Slaves to Do These Things*; Charles Bernstein's "War
Stories" and "The Ballad of the Girly Man" in *All the Whiskey in Heaven*;
Juliana Spahr's *Well Then There Now*; Rachel Zolf's *Neighbor Procedure*.
The list could go on with other works by each, and many more authors.

9
WELCOMING ALTERITY INTO THE HEART OF THE LOGOS

> I believe I summed up my attitude to philosophy when I said: really
> philosophy ought only to be written as *poetic composition* ... I was
> thereby acknowledging myself as someone who cannot quite do what
> he would like to be able to do.
>
> —Ludwig Wittgenstein, 1933–34[30]

WESTERN PHILOSOPHY, from Plato's robustly caricatured legacy on, has

consisted of language games with masculine identified rationalist rules
excluding poetic logics, aka the wiles associated with "flute girls" in
ancient Athens. The feminine in philosophy is always agonistic. The more
I've read Wittgenstein the more I've come to understand his inability
to comply with ordained philosophical rationalism as a struggle *of and
with* the agonistic feminine at the heart of his psychological and intellec-
tual being. (He loved poetry as defined by his aesthetic culture but took
contemporary characterizations of the "semitic races"—his genetic heri-
tage—as "unpoetic" to heart.[31]) The poetry/philosophy agon is apparent
in his strangely beautiful *Tractatus Logico-Philosophicus* (completed at age
twenty-nine)—a numerically ordered, quasi-axiomatic progression of
propositions demonstrating logical (and limiting) conditions for mean-
ing (what can be expressed) in language, but also full of aphorisms ("The
world of the happy is quite another than that of the unhappy" 6.43), reli-
gious yearning, and—yes—poetry. The work arrives at what Wittgenstein
claims in his preface to be "unassailable and definitive" truth, but more
strikingly at a spiritual apprehension of the immense reality (as he sees
it, *beyond* words) that he must leave out: "There is indeed the inexpress-
ible. This shows itself; it is mystical" (6.522). The final proposition of the
Tractatus is: "Whereof one cannot speak, thereof one must be silent" (7).

If these famous passages sound a bit off, it's because they are from the
first (1921) English translation by C. K. Ogden who strove to honor the
"peculiar literary character of the whole" with a rendering "very carefully
revised" by Wittgenstein himself.[32] (It was Ogden who initiated bilingual
editions in order to preserve the poetics and the frequent colloquialisms
of the original.) The Ogden-Wittgenstein version was "superseded" in
1961 (ten years after Wittgenstein's death) by a now standard transla-
tion for Anglophone academic use, aimed at making the philosopher's
thoughts more easily understood while sometimes subtly, sometimes
radically departing from his own poetics. What that means is that the
agonistic rationalist/poetic dialectic throughout the original is ironically,
silenced. In the early 1960s, when I began studying Wittgenstein as a
philosophy student, he was presented as a "linguistic analyst": aesthetic
and spiritual dimensions, ignored or dismissed. His repudiation of his

own "definitiveness" in the *Tractatus*, his performative challenge to the logical positivism of the incipient Vienna Circle—reading Tagore's poetry aloud (sometimes with back turned to his colleagues as they tried to make sense of the *Tractatus*)—was mentioned humorously, if at all, as anecdote documenting his eccentricity. Philosophy departments, preserving their academic rationalism, have attempted to save Wittgenstein's reputation as philosophical genius from himself.[33] But in the *Tractatus* he came close to composing philosophy like poetry as its scope and limits were understood in his aesthetic circle. If the model of a mathematical or philosophical poem is pre-Socratic: for example, Pythagoras or Parmenides; or modernist: for example, Stein's "Are There Arithmetics," or contemporary: for example, Oulipean or procedural investigative poetries, the *Tractatus* can be read as a philosophical poem that brilliantly fields tensions between rational-irrational, scientific-aesthetic, masculine-feminine polarities. (All of the postromantic models mentioned happen to share Wittgenstein's fin de siècle, early modernist sensibilities.)

Rosmarie Waldrop's gravely humorous engagement with Wittgenstein's work adds new dynamics to the agon. One might in fact call her 1987 prose poems in *The Reproduction of Profiles* a triumph of the agonistic feminine in its potential for sensual and intellectual intelligence and fun while fully entering a conversation about the relation between the world of happenstance experience and seemingly universal, if not eternal, ideas. For Wittgenstein the irrepressible agonistic poetics of the *Tractatus* had created a fascinating *logico ad absurdum*. He had demonstrated with propositions like "The facts in logical space are the world" (1.13) how, and perhaps why, what he most valued aesthetically, spiritually—possibly even sensually—had no place in the limited world of a scientifically precise philosophical method. In a sense both he and Waldrop ultimately rectify the project of the *Tractatus* with the concept of language as "form of life"—giving (and given) meaning by its very worldly uses in negotiating everyday experience. Wittgenstein does this in the *Philosophical Investigations*. Waldrop's "Reproduction" is in conversation with both the *Tractatus* and the *Investigations*. Sometimes directly, more often obliquely borrowing from the philosopher's "language games," she sets up her own

idiosyncratic relationship to "reality" and "truth" with implicit hypotheses
to be tested by poetic actions. Those stunningly sly actions swerve abstract
ideas out of inviolably logical space into humorously inflected domestic
or other commonplace situations, in which flourish a reverse exoticism
of commonsense observations. In passages that graphically mirror the
serial notes of the *Investigations*, metaphysics and epistemology continu-
ally make deliciously unsettling contact with concrete circumstances as
an unidentified "I" and "you" negotiate a sometimes dicey relationship.
Here is the first of a series of five prose poems under the heading "Facts."

> I had inferred from pictures that the world was real and therefore
> paused, for who knows what will happen if we talk truth while climb-
> ing the stairs. In fact, I was afraid of following the picture to where
> it reaches right out into reality, laid against it like a ruler. I thought
> I would die if my name didn't touch me, or only with its very end,
> leaving the inside open to so many feelers like chance rain pouring
> down from the clouds. You laughed and told everybody that I had
> mistaken the Tower of Babel for Noah in his Drunkenness." [34]

After the *Tractatus*, Wittgenstein addressed the Oxbridge philosophical
world with texts that refused the authoritative stance of a systematically
assertive, internally coherent through-structure, the staple of philosophical
argument. His interrogatively framed thought experiments are what have
made the work so inviting; suggestive fragments (silences of other kinds)
are productive of further thought. This approach was (still is, for anyone
else who tries it) an unnerving departure from the masculinized objectives
of consistency, coherence, conclusiveness, control—the QEDs that end
conversations. In his preface to the *Philosophical Investigations*, Wittgen-
stein writes ambivalently about the form his thought processes have taken.

> I have written down all these thoughts as *remarks*, short para-
> graphs . . . It was my intention at first to bring all this together in a
> book whose form I pictured differently at different times . . . After
> several unsuccessful attempts to weld my results together into such

a whole, I realized that I should never succeed. . . . my thoughts
were soon crippled if I tried to force them on in any single direction
against their natural inclination.—And this was, of course, connected
with the very nature of the investigation. . . . I should have liked to
produce a good book. This has not come about.[35]

This is a poignant reminder of the self-doubt instilled by deviance from
masculine rationalist norms. Wittgenstein's agon was an enacted resistance
to the academy's demand for rhetorics of persuasion, but he could not
help judging himself by its criteria. Wittgenstein wrote the *Philosophical
Investigation* preface in 1945, then withdrew the manuscript—already in
production—from his press. It was eventually published posthumously.
In 1947 he wrote, in a separate manuscript (posthumously incorporated
into *Culture and Value*), "Don't for heaven's sake, be afraid of talking
nonsense! But you must pay attention to your nonsense." [36]

For Wittgenstein, language as a form of life is played out in the
numerous language games that arise in the living experience of social
contexts. M. NourbeSe Philip's *She Tries Her Tongue, Her Silence Softly
Breaks* importantly models a poetics of the agonistic feminine in engage-
ment with language games of power—official grammars (secular and
religious) that enact violent historical logics of sexism and racism (white
supremacy) that continue to support long-embedded colonial structures.[37]
As history parsed Sappho into fragments, as history parses certainty into
thought experiments, essays and poems, as history is infernally reenacted
in the habitus—repository of all "legacies," as history parses persons into
docile/utilitarian minds and bodies, parses persons into bodies without
minds, parses bodies into cunts without persons, parses the whole of it
into property, what is one to do as poet? Philip's poetic agon is an act of
unflinching analysis and a fiercely moving linguistic reparation. Here is
an excerpt from "Universal Grammar."

Parsing—the exercise of dis-membering language into fragmentary cells that forget to re-member.

raped—regular, active, used transitively   the again and again   against women   participled into the passive voice as in, 'to get raped';   past present   future—tense(d) against the singular or plural number of the unnamed subject, man

when the smallest cell remembers—
how do you
how can you
when the smallest cell

                              remembers

lose a language

O homen alto, louro de olhos azuis esta a disparar
El blanco, rubio, alto de ojos azules está disparando
De lange, blanke, blonde, man, met der blauwe ogen, is aan het schieten
Le grand homme blanc et blond aux yeux bleus tire sur
Der grosser weisse mann, blonde mit bleuen augen hat geschossen
The tall, blond, blue-eyed, white-skinned man is shooting

                                        an elephant
                                        a native
                                        a wild animal
                                        a Black
                                        a woman
                                        a child

somewhere

Slip mouth over the syllable; moisten with tongue the word.
Suck   Slide   Play   Caress   Blow—Love it, but if the word
gags, does not nourish, bite it off—at its source
Spit it out
Start again

from **Mother's Recipes on How to Make a Language Yours or
How Not to Get Raped.**

NOTES

A short version of this essay was delivered as a talk for "Constructive Alterities in Feminist Ecological Poetics," a panel organized by Angela Hume, with Brenda Hillman and Evelyn Reilly, for "Poetics (The Next) 25 Years"— a conference sponsored by the Poetics Program at the University at Buffalo SUNY, April 2016.

1. *Feminist Measures: Soundings in Poetry and Theory*, edited by Lynn Keller and Cristanne Miller (Ann Arbor: University of Michigan Press, 1994). I later included "Rethinking" in my volume of interconversational essays, *The Poethical Wager* (Berkeley: University of California Press, 2004), along with further development of the idea of an experimental feminine in "The Experimental Feminine" and "The Scarlet Aitch: Twenty-Six Notes on the Experimental Feminine" (linked to Hawthorne's protagonist, Hester Prynne).

2. Theodor W. Adorno, *Aesthetic Theory* (1970), translated by C. Lenhardt, from the second German edition, 1972; edited by Gretel Adorno and Rolf Tiedemann (London and New York: Routledge & Kegan Paul, 1984), 8.

3. Adorno, "The Essay as Form" (written 1954–58), in *Notes to Literature*, vol. 1, edited by Rolf Tiedemann, translated by Shierry Weber Nicholsen (New York: Columbia University Press, 1991), 17, 23.

4. To mark a new epoch of disproportionate human effects on earth's geology and biosphere.

5. "In the nations of the Persian Gulf—Kuwait, Saudi Arabia, Qatar, Oman, and the United Emirates—women still remain disenfranchised [as well as] in Equatorial Guinea, Hong Kong, Suriname, and Taiwan. In Bhutan only one member of a household is allowed to vote. In practice, this rule has meant that few women exercise the suffrage." Elizabeth H. Pleck, "Women's Suffrage," *Encyclopedia Americana* (Grolier Online: http://ea.grolier.com. ezprox.bard.edu/article?id=0422610-00, accessed October 4, 2016).

6. See Pierre Bourdieu, *Masculine Domination*, translated by Richard Nice (Stanford, CA: Stanford University Press, 2001).

7. *The Logic of Practice*, translated by Richard Nice (Stanford, CA: Stanford University Press, 1990); see chapter 4, "Belief and the Body," 70–79. All quotations are from Book I.

8. Ibid. chapter 3, 55–56.

9. Gertrude Stein, *How to Write*, preface and introduction by Patricia Meyerowitz (New York: Dover, 1975), 133.

10. Ethos, logos, pathos: Aristotle's terms for the tri-partite dynamic equilibrium—of character, reason, and compassion (with its feminine associations)—that gives rhetoric both integrity and persuasive force.

11. Michel Foucault, *Discipline and Punish: The Birth of the Prison*, translated from the French by Alan Sheridan (New York: Vintage Books, 1979), 137–38.

12. Ibid., 136 ff.

13. Glossary notes: the "thorne" þ is the modern *th*, hence, *operhed*—otherhood, or otherness; *penne*—then. Thorneless *owe* can be read as ought. I owe this and other insights into Middle English vocabulary, spelling, and grammar to colleagues at Bard, particularly Marisa Libbon.

14. Composed from *OED* usage examples beginning with entries for *wont*.

15. Marianne Moore, *Collected Poems* (New York: The Macmillan Company, 1951), 69–70.

16. George Lakoff and Mark Johnson, *Metaphors We Live By* (University of Chicago Press, 1980), a text full of examples of the way we daily rehearse the links between language and our necessarily physical experience of the world. Sherry B. Ortner, "Is Female to Male as Nature Is to Culture?" in M. Z. Rosaldo and L. Lamphere (eds.), *Woman, Culture, and Society* (Stanford, CA: Stanford University Press, 1974), 68–87.

17. "Jimbo's Inferno" is part of my *Bosch Studies: Fables, Moral Tales & Other Awkward Constructions*, Litmus Press, 2018. The coda uses modified language from Henry Wadsworth Longfellow's 1867 translation of *Dante's Inferno*, widely available in the public domain.

18. Naomi Klein, *This Changes Everything: Capitalism vs. The Climate* (New York: Simon & Schuster, 2014). Epigraph to part 6 is taken from page 177.

19. Page duBois, *Sowing the Body: Psychoanalysis and Ancient Representations of Women* (University of Chicago Press, 1991).

20. Moore. Op. cit., 75.

21. Nietzsche, "Apothegms and Interludes" #86 in *The Philosophy of Nietzsche* (New York: The Modern Library, 1954). The epigraph to this section is #145.

22. In Seán Hand, *The Levinas Reader* (Oxford, UK and Cambridge, MA, 1992), 52–53. I cite other pages from the *Reader* as LR.

23. Levinas in *Time and the Other* crisscrosses from a necessarily womb-bearing feminine to feminine as cluster of characteristic traits—what he calls "mode of being." A question for French scholars, Why not two words—*femme* (woman) versus *féminin* (traits)? The word *féminin* that indicates gender in grammar, by the way, is amusingly a masculine noun. As I have indicated, I distinguish these importantly different ontologies by using different words—the biological *female* versus the *feminine* for traits, aesthetic properties, forms of behavior, strongly associated with the female but all of which can be expressed by persons of any gender.

24. Page duBois alerted me to this passage, in *Sowing the Body*, 33. She quotes the first four lines, to which I add the next three, from Richmond Lattimore's translation in *The Complete Greek Tragedies: Volume 1*, *Aeschylus*, edited by David Grene and Richmond Lattimore (University of Chicago Press, 1959), 158, lines 658–63.

25. Simone de Beauvoir, *The Second Sex* (New York & Toronto: Knopf, 1993), xiv, n3.

26. Jacques Derrida, "Violence and Metaphysics: An Essay on the Thought of Emmanuel Levinas" (hereafter referred to as V&M), in *Writing and Difference* (University of Chicago Press, 1978), 320–21n92.

27. Homer, *The Odyssey*, translated by Robert Fitzgerald (New York: Doubleday, 1963), 276.

28. In *Gertrude Stein: Selections*, edited and introduction by Joan Retallack (Berkeley: University of California Press, 2008), 264, 267.

29. I quote more of this passage, with more discussion, in *The Poethical Wager*, 146–47.

30. Ich glaube meine Stellung zur Philosophie dadurch zusammengefaßt zu haben indem ich sagte: philosophie düurfte man eigentlich nur *dichten* . . . Ich habe mich damit auch als einen bekannt, der nicht ganz kann, was er zu können wünscht. Ludwig Wittgenstein, *Culture and Value*, translated by Peter Winch. Bilingual Edition (Chicago: University of Chicago Press, 1984), 12, 12^e. I have slightly modified the English translation.

31. Ibid., 1930, 5^e.

32. Ludwig Wittgenstein, *Tractatus Logico-Philosophicus*, translated by C. K. Ogden, with an Introduction by Bertrand Russell (London: Kegan Paul, Trench, Trubner & Co., 1922). All quotations are from this edition. More about the difference in poetics between the Ogden-Wittgenstein English language *Tractatus* and the 1961 D. F. Pears & B. F. McGuinness version, will appear elsewhere.

33. In contrast to literary critics who, while remarking upon Wittgenstein's influence on contemporary poets, miss the agonistic import of his own transgeneric philo-poetics.

34. Rosmarie Waldrop, "Facts," from "The Reproduction of Profiles," in *Curves to the Apple* (New York: New Directions, 2006), 5.

35. Ludwig Wittgenstein, *Philosophical Investigations*, translated by G. E. M. Anscombe, 3rd ed. (New York: The Macmillan Company, 1958), ix^e, x^e.

36. Culture and Value, 56^e.

37. M. NourbeSe Philip, *She Tries Her Tongue* (Charlottetown: Ragweed Press, 1989), 66–67; reprinted in the Wesleyan Poetry Series, foreword by Evie Shockley (Middletown: Wesleyan University Press, 2015).

Precarity, Poetry, and the Practice of Countermapping

Adalaide Morris and Stephen Voyce

> The conceptual composition of "precarious" can be described in the broadest sense as insecurity and vulnerability, destabilization and endangerment.
>
> —Isabell Lorey, *State of Insecurity*

> the living were noisy
> crowding out the place
> the dead were marching through
> noone was paying attention
> thats when I started to
> —Caroline Bergvall, *Drift*

IN "BREATH AND PRECARITY," his keynote for the 2016 Buffalo Poetics conference, Nathaniel Mackey juxtaposes two historical, political, and aesthetic forces from the 1950s and 1960s: the post–World War II destabilization and endangerment epitomized by the threat of nuclear annihilation and the agitated, insecure, asthmatic breath that powered the black music of Charlie Parker, Dizzy Gillespie, Charles Mingus, Sonny Rollins, Cecil Taylor, and other mid-century composer-players, on the one hand, and, on the other, the New American Poetry of Charles Olson, Robert Duncan, Robert Creeley, Amiri Baraka, Allen Ginsberg, and other mid-century poet-performers.

As Mackey describes them, the anguished lines of these musicians and poets—their stutter, wail, and howl—are at once affective and

117

analytic. They come, as Olson put it, from the "heart" and from "the head." [1] As cries, they give voice to the prolonged and differential suffering of individuals and collectivities; as critiques, they give names to the institutionalized agents of that suffering. By whatever name—racism, nationalism, colonialism; capitalism, militarism, and other hierarchies of power; or, more bluntly, greed, hatred, and delusion—these are engines of death. In "Black Dada Nihilismus," Baraka identifies them as

> money, God, power,
> a moral code, so cruel
> it destroyed Byzantium, Tenochtitlan, Commanch. [2]

In "Howl," Ginsberg gives them the ancient name of "Moloch."

> Moloch whose mind is pure machinery! Moloch whose blood
>   is running money! Moloch whose fingers are ten armies!
>   Moloch whose breast is a cannibal dynamo! Moloch
>   whose ear is a smoking tomb! [3]

In their indictment of mid-century social, political, and economic forms of endangerment, the musicians and poets of breath and precarity are, as Mackey suggests, essential mentors for contemporary interpreters of the post-9/11 landscape of terror and unknowing, insecurity, and dread.

Our aim in this essay is not to minimize the need for the embodied forms of knowing characteristic of a poetics of breath and precarity but rather to bring into view an additional set of resources contemporary poetry might mobilize to address forms of precarity at work in the twenty-first-century's globally constructed information and surveillance culture. Not only has the precarity voiced by Parker, Gillespie, Baraka, Ginsberg, and their mid-century cohort not diminished, but, as Judith Butler, Isabell Lorey, and others have argued at length, the process of precaritization "[has been] transformed in neoliberalism into a normalized political-economic instrument." [4] How can contemporary poets and

critics join in this discussion—a discussion alert to disparities in access
to resources, proliferating wars, massive flows of refugees and migrants,
and accelerating ecological catastrophe—without falling into the abstract,
formulaic, or numbing rhetoric of a list that forfeits the pulse and urgency
Mackey emphasizes in his pairing of precarity and breath?

Along with Mackey, we advocate an expansion of poetry's purview,
but our focus in these pages is visual rather than aural. Along with the
other informational structures whose production Johanna Drucker calls
graphesis—diagrams, grids, charts, tables, timelines, flow charts, and
the like—maps are a crucial component of contemporary literacy. "The
screens on our hand-held and mobile devices, in public displays, and
connected to networked flows, not only flood us with images," Drucker
writes, "they structure our relation to knowledge visually." [5] Although
forms of spatially organized knowledge are among the most familiar ways
we access and interpret the world, like other language-oriented humanities
traditions, poetry has been slow to engage, incorporate, or contest them.

Increasingly available through digital capture, reproduction, and
dissemination, maps offer both a model and a resource for a poetics that
engages precarity. In the pages that follow, we focus on a lineage the crit-
ical geographer Denis Wood calls "counter-mapping." After surveying a
set of documents that illustrate some of the variants of countermapping
in twentieth- and twenty-first-century avant-garde and activist art, we will
conclude with a brief analysis of a multimedia performance poem that
incorporates satellite pictures and oceanographic mapping to trace the
trajectory of the so-called Left-to-Die Boat, a raft on which sixty-three
migrants lost their lives in an attempt to cross the Mediterranean Sea. [6]

Although primarily visual rather than linguistic, the countermaps
that follow—avant-garde maps, radical cartography and tactical maps,
embodied and locative maps, and forensic maps—are information struc-
tures available for use in a contemporary poetics of precarity. Like other
maps, countermaps draw on known conventions: most are aligned to
true north and framed by distinct margins; many use a familiar palette to
identify states, municipalities, networks of streets and paths, landmarks,

bodies of water, and open spaces; and a significant number incorporate linguistic elements—titles, labels, and embedded comments—that provide access to the cartographer's beliefs and attitudes. Countermaps developed since 1995 increasingly employ computational and algorithmic procedures to encode, present, distribute, and analyze data and generate dynamic, multimedia documents capable of embedding thick layers of linguistic information. The difference that divides a countermap from a map, however, is not a difference in medium but a critical cast of mind: the intervention countermaps make is pedagogical and political, activist and oppositional.

For Denis Wood and other radical geographers, the work of mainstream cartography is "[t]he ceaseless reproduction of the culture that brings maps into being."[7] As instruments of governmentality, Wood suggests, "maps blossom in the springtime of the state": they mark boundaries and set zones for voting, taxation, and other administrative functions and often include territories soon to be claimed in the name of the state.[8] For these geographers, maps are "engines that convert social energy to social work," to the production, in short, of social space, social order, and social knowledge.[9] For this reason, therefore, like other activist and innovative practices, countermaps attempt to disturb common representational conventions of shared environments. Although these documents critique many cartographic features, their primary target is an assumption so fundamental it easily escapes attention: for most makers and users, maps are understood to be representations of an objective and persistent world, a world as real and verifiable as rocks, trees, and city sidewalks.

As critical cartographers have long insisted, mimetic notions of mapping overlook the fact that most maps are two-dimensional abstractions of multidimensional space. For this reason, they are by necessity significantly less dense and detailed than the territories they represent. Hakim Bey makes this point more pungently: "The 'map,'" he writes, "is a political abstract grid, a gigantic *con* enforced by the carrot/stick conditioning of the 'Expert' State, until for most of us the map *becomes* the territory.... Hidden enfolded immensities escape the measuring rod. The map is not accurate; the map *cannot* be accurate" (italics in original).[10]

To interpret a map or countermap properly, it is crucial to understand the technologies and codes by which it has been produced, to see its affordances as part of larger ideological systems, and to ask what social spaces they promote, what forms of subjectivity they construct, what powers they serve, and, with accelerating urgency, how they position those who consult them within the global system. The countermap's warping of form—its fragmentation, superposition, polyvalence, zooming in, zooming out, and/or jamming of codes and scales—is driven by the cast of mind Barrett Watten calls negativity or critical alterity.[11] As a practice, its work is to expose the conventions through which space is claimed, zoned, and occupied and to propose new ways to navigate the precarities of the present. For Wood, "it is counter-mapping that shows us where mapping is headed" (111); for us, it also points in the direction of an emergent poetics of precarity.[12]

Perhaps the most efficient way to introduce the work performed by countermaps is to look briefly at two early aesthetic examples: "The Surrealist Map of the World," published in a special issue of the Belgian periodical *Variétés* in 1929, and "The Naked City," published by the Situationists Guy Dubord and Asger Jorn in 1957 (see figs. 1 and 2).[13]

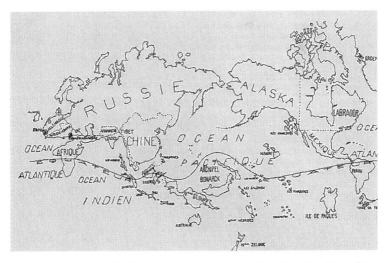

FIGURE 1. Anon., *Le Monde au Temps des Surrealistes* (The Surrealist Map of the World) (*Variétés*, Brussels 1929), 26–27.

As Wood suggests, this gleefully anticolonialist map, originally titled "Le Monde au Temps des Surréalistes," was probably composed by the poet Paul Éluard in the wake of his 1924 tour of Southeast Asia and parts of Indochina, sites of brutal colonial occupation by the English, Dutch, French, and Italians.[14] The convention this map interrupts is the Mercator projection, a standard mapping procedure devised by a Flemish geographer in 1569—the springtime of European colonialism—to transfer spherical surfaces onto two-dimensional mapping planes for use in navigation.

On Western maps using a Mercator projection, imperialist powers loom large: Europe appears to be twice the size of South America, Greenland is the same size as Africa, and the Atlantic sits in the map's center.[15] In a series of major counterwarps, the Surrealist map torques the equator, puts the Pacific at the center, and pushes Europe (and its ethnocentrism) to the edge of the page and end of the earth. Here, North America is swallowed whole by Alaska and Labrador; Ireland towers over England; and Paris pops up as the capital of Germany.

In a 1925 manifesto "The Revolution First and Always!," signed by a majority of the artists and writers in *Variétés*, the French and Belgian Surrealists described the world as "a crossroad of conflicts." The previous

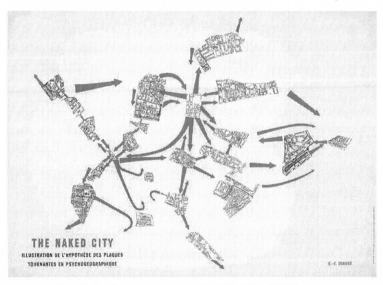

FIGURE 2. Guy Debord and Asger Jorn, *The Naked City* (1957).

year, France had joined Spain's colonial repression of the Berber rebellion in Morocco's Rif region, an incursion that prompted Surrealists to consolidate their ties with the French Communist Party (PCF). "We vigorously and in every way reject the idea of this kind of subjugation," the manifesto's authors declare; "... for us France does not exist." [17] And, in "Le Monde au Temps des Surrealistes," France vanishes, its capital moves to Germany, and the Soviet Union, energized by its 1917 revolution, expands eastward across the globe.

The point, as Debord and Jorn knew, is to imagine otherwise. Like the "temps" of the Surrealists, Situationist time is a time of possibility. Rather than reiterating known representations, their maps are abstractions of the lived complexities of the drifts or *dérives* they made through the streets of Paris. "From a dérive point of view," Debord explains, "cities have psychogeographical contours, with constant currents, fixed points and vortexes that strongly discourage entry into or exit from certain zones." [17] "The Naked City" maps a Paris that appears when explorers swerve away from zones of conventionality into spaces of psychological, social, political, and artistic freedom.

To make their countermap, Debord and Jorn used an X-ACTO knife to excise from two municipal tourist maps sections of Paris not yet ruined by capitalism, bureaucracy, and postwar urban planning. [18] The remaining zones of potential were set into a swirl and struck through with arrows to mark junctions and transfer points—"slopes," in Debord and Jorn's terminology—into and out of territory conducive to the aleatory practice of the drift. The result is to transform two static state-sponsored maps into a dynamic and transgressive event-space. Proleptic rather than descriptive, their countermap is a cognitive space of breached borders, incursions, and recalibrations, a heterogeneous terrain to be traversed and remapped according to the communal desires of roaming fellow travelers.

RADICAL CARTOGRAPHY AND TACTICAL MAPPING

IN 1968, the year after Debord published *The Society of the Spectacle*, a geographer by the name of William Bunge cofounded with Gwendolyn

Warren, an African American public sector administrator, the Detroit Geographical Expedition and Institute (DGEI). Initially drawing support from Michigan State and Wayne State Universities, they described their venture as "an experimental community college" and provided free courses to inner-city residents in cartography, geography, community activism, and urban planning.[19] The countermaps they produced are a model for a practice activist geographers call "radical cartography."

In place of the Situationist psychogeographical and aesthetic *dérive*, radical cartography is conducted in the name of justice.[20] Introducing their *Atlas of Radical Cartography*, Alexis Bhagat and Lize Mogel define this term as a "practice of mapmaking that subverts conventional notions in order to actively promote social change. The object of critique," they continue, "is not cartography *per se* (as is generally meant by the overlapping term *critical cartography*), but rather social relations."[21]

Just as Deborn and Jorn started with municipal tourist maps, the DGEI began with official state and municipal data sets. Working with

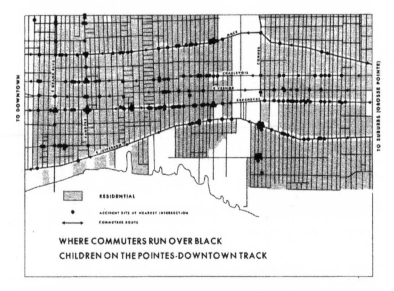

FIGURE 3. William Bunge, "Where Commuters Run Over Black Children," Detroit Geographical Expedition and Institute, *Field Notes: Discussion Paper No. 3*, "The Geography of the Children of Detroit," Detroit, 1971.

the statistics in a police report titled "Citywide Pattern of Children's Pedestrian Deaths and Injuries by Automobiles," a team of DGEI geographers made a map titled, in block letters, "Where Commuters Run Over Black Children on the Pointes-Downtown Track" (see fig. 3). "Any Detroiter," Wood comments, "would have known that these commuters were white and on their way between work downtown and home in the exclusive Pointes communities to the east. That is, [the DGEI map] is a map of where white adults kill black kids. It is a map of racist infanticide, a racial child-murder map." [22]

Unlike colonialist geographical institutes, which sent teams of experts outward from Europe's capitals toward territories marked for expropriation, the DGEI's team of amateur geographers moved inward to chart a pattern sixties activists called *interior colonialism* and theorists now describe as *governmental precaritization*. If precarity is a social positioning of endangerment, differential access to resources, and, in Lorey's words, "the hierarchization of being-with that accompanies the process of *othering*," the DGEI's "Where Commuters Run Over Black Children" exposes its construction as a systemic split between wealth and poverty, owners and workers, whites and blacks, suburbs and inner city. [23] The basis for this interpretation was present in the Detroit police report, "[b]ut," as Wood remarks in reference to Google's Streetview, "all disaggregated, inchoate. Something's missing, maybe the poetry." [24]

Bunge and the DGEI cartographers are key precursors of tactical mapping in a post-1995 digital environment. The term *tactical mapping* draws on three related sources: Michel de Certeau's use of the adjective *tactical* to describe the situational, makeshift activism of groups that "compose the network of an antidiscipline;" the Critical Art Ensemble's definition of *tactical media* as "situational, ephemeral, and self-terminating" art that "engage[s] a particular socio-political context in order to create molecular interventions and semiotic shocks that collectively could diminish the rising intensity of authoritarian culture;" and Rita Raley's *Tactical Media* (2009), which draws on these and other theoreticians and practitioners to survey artistically driven forms of digital resistance. [25]

Tactical mapping remakes the lineage of radical cartography through the use of contemporary digital technologies such as global positioning systems on smartphones, cameras, Bluetooth devices, and handheld receivers (GPS); geographical information systems that query, index, and map large quantities of data in a single database (GIS); imagery obtained over decades by networks of government, military, and private remote sensing satellites; application programming interfaces (APIs) constructed by such sites as Google Earth, HyperCities, OpenStreetMap, and Harvard World Map; and, not least, an array of gaming platforms in wide circulation.[26]

The Institute for Applied Autonomy, whose "Routes of Least Surveillance" (2001) first appeared in Bhagat and Mogel's *Atlas of Radical Cartography*, identifies tactical mapping's target as the authoritarian structures that oversee all levels of contemporary life. "In taking up the term 'tactical' in an arts context," they write, "we link cartography with 'tactical media' . . . [and] claim that 'tactical cartography' refers to the creation, distribution, and use of spatial data to intervene in systems of control affecting spatial meaning and practice."[27] Although tactical mapping is especially powerful in exposing systems of precarity that involve the workings of race, class, and ethnicity in urban contexts,[28] our examples below come from materials that expose covert systems at work in a global context.

The first is a map of the operations of "Boundless Informant," a top-secret NSA data-mining program exposed by whistleblower Edward Snowden (see fig. 4). Like the DGEI's "Where Commuters Run Over

FIGURE 4. "Boundless Informant," National Security Agency, the *Guardian*, June 11, 2013. Courtesy of Edward Snowden Archive.

Black Children," this map requires only a shift in audience from the agency to the public at large to function as a readymade countermap.

Information graphics like this one are crucial to comprehending the operations of mass-surveillance programs like Boundless Informant, XKeyscore, or Prism. Color coded to show areas least-to-most surveilled (green, yellow, orange, red), this map sorts metadata from close to 3 billion computer and telephone interactions over a thirty-day period ending in March 2013.[29] Among other patterns in the aggregation Wood might call its "poetry" is the fact that while the United States spied on Iran most often, its second- and third-ranked targets were Pakistan and Jordan, putative U.S. allies in the Arab World.

In a twist on tactical mapping, photographer and social geographer Trevor Paglen uses print journalism, experimental cartography, and conceptual art to document entities that are not supposed to exist. Among other examples of his practice, Paglen's photographic series *The Other Night Sky* captures images of classified American satellites; *Limit Telephotography* pictures restricted military bases and installations; and a third, untitled series depicts the headquarters' of the three largest U.S. intelligence agencies—the NSA, the National Reconnaissance Office (NRO), and the National Geospatial-Intelligence Agency (NGA).[30] Published in partnership with the websites "Creative Times Reports" and "The Intercept," these images are now in the public domain on Wikipedia's free media repository.

Paglen's most radical gesture, however, is to link graphic evidence to discursive interpretations. Maps such as "Selected CIA Aircraft Routes" (see fig. 5) or "Terminal Air" (produced with the Institute for Applied Autonomy) are most effective read in conjunction with Paglen's books *Torture Taxi* (2006) and *Blank Spots on the Map* (2009), both of which meticulously trace rendition flights to and from a network of secret prisons throughout the world.

Paglen's radical cartography amounts to a digitally powered Situationist drift across the most guarded terrains on earth. The covert systems of power disclosed by Snowden, Paglen, and others expose the activities of the NSA's web of surveillance programs, the NRO's operation of U.S. spy satellites, and the NGA's interpretations of geographic information

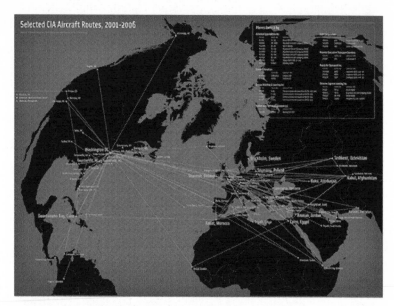

FIGURE 5. Trevor Paglen and John Emerson, "Selected CIA Aircraft Routes, 2001–006," *An Atlas of Radical Cartography* (Los Angeles: Journal of Aesthetics & Protest Press 2007).

coordinated with surveillance data collected by other agencies. Together they map classified landscapes, funded from a "black budget," operating in support of CIA-directed black-ops programs, whose illegal rendition program flew detainees to face torture in a black site in Kabul informally known as the Dark Prison.[31]

EMBODIED AND LOCATIVE MAPPING

MOST MAPS ARE scratched, traced, drawn, stitched, or plotted on one or another material substance, and all, if they are readable, locate things in relation to other things. What might it mean, then, to distinguish a cartographic practice as "embodied and locative"? In its depiction of a constitutive separation, a distance between map and viewer, Wisława Szymborska's poem "Map" suggests how post-Enlightenment cartography might be thought to have lost its body.

The map, the poem begins, is

> Flat as the table
> it's placed on.
> Nothing moves beneath it
> and it seeks no outlet.
> Above—my human breath
> creates no stirring air
> and leaves its total surface
> undisturbed.[32]

Szymborska's map takes a perspective de Certeau labels bird's-eye or top-down: its effect is abstract and totalizing.[33] Separated by a distinct distance, the map and viewer co-construct each other as static and objective. No air stirs. "Mass graves and sudden ruins / are," Szymborska notes, "out of the picture."

A map that has lost its body, a viewer whose breath stirs no air, a territory that yields no trace of death, no hint of life: this is the landscape Nathaniel Mackey identifies as sign and symbol, "diagnostic and symptomatic both" (3), of collective precarity. Multivalent and multicausal, the dread it signifies takes many forms: in "Breath and Precarity," Mackey locates it in particular in the post–World War II threat of nuclear annihilation and the ongoing chokehold of racism that makes Eric Garner's last words—"I can't breathe"—so resonant.

In the fifties and sixties, as Mackey argues, this dread generated the counterforce of "radical pneumaticism" in black jazz by musicians such as Dizzy Gillespie, Charlie Parker, and Cecil Taylor and the "poetics of breath" of New American Poets such as Olson, Creeley, Ginsberg, and Williams. In the radical pushback of this work, Mackey writes, "[b]reath becomes tactical, tactile, textile, even textual, a haptic recension whose jagged disbursements augur duress" (7). In the poetics of countermapping, an apprehension of mass graves and sudden ruins, dislocation and dread, disturbs the static and abstract perfection of conventional mapping through the exaggerated mobility, limited perspective, and productive confusion characteristic of embodied and locative mapping.

Embodied and locative countermaps are constructed and experienced from the bottom up; they are often collectively assembled; and they are not still but fractious, multiple, mutable, and contingent. The viewers this form of countermapping imagines are thrown into the thick of things, asked to rely on their own intuitions, and situated, like Debord and Jorn, as participant-cartographers who are eager to get lost. Sometimes described as "thick" or "deep," such maps are extensible, polyvocal, and open-ended in their accretion of layer on layer of place-specific data.[34]

Although GIS tools facilitate the construction of deep or thick maps, the difference between top-down and bottom-up cartography is not technologically determined: many hand-drawn or print maps are as multiple and contingent as maps constructed with GIS technology, and, as Jordan Crandall forcefully argues, many digital maps present themselves as objective depictions of fixed space.[35] In a culture in which every person, thing, and behavior "can be watched, monitored and tracked," furthermore, "thick maps" may carry, as Todd Presner, David Shepard, and Yoh Kawano point out, not an air of openness but "an underbelly

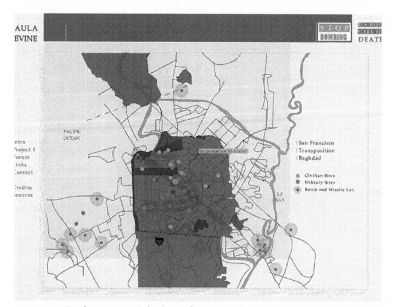

FIGURE 6. Paula Levine, "Shadows from Another Place: San Francisco <-> Baghdad," http://shadowsfromanotherplace.net, 2004.

of unmitigated paranoia and unchecked control."[36] But that's not—
or doesn't have to be—the end of the story.

Paula Levine's embodied and locative new media poem "Shadows
from Another Place: San Francisco <-> Baghdad" (2004) suggests alter-
native possibilities facilitated by GPS, GIS, and high-resolution satellite
surveillance (see fig. 6).[37]

Levine's dynamic multimedia poem superimposes on a georecti-
fied map of San Francisco the sounds, statistics, and spatial plotting of
bombs dropped on Baghdad on March 19, 2003, the first day of the U.S.
invasion. Listening in real time to radio reports of the invasion, Levine
writes, "This was the feeling I had. . . . I expected to feel the impact, hear
bombs, feel shock waves, see bright lights in the sky outside my studio
window similar to those described on the radio."

> Thousands of miles separated the site of the invasion from where
> I sat witnessing, and the only things that seemed fixed were the
> relative positions of perceiver and perceived and the impossible con-
> junction of both presence and absence. Two things became apparent.
> First, a spatial fear—a disjuncture, disorientation, and a sense of
> being unsettled. . . . Second, in spite of being immersed in informa-
> tion, I wasn't able to *get it*.[38]

As an act of empathic imagination, Levine's poem is an attempt to use
digital mapping affordances to overcome physical distance, inhabit the
moment's precarity, dislocation, information discord, and geographic
estrangement, and *get* the damage—Szymborska's "mass graves and
sudden ruins"—even at a distance. The effect is to transpose a war on a
designated *other* onto American terrain.[39]

Levine's poem bundles maps of Baghdad and San Francisco with
recorded bombing noises, records of the latitude and longitude of both
cities, a timeline, a forum for debate, a button a viewer can click to STOP
BOMBING, at least in the poem's simulated world, and, in a real world
for pedestrian-cartographers navigating by her map, geocaches at super-
imposed Baghdad/San Francisco sites of missile strikes that contain the

names of U.S. personnel killed in the year that followed the spectacle of President Bush's declaration of the end of major combat operations.[40]

"San Francisco < - > Baghdad" is a radical attempt to collapse the binaries—*here* and *there*, *us* and *them*, *domestic* and *foreign*—that sustain the rhetoric of war. For implicated American viewers, the poem offers, for a moment at least, an entry into the ethical complexities of a destabilized and endangered world.

FORENSIC MAPPING

THE FINAL SECTIONS of this essay focus on a pair of projects—one expository, the other poetic—that combine cartographic, linguistic, diagrammatic, and photographic evidence to document the journey of a motorized rubber boat that departed Tripoli on March 27, 2011, carrying seventy-two sub-Saharan migrants; ran out of fuel on March 28th; drifted in distress without food, water, or meaningful assistance through an intensely surveilled area of the Mediterranean Sea; and beached April 10th to the southeast of Tripoli carrying eleven survivors, two of whom died shortly thereafter.

Centering on the flow of refugees that has become increasingly emblematic of global precaritization, Forensic Architecture's case of the "Left-to-Die Boat" presents the research of a team of activist scholars, scientists, artists, architects, and lawyers based at Goldsmiths College, University of London.[41] Incorporating materials from that report, Caroline Bergvall's *Drift* is a collaborative multimedia performance piece, gallery installation, and poem that turns linguistic and aesthetic tools to forensic ends.

The critical practice of Eyal Weizman and his colleagues at Forensic Architecture is to reconstruct global conflicts using an array of maps, geospatial data, satellite imagery, aerial footage, and digital modeling tools. "These technologies," Weizman writes, "have expanded the capacity to bear witness, but they have also transformed the meaning of testimony, and to a certain extent eroded its sanctity. Today there are many photographers and spectators but only a few witnesses in the traditional sense." [42] Their aim is double: to investigate the violent actions of states and corporate actors and to lend their findings to "NGOs, activist groups, and prosecutors" for presentation and adjudication in various legal and political forums. [43]

Among the group's past projects are "Guatemala: Operacion Sofia," an analysis of environmental violence in the Ixil Triangle, 1980–1983; "Bil'in," a reconstruction of the death of a Palestinian demonstrator via video analysis; and "Unmanned Aerial Violence: Covert Drone Strikes in Pakistan, Yemen, and Gaza, 2008–present," a report that maps U.S. drone warfare in areas outside the effective control of sovereign states. Like the waters through which the Left-to-Die Boat drifted, each of these investigations scrutinizes a frontier zone—a place of murky jurisdiction—in which regulatory agencies have disintegrated or been suspended indefinitely. "In these places," as Weizman rightly notes, "powerful states can both inflict violence and deny they have done so." [44]

To hold state-sponsored actors accountable, Weizman and his colleagues practice a kind of *counterforensics*. [45] If the history of forensics has been "the history of the techniques by which states police individuals," Weizman notes, Forensic Architecture was "committed to the possibilities of reversing the forensic gaze, to ways of turning forensics into a counter-hegemonic practice able to invert the relation between individuals and states, to challenge and resist state and corporate violence and the tyranny of their truth." [46] Like other forms of countermapping, counterforensics uses the affordances of GIS, GPS, and satellite imaging to present evidence of state violence, armed conflict, and global precaritization.

The extensive research that generated the Left-to-Die report includes interviews of the surviving passengers and the military personnel, merchant seamen, and others in its vicinity; contact with previous migrants, immigration lawyers, governmental representatives, and international investigative bodies; and oceanographic and meteorological calculations capable of predicting the path of the boat and the positions of nearby commercial and military ships, helicopters, and fishing boats. Signed by Charles Heller, Lorenzo Pezzani, and SITU Research, the report is a graphically documented spatiotemporal account of the journey of the migrants and those who might have—but did not—intervene to avert their deaths.[47]

From the Surrealists forward, countermappers have employed aesthetic means as investigative procedures to think about political processes and their consequences. In tandem with a multiplicity of on-the-ground tactical and embodied approaches both discursive and graphic, these means have been important facilitators for the practice the Critical-Cartographies Collective has called "militant research."

Our aim here is to argue that a significant group of contemporary poets can be understood as participants in this forensic engagement of precarity. Like the mid-twentieth-century poets whose breath-driven lines Mackey hears in the context of the black music to which they were listening, these poets write in tandem with the work of artists and activists who make it their focus to document precarious life in a variety of geo-political locales. Indeed, what we call the *tactical, embodied-locative*, and forensic features of an evidence-collecting new media art comprise core facets of twenty-first-century poetry, its incorporation of aesthetic, political, and legal materials in search of public truth and ethical accountability. To this end, we close with a brief look at a long poem that extends the findings of Forensic Architecture's report on the Left-to-Die Boat.[48]

Bergvall's *Drift* is an information construct that is, in Marjorie Perloff's sense, a "differential text": it exists, that is, as language printed in a book, letters in motion on a screen, a series of gallery installations, a set of multimedia collaborative performances, and, at this moment in time, a number of partial recordings, all relevant but none definitive.[49] It is also, like the forms Drucker groups as instances of graphesis, a visualization of cultural knowledge and a witness to the events of its moment. Its lineage, in this sense, includes not only the literary documents it engages—most importantly, the Anglo-Saxon poem "The Seafarer," the Old Norse poem "Hávamál," and the Icelandic *Vinland Sagas*—but also maps, nautical charts, and line drawings that put it in conversation with the countermaps of the Surrealists and Situationists, William Bunge and the DGEI geographers, the new media poet Paula Levine, and the researchers at Forensic Architecture.

Forensic Architecture's report has two interlocking audiences. The first, bound by professional protocols, is a legal community charged with enforcing international conventions; the second, bound by broader humanistic principles, is a public committed to discussion of justice for populations that are or have been, in Butler's words, "differentially exposed to injury, violence, and death." [50] Bergvall and her performance team—Norwegian percussionist Ingar Zach, Swiss programmer and artist Thomas Köppel, and Swiss dramaturge Michèle Pralong—belong to the second community. If the heart of a Situationist drift is the psychogeography of urban landscapes, the core of Bergvall's *Drift* is an etymologically and aurally resonant sound-sense embedded in the poems of seafaring peoples. Her method, she tells us, was "archaeological or forensic" [51]: to explore multilinguistic "messengers, root-words, stem-sounds" [52] that convey centuries of northward journeys, migrancy, peril, desolation, and abandonment.

> What one doesn't know fact nofool knows
> that nowind filled my sails gold holds nogold
> breath nobreath . . . There are
> abandoned vessels ok heart sightings ok lifted
> anchors ok sky showers ok allround vanysshyng. [53]

Among the poem's fields of investigation, two of the most powerful are the terror of the condition the Vikings called *hafvilla*—an "allround vanysshyng" in a wilderness of sea—and its counterforce, the obligation, iterated in the Old Norse *Håvamål* and reiterated in the United Nations Convention on the Law of the Sea, to assist the distressed.

Like the moan, wail, howl, stumble, and stutter of the music and poetry Mackey discusses, the lexicon of *Drift* is valuable not for its denotative or legal purchase but for its multivalent, layered, sedimented generativity, for its resonance, ambiguity, inference, and ethical weight. The countermaps that accompany this language in the book,

the installation, and the performance of the poem enhance the burden
of its sound-sense.

This map of the Left-to-Die Boat's route, created by the Boats4People
Network, is easy enough to read, but it's not part of Bergvall's compo-
sition (see fig. 7).

These two graphics—a constellation of dots and a line drawing
—are Bergvall's countermaps, featured in two graphic portfolios embed-
ded in her text and displayed in its installations and performances
(see figs. 8 and 9).

The white dots against a black background location mimic the
oceanographic data captured by various governmental surveillance units
throughout the days the migrants were left to die. They look like stars in a
"[s]ealike sky [that] falls into skylike ocean," reflections of the same shim-
mering constellations by which Old Norse, Icelandic, and Anglo-Saxon
voyagers navigated northward the open seas.[54] They also mark, elegiacally,
some of the over 14,000 deaths in these seas across the last twenty years.

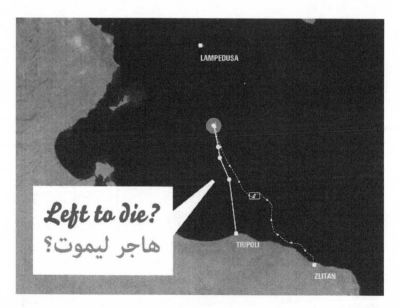

FIGURE 7. Boats4People Network, Meeting of the World Social Forum, Monastir,
Tunisia, July 2012.

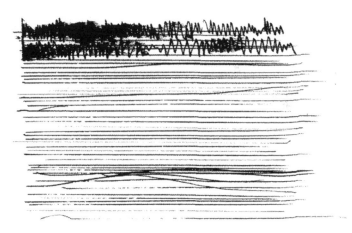

FIGURES 8 AND 9. Caroline Bergvall, *Drift* (Brooklyn, NY: Nightboat, 2014), 84–85, 7.

By the same token, the line drawing is one of a suite of sixteen that opens the poem, a tracing of disappearing oscillations, sound waves, apparitions, or contact ripples—"Everything," Bergvall writes, "ripples at contact"—at sea, in space, through the air, on a page.[55] The lines and swerves replicate one of the many paths of language charted on screen in the palimpsested poem that moves behind Bergvall as she performs. Viewers of the performance wander through a "textual scape" of *Drift*'s etymological dimensions, bringing historical language, writing's "tracks and traces and lines," into contact with the coordinates of spatial navigation. In these drawings, we move without predetermined route, "joining the dots, writing up the oscillations and the coastlines any way we can."[56]

We propose that critical cartography's graphic representations of direction, method, and place can also be used to describe a multimedia poetry that troubles the distinction between close and distant reading, depth and surface models, micro- and macroanalysis. This expanded poetics zooms in and zooms out, moving slantwise in a form of creative research that aims, like Gilles Deleuze and Félix Guattari's rhizomatic thinking, "to lay everything out on a plane of exteriority of this kind, on a single page, the same sheet: lived events, historical determinations, concepts, individuals, groups, social formations."[57] To wander through Bergvall's layered, multifaceted document is to be cocreated as an embodied, locative, and ethically alive being amid the knowledge practices, affects, and information structures of our time.

NOTES

1. Charles Olson, "Projective Verse" *Collected Prose: Charles Olson*, eds. Donald Allen and Benjamin Friedlander (Berkeley, CA: University of California Press, 1997), 242.

2. Amiri Baraka, "Black Dada Nihilismus," *The LeRoi Jones/Amiri Baracka Reader*, ed. William J. Harris (New York: Thunder's Mouth Press, 1991), 73.

3. Allen Ginsberg, "Howl," *Collected Poems, 1947–1980* (New York: Harper Perennial, 1984), 654.

4. Lorey, *State of Insecurity*, 39. See also Judith Butler, *Precarious Life: The Powers of Mourning and Violence* (New York: Verso, 2004) and *Frames of War: When Is Life Grievable?* (New York: Verso, 2009); Wendy Brown, *Undoing the Demos: Neoliberalism's Stealth Revolution* (New York: Zone, 2015); and Francesco Di Bernardo, "The Impossibility of Precarity," *Radical Philosophy* (July/August 2016), available at https://www.radicalphilosophy.com/commentary/the-impossibility-of-precarity.

5. Johanna Drucker, "Overview," *Graphesis: Visual Forms of Knowledge Production* (Cambridge, MA: Harvard University Press, 2014), n.p.

6. For a full account of this widely reported incident, see http://www.forensic-architecture.org/publications/report-on-the-left-to-die-boat.

7. Denis Wood, *Rethinking the Power of Maps* (New York: Guilford Press, 2010), 1.

8. Ibid., 15.

9. Ibid., 1. "Once a map has been published," Wood concludes, "it is pretty much taken for a description of the way things actually *are*. . . . The map's *propositional* character becomes . . . hard to see" (2–4, second ellipsis in text).

10. Hakim Bey, *T.A.Z.: The Temporary Autonomous Zone, Ontological Anarchy, Poetic Terrorism*, 2nd ed. (Brooklyn, NY: Automedia, 2003). 101. Once "it becomes clear that there can be no true maps," Fredric Jameson has observed, "it also becomes clear that there can be . . . a dialectical advance, in the various historical moments of mapmaking." See Jameson, *Postmodernism, or, The Cultural Logic of Late Capitalism* (New York: Verso, 1991), 52.

11. Barrett Watten, *Questions of Poetics: Language Writing and Consequences* (Iowa City, IA: University of Iowa, 2016), 8–9.

12. Wood, *Rethinking*, 111.

13. Anon., *Le Monde au Temps des Surrealistes* (The Surrealist Map of the World), *Le Surréalisme en 1929*, ed. P. G. Van Heck, *Variétés* (Brussels 1929), 26–27. The special issue of *Variétés* featured works by René Crevel, Paul Éluard, Louis Aragon, Robert Desnos, and André Breton, alongside Belgian writers and artists Paul Nougé, E. L. T. Mesens, and others. See Guy Debord and Asger Jorn, *The Naked City*, in Simon Sadler, *The Situationist City* (Cambridge, MA: MIT Press, 1998), 60.

14. Wood, Rethinking, 198. As Wood goes on to note, "Éluard had recorded his route on a map, *Les Cinq Parties du Monde, Planisphère, Comprenant toutes les Possessions Coloniales*, a classic of the era that displayed, on a Mercator projection, English colonial possessions in yellow, French in pink, Dutch in orange, Italian in mauve, and so on" (199).

15. In actuality, South America is twice the size of Europe, Africa ten times the size of Greenland. For a clearer picture of things, see the world rendered by the Peters projection, available at https://en.wiki pedia.org/wiki/Gall%E2%80%93Peters_projection.

16. Louis Aragon, Antonin Artaud, Andre Breton, Max Ernst, Robert Desnos, et al., "The Revolution First and Always," *Surrealism*, ed. Mary Ann Caws, trans. Michael Richardson and Krzysztof Fijalkowski (London: Phaidon, 2004), 201–2.

17. Debord, "Theory of the Dérive," *Situationist International Anthology*, trans. Ken Knabb (Berkeley, CA: Bureau of Public Secrets, 2006), 62.

18. The Situationists' immediate target was, of course, the rationalized Paris of Le Corbusier's steel-framed, glass-enclosed housing blocks; prefabricated, mass-produced office and manufacturing complexes; and networks of ring roads, shuttle stops, and pedestrian "circulation paths" designed to bind them together.

19. Wood, *Rethinking*, 166 ff.

20. For examples of contemporary radical cartography, see maps by such groups as Hackitectura, the Institute for Applied Autonomy, and the Counter Cartographies Collective.

21. *An Atlas of Radical Cartography*, ed. Lize Mogel and Alexis Bhagat (Los Angeles, CA: Journal of Aesthetics and Protest Press, 2010), 6–7.

22. Denis Wood and John Krygier, "Maps and Protest," *International Encyclopedia of Human Geography*, vol. 1 (Oxford, UK: Elsevier, 2009), 438.

23. Lorey, *State of Insecurity*, 12.

24. Denis Wood, *Everything Sings: Maps for a Narrative Atlas*, 2nd ed. (Los Angeles: Siglio, 2013), 29. In explaining its "poetic specificity," Wood compares this compendium of maps of the suburb of Boylan Heights, North Carolina, to Ezra Pound's "In a Station of the Metro" and William Carlos Williams's "Red Wheelbarrow," 19.

25. Michel de Certeau, *The Practice of Everyday Life*, trans. Steven Rendall (Berkeley, CA: University of California Press, 1984), xv; Critical Art Ensemble, "Tactical Media," http://www.critical-art.net/TacticalMedia.html; and Rita Raley, *Tactical Media*, Electronic Mediations 28 (Minneapolis, MN: University of Minnesota Press, 2009).

26. For discussion of these and other digital systems, see Laura Kurgan, *Close Up at a Distance: Mapping, Technology, and Politics* (New York: Zone Books, 2013), 39–54.

27. Institute for Applied Autonomy, "Tactical Cartographies," eds. Alexis Bhagat and Lize Mogel, *An Atlas of Radical Cartography* (Los Angeles: Journal of Aesthetics and Protest Press, 2008), 29.

28. See, for example, Bill Rankin's "Chicago Boundaries," an interactive map that draws and redraws the city's class, racial, and ethnic enclaves, available on Rankin's website, www.radicalcartography.net.

29. The 2007 date in the image refers not to the map but to the document authorizing its top-secret classification. For the map, see https://www.theguardian.com/world/2013/jun/08/nsa-boundless-informant-global-datamining.

30. These works from 2006 to 2009 document programs and practices later confirmed by the U.S. Senate Select Committee on Intelligence's "Torture Report," approved December 13, 2012.

31. For information regarding Edward Snowden's disclosure of the "Black Budget," see the *Washington Post*'s interactive data visualization, available at http://www.washingtonpost.com/wp-srv/special/national/black-budget/.

32. Wisława Szymborska, "Map," *The New Yorker*, April 14, 2014. Available at http://www.newyorker.com/magazine/2014/04/14/map.

33. de Certeau, *Practice*, 91–93.

34. For a description of "deep" mapping, see David J. Bodenheim, "The Potential of Spatial Humanities, *The Spatial Humanities: GIS and the Future of Humanities Scholarship*, eds. Bodenhamer, John Corrigan, and Trevor M. Harris (Bloomington, IN: Indiana University Press, 2010), 27–28; for "thick" mapping, see Todd Presner, David Shepard, and Yoh Kawano, *Hypercities: Thick Mapping in the Digital Humanities* (Cambridge, MA: Harvard University Press, 2014), for whom depth models seem to imply "deep, total, and utopian 'solutions.'" Their term, *thickness*, by contrast, is

intended to suggest "diachronic and synchronic, temporally layered, and polyvalent ways of authoring, knowing, and making meaning," 17–19.

35. Jordan Crandall, "Operational Media" (2005), available at http://www.ctheory.net/articles.aspx?id=441.

36. Presner, Shepard, and Kawano, *Hypercities*, 17.

37. Paula Levine, "Shadows from Another Place: San Francisco <-> Baghdad" (2004), available at http://shadowsfromanotherplace.net.

38. Levine, "Shadows from Another Place: Transposed Space," unpublished conference paper, *Media in Transition 4: The Work of Stories*, May 6–8, 2005, 4. Available at http://web.mit.edu/comm-forum/mit4/papers/levine.pdf.

39. Rita Raley points out that in new media poetics the term *locative* "comes from a workshop hosted by a Latvian media arts center (2002) and is said to derive from the locative noun case indicating position in Balto-Slavic languages (akin to English pronouns 'in,' 'by,' and 'on')." See "On Locative Narrative," *Genre* 41 (Fall/Winter 2008), 125.

40. "In its methods," Bodenhamer explains, "deep mapping conflates oral testimony, anthology, memoir, biography, images, natural history, and everything you might ever want to say about a place.... [I]ts best form results in a subtle and multilayered view of a small area of the earth," 27.

41. The Missing Migrants Project documents the death of 3501 migrants in attempted crossings of the Mediterranean in 2016, more than double the number who died in 2011. See http://missing migrants.iom.int/.

42. Eyal Weizman, "Introduction: Forensis," *Forensis: The Architecture of Public Truth* (London: Sternberg Press and Forensic Architecture, 2014), 12.

43. Ibid., 11.

44. Ibid., 11.

45. Ibid., 13.

46. Ibid., 11.

47. For the full report, see Charles Heller, Lorenzo Pezzani, and SITU Research, "Forensic Oceanography: The Deadly Drift of a Migrants' Boat in the Central Mediterranean Sea, 2011," *Forensis*, 638–55.

48. Examples published in the past fifteen years include Claudia Rankine's *Citizen* (Graywolf, 2014), Mark Nowak's *Shut Up Shut Down* (Coffee House, 2004) and *Coal Mountain Elementary* (Coffee House, 2009), Cheena Marie

Lo's *A Serious of Un/Natural/Disasters* (Commune, 2016), Evelyn Reilly's *Styrofoam* (Roof, 2009), Stephen Collis, *Once in Blockadia* (Talonbooks, 2016), Rachel Zolf's *Neighbour Procedure* (Coach House, 2010), Robert Fitterman's *Holocaust Museum* (Counterpath, 2011), Amy Sara Carroll's *Fannie + Freddie* (Fordham, 2013), Philip Metres's *Sand Opera* (Alice James, 2015), and numerous other long poems and poetic projects that détourne documents from the public sphere to expose and condemn habits of thought and turns of language that undergird labor exploitation, racial violence, systematic torture and abuse, and the massive intensification of precarity and governmental precaritization in the twenty-first century.

49. Perloff, "Screening the Page / Paging the Screen: Digital Poetics and the Differential Text," *New Media Poetics: Contexts, Technotexts, and Theories*, eds. Adalaide Morris and Thomas Swiss (Cambridge, MA: MIT Press, 2006), 143–65. For samples of the various instantiations of *Drift*, see Callicoon Gallery's website at http://callicoonfinearts.com/exhibitions/caroline-bergvall/, performance stills at http://www.caroline-bergvall.com/drift-performance.php, and a brief video trailer at https://vimeo.com/86554191.

50. Butler, *Frames of War: When Is Life Grievable*, 25.

51. Bergvall, *Drift*, 143.

52. Ibid., 128.

53. Ibid., 55.

54. Ibid., 58.

55. Ibid., 135.

56. Ibid., 153, 147.

57. Gilles Deleuze and Félix Guattari, *A Thousand Plateaus: Capitalism and Schizophrenia*, trans. Brian Massumi (Minneapolis, MN: University of Minnesota Press, 1987), 9.

Supine, Prone, Precarious

Sarah Dowling

FOR SEVERAL DECADES NOW, scholarship in poetics has engaged questions of sovereignty and personhood primarily through debates about the "I" and its relative degree of unity or dispersal. In one camp, scholars of modern and contemporary experimental poetry (as well as experimental poets) have critiqued the fiction of unified subjectivity, often encouraging a rejection of the "I" or of the "lyric" poetry where it seems most prevalent. Partly in response to this critique, theorists of the new lyric studies have sought to historicize the notion that poems encode and reveal private, introspective, or meditative subjects, arguing that this idea is more representative of twentieth-century reading practices than it is of any particular genre of poetry.[1] What is less often discussed are the ways in which questions about the "I" and its imputed instability or disunity resonate with theories of precarity, which also tend to rely on the idea that a previously whole subject has, under contemporary conditions, suffered a fundamental disaggregation. Psychoanalytically derived accounts of precarity, such as Judith Butler's, describe an "undoing" of a previously whole or stable self, framing this as a response to witnessing another's spectacular vulnerability.[2] Relatedly, theories of precarity that emphasize its economic basis, such as Angela Mitropoulos's, describe a post-Fordist indistinction between work and life that enables the movement of exploitation into every aspect of the worker's personhood, enjoining the worker to treat him- or herself as a commodity all of the time, not just from nine to five.[3]

While I am obviously sketching a very broad theoretical terrain in very light strokes, this essay responds to a variety of contentions that the pressures of the present have put the "I" in a precarious position. I want to shift attention away from the "I," though, in order to attend more carefully to the material that remains after its undoing: to bodies, to the postures that they take, and to the ways in which they are described. Rather than the abstractions of legal or lyric personhood—of the subject or the worker—rather than the abstraction of *the* body as a generalized site or object of theoretical inquiry, this paper focuses on a single gesture, lying down. In analyzing this gesture, I want to think about how bodies on the ground, as remnants left after the undoing of the "I," might serve as representative figures for our time.

In contemporary poetry, fiction, performance, and film, supine and prone bodies are ubiquitous, disrupting and rearranging the scenes in which they appear, and offering disturbing notations of the present that contest dominant narratives of liberal individual agency, postracial harmony, meritocratic individualism, and the like.[4] While bodies on the ground often seem flatly to suggest victimization, lying down carries a number of connotations that are more *and* less agential: acts of withdrawal such as taking to one's bed mean something different from iconic protest tactics such as the die-in, and neither can be equated with the unfortunate or even comical results of unintentional stumbling and falling. Lying down is often a feminized gesture, and as such it frequently carries connotations of sexual passivity.[5] In this way, lying down can encompass questions of public and private, of engagement and disengagement, of going on and not-going on, of ability and sexuality. Because of its close association with victimization and with protest, though, lying down also draws attention to the social structures through which violence is distributed, particularly racism, sexism, and their various entwinements. Supine and prone bodies raise questions of periodization in their vivid evocations of the divide between modernist break, rupture, or resistance, and the post-modernist depression and resignation that derive from the suffocating exhaustion brought on by the neoliberal reconfiguration of work; by the shrinking and atrophy of social welfare programs; by the length of your commute and the rising costs of housing and child care; by the necessity of taking on debt and the inability to pay it off; by routine and overwhelming racism, sexism, transphobia, classism, and ableist micro- and macroaggressions; by the toll and necessity of performing emotional labor . . .

In this essay, I will examine contemporary representations of lying down through comparisons with two related figures: first, I want to consider the supine and prone bodies in contemporary literature in contrast with the Euro-modernist flaneur, the representative figure of the nineteenth and twentieth centuries who, in Baudelaire's view, also served as the prototype for the lyric "I." [6] Equally, I want to consider such bodies in relationship to the bodies of protesters engaged in a die-in. The die-in became an iconic protest tactic during the 1980s and early 1990s, when the AIDS Coalition to Unleash Power (ACT UP) deployed it in carefully orchestrated and highly publicized acts of resistance against state violence toward persons with AIDS. Unlike the flaneur, the singular and mobile consciousness whose unique perspective filtered and shaped the representation of the city through which he moved, the protester dying-in momentarily halts his or her own mobility, and ideally also draws to a halt the portion of the city in which he or she is located. By lying down with others, protesters engaged in a die-in use their bodies to represent a collectivity of persons impacted in various ways by structural violence. ACT UP die-ins aggregated the bodies of persons with AIDS and their allies, using passive noncompliance to frustrate police access to any individual body and to prevent the removal of protesters from the street. [7] In this way, I understand the protester dying-in as a counterfigure to the flaneur: intentionally un-unique, protesters work together to repeat the postures and gestures of many others; their immobile nonconsciousness represents an experience that they either share with others, or that is not even their own. In this essay, I want to think of supine and prone bodies in contemporary literature as engaging in acts akin to miniature die-ins—acts that annihilate mobility and consciousness in demonstration of state and interpersonal violence. However, these acts are, in their small size and lack of collective ambition, stripped of the power of scale that the die-in achieves.

I will focus, then, on just one text in which lying down forms an especially prominent motif, Bhanu Kapil's *Ban en Banlieue* (2015).[8] This book of poetic prose, which Kapil describes as a novel, combines various genres and moments of crisis, laying these one on the other through photographs, notes, instructions, vignettes, lists, reflections on the failures of the writing process, and documents for and from the performances that constellate around the book. In *Ban en Banlieue*, supine and prone bodies act as stumbling blocks to narrative completion, and also break any arc toward closure or repair. The gesture of lying down (or laying down, as I will describe) is staged as a critical response to the pressures of the present, which chip away at the viability of life for women of color in particular, and at the viability of traditional genres and models of completion.[9] In Kapil's book, lying down is not a matter of personal comfort but a historical condition: bodies on the ground are primarily feminized, primarily of color, and have been made extraneous to the economic order. These bodies have been brought low through specific, traceable processes, which her book elliptically documents. Although *Ban en Banlieue* relies heavily on a certain impression of autobiography, Kapil's first- and third-person narration breaks with the grammatical conventions for rendering singular subjectivity and instead her book's many supine and prone bodies are caught up in what Lauren Berlant has described as "a circuit of adjustment and gestural transformation."[10] That is, these bodies do not resist their social and structural conditions but respond in other ways to what they have to face. I argue that *Ban en Banlieue* calls for a materialist reconception of suffering, one that is not oriented toward notions of recognition, redress, or repair, but that is motivated by a desire to be with, to be near, and to be like those who have suffered and are suffering in order to understand their condition in a bodily (and perhaps not a strictly intellectual) way.

But first, the flaneur.

This upright, ambulatory figure moved through the city, undertaking modes of scanning and collecting that relieved him from the crisis of urban anomie and allowed him access to the milling crowd, as well as a compensatory mental distance from it. The flaneur (and, to a lesser extent, the flaneuse, whose movement was much more encumbered than that of her masculine counterpart) was a mobile agent of perception, exercising control over his sensory impressions and choosing what to record and convey. While the flaneur's progress through and observations of the city emblematized the shock of modernity and its new forms of urbanization, the vast majority of the world's population now lives in cities (or in their surrounding *banlieues*, as I will discuss) and has access to mass culture via multiple technologies. The gestures that provided relief for the flaneur are, in our moment, part and parcel of mass culture: scanning and collecting have been fully assimilated into the processes of data mining and surveillance. Theorists of everyday life argue that the shock of the urban that characterized the sensorium of the previous century no longer describes how most people live and feel today. So how, then, are we responding to the pressures of the present?

Supine and prone bodies vividly convey a common emotional response to the contemporary moment. They lie still and are bombarded. They take it lying down, and make a display of their own having to do so. They demonstrate the racial and classed hierarchies through which people are variously made to live and die. Certainly, the gesture of lying down might at times provide compensation or relief (as it would in the case of taking to one's bed, to one's couch, or to one's bath), but it is more often—and more significantly—a result of being made extraneous to or expendable by the social order. As I indicated, in *Ban en Banlieue*, the solitary gesture of lying down, so often repeated, has another important precedent: it shares something with the structure of the die-in, a protest tactic that became iconic with ACT UP's spectacular militancy against AIDS and that has once again come to prominence in the Black Lives Matter movement.[11] The die-in makes a large-scale display of the effects of structural violence, vividly representing a particular group's precarious condition by making a public performance of mass casualty. Spurred by the writings of artist David Wojnarowicz, ACT UP's die-ins sought to make private, individual deaths public and visible. Activists jumbled the streets of lower Manhattan, mingling the bodies of healthy allies pretending death with the bodies of the dying in stark demonstrations of the virus's impact.[12] Placing hundreds of prone forms on Wall Street, at the gates of the White House, in and around New York's St. Patrick's Cathedral, and outside the headquarters of the Food and Drug Administration and New York City Hall, ACT UP's die-ins used ill and well bodies to create interference at precisely the sites where their own lives and the lives of their loved ones were being interfered with. The individualized acts of lying down in *Ban en Banlieue* similarly evoke the postures and fates of those who have fallen victim to or are trying to survive racialized and gendered violence, with the important difference that in Kapil's book the posture does not contribute to the making of a collective. Unlike the public gesture of solidarity that is the die-in, the individual gestures of lying down narrated in *Ban en Banlieue* are more evocative of private, even sexual refusal, although they too take place in public streets: "I don't have to lie down with you," her narrator says, in one moment of oblique apostrophe, "And I don't" (62).

This refusal begins to suggest the ways in which *Ban en Banlieue* is not reparative in its aims. Rather than seeking to humanize the figures she describes, Kapil's descriptions of single bodies on the ground have a distinctly nonspectacular quality, which is remarkably continuous with the grammar of violence that would deny the subjectivity of her narrator, Ban (who is ambiguously autobiographical in her possession of Kapil's own childhood nickname). Importantly, Kapil does not resist this denial, even describing Ban as "a vaginal opening . . . a blob of meat on the sidewalk" (20), "a monster" and "a desiccating form" (21). In addition to this dehumanizing imagery, her prose toggles between third- and first-person perspectives that at once multiply and minimize the narrator/protagonist. In the third person, her descriptions of lying down are straightforward, although they have a dispassionate, distancing effect: "A girl stops walking and lies down on a street in the opening scene of a riot" (32); "Ban lying down in a sidewalk in London" (45); "she simply did this (lie down), then stood up with a long stick torn from a nearby tree, though the area is desolate, marked the outline that was left" (57). The uses of the first person intensify the passivity of the gesture as the narrator's body becomes the direct object of the grammatical phrase: "As a child, I lay down on the bed like a sentence not written yet" (62); "I think of how I lay down on the ground for him, thinking he would come, with coffee, and a blanket, but how, when morning came, I had frozen into a new position" (63); "And there I lay down" (47). Slipping between narrative points of view that seem to overlap, and between activity and passivity, this grammatical intensification of the gesture(s) of lying down and of laying oneself down as one would an object creates the impression of a disunified and dispersed narrator/protagonist, diminishing Ban's agency and individual subjectivity. But it is this that the book calls for: its narration leaves Ban as a passive and inert object, prone at the side of the road.

This "auto-sacrifice" (7) of subjectivity takes place in response to social denials of subjectivity, extending rather than repairing their violence. It is precisely from the physical space and gesture of this annihilation that the narrative proceeds: the conceit that shapes the book is that Ban, a young "brown [black] girl"[13] is walking home from school when she hears

> the sound of breaking glass, and understands the coming violence has begun. Is it coming from the far-off street or is it coming from her home? Knowing that either way she's done for—she lies down to die. A novel is thus an account of a person who has already died, in advance of the death they are powerless. To prevent. "There are no angels." What will it take to shed off, to be rendered, to incarnate, to never be there in the same way again? (20)

The book grapples with the possibility of narration from the position of the girl on the ground, who has placed herself there in response to multiple threats: violence at home, an incipient race riot. She is "powerless" to prevent her own death, but Kapil's prose blurs Ban's agency with the novel's—instead of construing the work as an imaginative space in which a young girl like Ban can save herself or be saved from external forces of violence, Kapil suggests that "there are no angels." Her book constantly returns to the space where Ban was, and gives instructions—which seem to address Kapil as well as readers—to lie down in it, to follow Ban's example. In reading the book we are "there" again and again in the places where Ban responded to her own or to others' victimization, although not in "the same way" that she was, or that they were.

Kapil's suggestion that "to never be there in the same way again" is a broad goal belies the significance of the repetition of being "there" on the ground throughout her book. Her emphasis on the sexual connotations carried by the gesture of lying (or laying) down suggests an intimacy with, or a desire to be physically close to, those who have suffered, those who have been brought low. In addition to the oft-stated desire to "lie down in the place I am from: on the street I am from" (31), Kapil explains that she "wanted to write a book that was like lying down" (42). In addition to Ban, four fallen figures haunt the text, offering evocative suggestions as to what this similarity to lying down might mean or do. The book is dedicated to Blair Peach, a teacher and an activist killed by police during an anti-Nazi demonstration in Southall, England, on April 23, 1979. Its disrupted and disruptive rituals are indebted to two radical artists of color, Theresa Hak Kyung Cha and Ana Mendieta, both killed in New York (in 1982 and 1985, respectively). Perhaps most overtly elegized in the text is Jyoti Singh, a young woman who was gang raped and mutilated in Munirka, South Delhi, India, on December 16, 2012, and whom Kapil's narrator most explicitly seeks to memorialize and emulate. These four figures' bodies appear in the text in direct and indirect ways: describing a 2014 performance in New Delhi, Kapil writes, "I walk—naked, bare-foot, red—from the cinema in South Delhi where she watched *The Life of Pi*. Then caught a bus. To this spot. The antirape protesters make a circle around my body when I lie down. What do they receive? An image. But what happens next?" (16). In this intimate, confessional first-person narration, Kapil describes repeating Singh's bodily posture and occupying the location in which she suffered, asking what happens when one's physical posture is imagined or framed as a repetition of the results of violence. She describes her action as a "performance" and a "memorial" that produces "hormones," suggesting that it alters the physical composition of the bodies of those who participate in or observe its rituals (16). At a minimum, such reenactments serve as a way of showing "how some bodies don't disseminate; they don't degrade. Are never washed away" (90). Though their suffering seems small, even invisible, through performative repetition these bodies become monumental.

Lest this description suggest that the bodies whose postures Kapil repeats are in any way singular, she also emphasizes the structural character of the violence that they have suffered. To write the supine or prone posture as suffused with the histories of those who have previously taken or been forced into it, she explains, is "a way of marking, too, the violence received by the bodies of women in the place that I am [was] from" (90).[14] To be absolutely clear, that place (or at least one of those places) is London, particularly its lesser-known immigrant and working-class enclaves. If the flaneur wandered more or less freely through the metropolis, the central figure of Kapil's *Ban en Banlieue* is largely restricted to the suburbs, the *banlieues* of her title. The term *banlieue* not only echoes the names of the author and her narrator/protagonist, it also carries a racial connotation in that *banlieues* are the outer rings of contemporary global cities, and are generally home to racialized populations whose access to the city center and its resources is limited. Kapil's insistence on this economically disadvantaged and disconnected setting locates the action of her text in regions often perceived as peripheral or irrelevant within the metronormative imaginary of global capitalism.[15]

The frequently expressed desire to be close to the prone or supine bodies on the ground—to occupy their same position, to acknowledge a shared positionality, or to repeat their position in demonstration of it —traces trajectories of migration that angle away from the most urban sites, or indicate failure and suffering within them.

2. Street: Lie down on sidewalk next to the ivy in the exact spot that the novel is set, somewhere between Balmoral Avenue and

Lansbury Drive. Observe the sky. Install circular mirrors in the vines. Nervous system notes. Descriptions of weather and neighborhood. Similarly, at other sites in West London, crumple aluminium foil, make a daffodil ikebana as a late April shrine. Hayes, Middlesex, England, 2012. (16)

These numbered, Fluxus-inspired instructions are only one of Kapil's poetic challenges to the genre of the novel, as well as to the lyric's connotations of individual singularity. Evoking the radical performance traditions of Yoko Ono and others, as well as the protest tactics and histories that I have described, Kapil's repeated (instructions for a) performance of lying down is a way to be "there," where some victim was, not in "the same way" that they were, but in a way that maintains and insists on their presence within a given scene. Moreover, the distribution of performative acts that occurs, if only through suggestion and through the use of the imperative mood, proposes that bodies on the ground will proliferate—if only imaginatively—as readers picture themselves "[lying] down on the sidewalk next to the ivy in the exact spot where the novel is set." The supine and prone positions described in the text are, then, positions into which one might be forced through structural and interpersonal violence, but they are also poses that can be struck intentionally, with volition, in order to make visible the structural conditions of the present, the ways in which our collective moment is conditioned by its histories.

In *Ban en Banlieue*, then, bodies on the ground expose the historical present as suffused with and constituted by its pasts—of post- and neocolonial racism, and of gendered violence. The postures of these supine and prone bodies suggest that all one can do in the encounter with the present is to be overwhelmed and to lie still. While Kapil directly connects her instructions for and evocations of supine bodies to the prone forms of Peach, Cha, Mendieta, and Singh, the bodies in her book also evoke other histories, which seem encapsulated or miniaturized in the singular form of a body on the ground.

Ban is a desiccating form on the sidewalk—her teeth, in contrast, are so white—turn indigo: when the headlights of oncoming cars strobe over her prone, barely visible/dark face. And hair. I should have written the alien body as a set of fragments, a ghazal with an omega mouth and a healing cry; instead, I went with *historical fiction*—the narrative of a riot that had receded by 1983, to be overlain by other riots. The riot is a charnel ground in this sense—overlain—in the present—by concrete—poured right down—over the particular spot on the sidewalk I am speaking of—as well as—migrations—from Eastern Europe—and beyond. . . . I wanted the fragments to circulate then ebb, just as immigrant memory is fragile, replaced by the next incoming wave of life; . . . later, in Arabic, Polish, and Tamil script printed right on the glass, the words for goat, electronics, the fruit with the little black spots below the anus of the stem. (21–22)

Kapil's images of layers—of poured concrete, of "incoming waves," and of the palimpsest of languages—suggest a thickened historical present in which a body on the ground might be suffering from or calling attention to any number of threats and kinds of violence that have accreted over time. Kapil's repetition of the small girl Ban's gesture takes her wise passivity and places it within a network of related postures that manifest a politically depressed position, without necessarily seeking repair or any form of further action. In this respect, the gesture of lying down that appears in *Ban en Banlieue* differs from the die-in, although both expose the vulnerability to structural violence that is sometimes called "precarity." Whereas in a die-in the supine posture that protestors strike is inhabitable and shareable, constituting a momentary "we" who are united in protesting against the conditions that some group of people is made to suffer, in *Ban en Banlieue* the self-contained, individual body demonstrates the repetitive quality of violence, without constituting a collective, and without preserving its own individual subjectivity while striking the pose. The supine and prone positions struck by characters and narrators, and perhaps by the author and her readers, differ in their degrees of violation and in their causes, but they share a capacity to be annihilated, or to point to the annihilation of the capacity of the body to carry its own distinctive "I."

What I am proposing in this essay, then, is a shift in critical emphasis: from the psychological precarity of the "I" and the economic precarity of the worker, to the physical precarity of the body as matter and as flesh. What I find so significant about Kapil's emphasis on imitation and performance is that its descriptions of lying down—especially the gestures of lying down that repeat someone else's bodily position—completely undercuts the mastery and singularity associated with a flaneur-type commentator, who might curate and select the city's sights and sites for readerly consumption. In this sense, I understand her book as calling for a materialist reconception of suffering that is not oriented toward recognition, redress, and repair, but that is focused on repetition and annihilation as mutually constituting structural forces.[16] Lying down does not offer a unique perspective on these conditions, but simply evidences their material effects by showing the exhaustion, the hurt, and the death that they produce.

In response to a pervasive crisis in which such annihilation streams from multiple sources, perhaps lying down is all we can do. And in this respect, we might think about lying down as a way of doing nothing that does something: it might be a way of going self-protectively catatonic; it might be a way of rearranging a scene in order to demonstrate what goes unnoticed or unseen within it. Lying down can be a way of *not* going on, an auto-sacrifice in which one's individuality is snuffed out, whether for a moment (as is the case in a die-in) or forever (as is the case when one dies). The supine or prone body lies in the path of the neoliberal presumption of progress that explains away structural inequalities and the distribution of violence that structure the present, tripping up easy stories of postracial meritocratic liberal progressivism. In this sense, representations of bodies on the ground point to the limitations of critiques of the lyric "I," of work in the new lyric studies, and with much new work on precarity, as they vividly demonstrate the limitations of critical preoccupation with subjectivity and personhood. Such representations reveal the necessity of accounting for bodies in their fleshly specificity, and of developing a critical language capable of describing the structural processes through which some bodies are brought low.

Ban en Banlieue begins from the assumption that when one suffers these processes, one will be unable to go on—or, from another, perhaps more privileged standpoint, that when we really look at them, we will decide that we oughtn't. The layered crises of the present have made and are making other responses impossible. I am arguing that criticism ought to follow its object in attending to this politically depressed position (where depression is "postmodern" in the sense that it is apposite to the "activity" of modern rupture). We ought to view lying down as a periodizing gesture insofar as it reveals the somatization of historical harms—the hurt that accretes in our bodies over years or even generations. The repeated encounters with bodies on the ground—how many did you see on your way to work this morning?—that are staged in *Ban en Banlieue* and other works ask us to rethink the terms through which we imagine the period in which we are living. They ask that we attend to the consequences of suffering in their materiality, to look carefully at who falls and to describe how much energy it takes to walk away.

NOTES

1. For examples of the resistance to the lyric "I," see Bruce Andrews and Charles Bernstein, eds. *The L=A=N=G=U=A=G=E Book* (Carbondale: Southern Illinois University Press, 1984). For thorough discussions of the new lyric studies see Virginia Jackson and Yopie Prins, *The Lyric Theory Reader: A Critical Anthology* (Baltimore: Johns Hopkins University Press, 2014), and Stephen Burt, "What Is This Thing Called Lyric?" *Modern Philology* 133.3 (2016), 422–40.

2. Judith Butler, *Precarious Life: The Powers of Mourning and Violence* (London: Verso, 2006).

3. Angela Mitropoulos, "Precari.Us?" *EIPCP.net* (2005). http://eipcp. net/transversal/0704/mitropoulos/en.

4. There are an almost infinite number of works in which lying down features prominently. A few key examples include: Virginia Woolf's *On Being Ill* (1930); Ana Mendieta's *Silhuetas* series; Agnes Varda's *Vagabond* (1984); Robert Kroetsch's *The Studhorse Man* (1969); Gail Scott's *Heroine* (1987); Luisa Valenzuela's *Realidad nacional desde la cama* (1990); David Wojnarowicz's *Close to the Knives: A Memoir of Disintegration* (1991); and Dawn Lundy Martin's *Life in a Box Is a Pretty Life* (2014).

5. A trove of examples can be listed here, from Bob Dylan's grammatically incorrect "Lay Lady Lay" (1969), to Eric Clapton's equally incorrect "Lay Down Sally" (1977), to the iconic image of the nude teen Angela (Mena Suvari) reclining on a bed of rose petals in Sam Mendes's *American Beauty* (1999), to the cover of Nicki Minaj's album *Pink Friday* (2010), or any of the multitude of contemporary odalisques populating magazine editorials and print ads.

6. While it may seem anachronistic to associate the flaneur and flaneuse with the twentieth century as a whole, a number of writers and art historians have recently argued for the ongoing significance of flanerie, even into the present moment. See Rebecca Solnit's *Wanderlust: A History of Walking* (New York: Penguin, 2001); Lauren Elkin, *Flâneuse: Women Walk the City in Paris, New York, Tokyo, Venice and London* (New York: Farrar, Strauss & Giroux, 2016); and Judith Rodenbeck's project in progress, *Bipedal Modernity*, which examines the biopolitics of modernity through its configurations of human and robotic bodies, and their ability (or inability) to walk. For more on Baudelaire and flanerie see Walter Benjamin, *Charles Baudelaire: A Lyric Poet in the Era of High Capitalism* (New York & London: Verso, 1997).

7. Susan Leigh Foster, "Choreographies of Protest." *Theatre Journal* 55, no. 3 (2003) 395–412.

8. Bhanu Kapil, *Ban en Banlieue* (New York: Night Boat, 2015).

9. For an excellent take on the grammar of l(a)ying down in this book, see Amy De'Ath's "L(a)ying Down in the Banlieue," *Mute Magazine*, September 16, 2016 http://www.metamute.org/editorial/articles/laying-down-banlieue.

10. Lauren Berlant, *Cruel Optimism* (Durham, NC: Duke University Press, 2011), 249.

11. See Nicholas D. Mirzoeff, "#BlackLivesMatter Is Breathing New Life into the Die-In." *New Republic* August 10, 2015. https://newrepublic.com/article/122513/blacklivesmatter-breathing-new-life-die.

12. Eventually, when death rates climbed, ACT UP shifted to the tactic of the "political funeral," moving from the symbolic to the actual by incorporating the bodies of their beloved dead into their actions.

13. The brackets in this quotation are Kapil's. Her copresentation of the terms *brown* and *black* simultaneously evokes different ethno-racial classifications: the term *brown* generally refers to people of color not of African descent (in this case, most likely South Asians), while the term black in this case seems to refer to the British use of the term. Unlike the U.S. American term *black*, which refers specifically to people of African descent, in the U.K. the term *black* has been used to refer to people of color in general. More recently, the term *black* in the U.K. has been replaced by the phrase "black and minority ethnic" or "B.A.M.E.," although this too has come under criticism. Kapil's simultaneous use of both terms implicates her U.S. American and British readerships, as both *black* and *brown* seem to be attributions rather than terms that Ban uses to refer to herself.

14. The square brackets in this quotation are Kapil's.

15. While U.S. readers of *Ban en Banlieue* may be more accustomed to imagining that people of color tend to live in city centers and that suburbia is the quintessential space of whiteness, it is important to keep in mind the contexts of *Ban en Banlieue*, which are specifically and insistently English and European. Moreover, *Ban en Banlieue* is framed in moments as a response to the rioting in the suburbs of Paris in 2005. It is worth considering, however, that the patterns of white flight that created white suburbia have been significantly reversed in many North American cities. American suburbia, like its European counterparts, is now home to many communities of color, and U.S. inner cities' populations of color are in significant decline. See Jeff Chang's "Vanilla Cities and Their Chocolate Suburbs: On Resegregation" in *We Gon' Be Alright: Notes on Race and Resegregation* (New York: Picador, 2016) and Karen Tongson's *Relocations: Queer Suburban Imaginaries* (New York: NYU Press, 2011).

16. Another critic who calls for a materialist reconception of suffering is Alexander Weheliye. His book, *Habeas Viscus*, while much different than Kapil's, seems sympathetic to her aims. See *Habeas Viscus: Racializing Assemblages, Biopolitics, and Black Feminist Theories of the Human* (Durham, NC: Duke University Press, 2014).

The Opening of the (Transnational Battle) Field

Heriberto Yépez

/// 1 ///

Concept plus its other, poetics
Feels
   Like a program
Poets' theory is case-based wish-form
Wish-faulted
     Caged-thinking
     Precarious prophecy
Poetics
Paper Prayer Pamphlet

In a gathering of poets-professors wishing
To exercise poetics-as-prefiguration
I want to point-at
     And
      Constellate
The entanglement of revolution and coloniality
(Re)animating
      The opening of the (transnational
Battle) field

/// 2 ///

WILLIAM BURROUGHS, or, as he liked to called himself, "el Hombre Invisible" went to Mexico at the middle of the last century, where he reported a fuller freedom. He wasn't the only North American experimental writer who thought the "American Dream" was located in Mexico. Most famously, Olson and Kerouac had also Mexican episodes in the fifties.

Burroughs attributed the killing of his wife to the influence of an "Ugly Spirit" and described it as a "hateful parasitic occupation ... a possession ... a definite possessing entity" that he considered closer "to the medieval model than to modern psychological explanations, with their dogmatic insistence that such manifestations must come from within and never, never, never from without." [1]

There is strong evidence that one key ingredient in the "Ugly Spirit" was Burroughs's imperial contact with Southern cultures. The cut-up of drugs, Northern experimental machismo and Mexican urban culture triggered the formation of the "Ugly Spirit," a language-centered psychosomatic transnational entity.

Now let us see how this ethopoetical process evolved.

Goldsmith Goes Global.

FIGURE 10. "Printing Out the Internet." Marisol Rodríguez, Mexico City, 2013.

Here we have Kenneth Goldsmith enjoying white control of global archives in the age of electronic inequality. The photo was taken in Mexico City in 2013 by Marisol Rodríguez on the occasion of the *Printing Out the Internet* exhibition.

This portrait shows how the "electronic revolution" (to use Burroughs's viral words) helped this ethopoetic subject to avoid the formation of the "Ugly Spirit." Goldsmith has cocreated *here* (but not at Brown University) a scene where the hubristic macho xenophobic assymmetrical intercultural dominator self-expresses in cooler ways.

Goldsmith's pleasant day at the remediated beach was made possible by NAFTA, nonexistent at the time of Burroughs's transnational crisis. Another element that eased Goldsmith's status is the solidification of the "Colonial Library," defined by the Bolivian poet-professor Silvia Rivera Cusicanqui as the "colonial appropriation" and management of centralized collections of Latin American primary and secondary sources by North American universities.

Rivera Cusicanqui describes her experience at the "Colonial Library" as a series of "intense and contradictory emotions" running from "amazement to despair" and simultaneous "feelings of expansion of the intellectual horizon" and a "deep sense of frustration." [2]

In order to talk about the "Colonial Library," Rivera Cusicanqui says she needs both to *reflect* and *feel*. I return, then, to my point of departure: a poetics that is only concept reduces itself to rational, instrumental "Enlightenment." Poetics should at least be *concept* plus its *other*, and that is why I will further exit the "paper"-form for the remaining space available.

/// 3 ///

The Oniro-NAFTA region desires
An active transnational writing
But this libidinal surge does not intend to abandon

Monolinguism. It wants new markets, new archives
To solve domestic crises. Appropriating and subsuming others—
It's still an expansionist-colonial desire. It's Empire

(Mostly) white cultural elites ping-pong Capital Aesthetics
Across the colonial axis. "Cosmopolitan" Eurocentric inertia
Is transnationalism's undercurrent. Another somatic
Transnationalism comes from working class migrants
Using more than one language and remaking culture
Outside law, peace and citizenship. The inventive
Is coming from these peoples.

Fights between transnationalisms will define
Tomorrow's poetries of risk. The question is not
To be or not to be transnational but in which way?

Today neoliberalism has refurbished
Experimentalism into varieties of resilient job experience
Neoliberal poetics doesn't mean writers are sinners
It means they are embedded

Goldsmith's old concept reframed
Reaffirmed colonial structures on the other side
Of Bill Clinton's border fence. Goldsmith's appropriation
Of experimentalism strengthened official verse culture's apoliti-
    cal predisposition
Upper-class aesthetic elegance and neutralization of leftist poetics
Northern conceptualism proved to be counterinsurgent
    in the South—Also

Before and after the conceptual implosion
Previous Latin American conceptualisms here and there
Have been co-opted, put at the service of the Master-
Slave blood bank supply

Where the conceptual slave enters the stage
When the conceptual master grows weak

Transnationalizing experimentalism does
Not necessarily produce innovation
Although the geopolitical gaze does endanger the spell

Unexpectedly for the now dead Buddhist and anarchist spirit
À la John Cage, neoliberal experimentalism
May precisely be the driving force of its transnationalization
Across the Americas today

If setting patterns of aesthetic dissent
Is one ingredient in the contradiction which is poetics
We can try preventing the transnational from turning
Into the most appealing ideology only if we remember
The transnational is also a nonhuman agency and will
Trump us

I read Marx's diagnosis of a "world-literature" along these lines
Including his own Eurocentric-biopolitical pilot-plan

If transnational poetics take decolonial forms
We might co-ignite change. As of now "experimentalism"
Aestheticizes the *leukotropic*
What tends toward "whiteness," the so-called fine, ratio-
      nal, beautiful, cool
Eunoian, harmonic and superior
And marginalizes the *melantropic*, the dark, disorderly, cacopeian
Dangerous, deficient, vulgar and inferior

Experimentalism chained itself to the leukotropic rules of D*E*S*I*G*N

North American experimentalism mostly lives

In denial of how its nation-centered procedures
Have much to do with xenophobia, the job market and imperialism
But as it encounters other innovative networks
And traditions in the DysGlobal South
Experimentalism will lose its national patriarchal and matriarchal
Bodyguards and linear avant-garde master narrative
Coming out of these struggles enriched by a state
Of partial memory loss, archive fever, inappropriate
Behavior, mistranslation, forced displacement and acute fragmentation

The transnational could become the ultimate paratactic rearrangement
Disabling poets to shape and re-produce themselves
Through national entitlements
Never ecological in relation to a larger geopoetics

To separate experimentalism from national leukotropisms
Is historically impossible. The (Neo)Avant-Garde
And the Colonial Library are intertwined

Only if experimentalism expands leukotropically can it survive

Once postnational and postexperimental
Ethopoetics take charge of new-writer's bodies
"Experimentalism" will not be the driving force of innovative poetics

Currently, in ceasing to be an influential *network*, Language
Poetry begins to fully operate as a *tradition*
A militant participant in curated history
A collective and disjointed body able to be reanimated
And mobilized by other agents in other times and sites

Today we imagine the transnational as spreading
Through synchronic networks
But the transnational also involves diachronic engagements

With foreign lineages and discontinuous periods
Disruption thus may occur through tradition-work

We can't say the revolution will be networked
But we can be sure it will be fueled by archives

Traditions in a transnational field of writing will not necessarily work
As they do in national literatures, where they preserve legacies
And erase alterities. At the transnational level, alien traditions may play
A destructive role against other sets of masters

Against intentions of nonexpressiveness, Language
And Post-Language white poetics will become problematic
"Demons" for others
						Like Stein or Pound
These demonic voices will probably creep
Into cultures that do not hate speech
Or deals with foreign colonial specters

The transnational is all about demonology						⟩

This revolutionary agency will increase
In the case of powerful melantropic, underground, peripheral
Indigenous, Black, mongrel, non-Western traditions
And networks only if they are radically decolonial

In sum, transnational conditions already shape our writing
And the lack of a transnational consciousness
Allows Marx's and Whitman's
Olson's and Goldsmith's ultra-modernistic
Expansionist projects to crystallize
Our growing transnational desires
Into the form of an irresistible COLONIAL REVOLUTIONARY
		seduction

All our poetic-epistemic desires occur inside the Colonial Library

The transnational of the now-future
Is being propelled and accelerated
Through this COLONIAL REVOLUTIONARY program

But some Souths desire to unrest the transnational

And force the "experiment"
To become a program of world revolution
Without world coloniality

NOTES

1. William Burroughs, "Introduction." *Queer* (New York: Penguin Books, 1987), XIX.

2. Silvia Rivera Cusicanqui, "Un paseo por la biblioteca colonial." *Hambre de huelga* (Mexico: La mirada salvaje, 2014), 99–100.

Poetry in the Making

A Bibliography of Publications by Graduate Students in the Poetics Program, 1991–2016

A PERSONAL INTRODUCTION TO A PUBLIC HISTORY

FROM ITS BEGINNING in the fall of 1991 up through today, the University at Buffalo English Department's Poetics Program has been largely organized around a single question: *what is poetics?* While far from the first to orient itself around such a pursuit, what has distinguished the program over the years is its assumption, shaped entirely in the image of its founders and continuing core faculty, that all answers to this question must invariably be experimentally derived, historically and culturally situated, and always plural. The defining vision of the program is based on an antifoundational understanding of poetry—that is, the processural activity of *poiesis*—as a liminal field always evolving out of its multiform past in response to the overlapping aesthetic, social, and political needs of the present. Its approach to poetry is a radical praxis in both senses of the word: rooted in particular theories and traditions and yet constantly branching out into progressively new and unforeseen directions. Pedagogically, the program has been heavily informed by former UB English Department Chair Albert Cook's practice in the 1960s of hiring poets and writers to teach literature classes based on their experience as practitioners of language as well as by those poets (both on faculty and visiting) who had previously been associated with that other great educational experiment Black Mountain College. It is no coincidence that the Poetics Program developed in a Rust Belt city that historically has been welcoming to experimentation across the arts. Encouraging an interdisciplinary study of poetries often within and between different cultures and time periods, the program's ethos from inception has included an openness to formal innovation, a general respect for all forms of linguistic alterity, ethnopoetics' insistence on the significance of sound and oral performance, and an emphasis on writing as social practice.

But, to be more specific, *what has been / is the poetics of the UB Poetics Program?* Certainly one answer lies in the program's dedicated and engaged faculty who have each left an indelible mark on the students like me who have been fortunate enough to study with them, so much so that it is impossible to think of the program without thinking of its core faculty Charles Bernstein, Robert Creeley, Raymond Federman, Judith Goldman, Susan Howe, Myung Mi Kim, Steve McCaffery, and Dennis Tedlock; its extensive group of affiliate faculty in English and other departments; and the curators of the Poetry Collection who have been longtime collaborators and participants, not to mention the hundreds of writers—some of the most interesting and significant poets and prose writers and critics and theorists from the latter half of the twentieth and beginning of the twenty-first centuries—who have visited over the years to give readings and guest lectures. But in my experience, biased as it surely is, I've always believed that the best indicator of the program's evolving poetics, not to mention its long-standing vitality, can be found in the activities of its students and especially their publications. And this is as true today in 2016 as it was in 1991. When I first arrived in Buffalo as a new poetics student in the summer of 2001, it seemed to me like everyone I met here was publishing a magazine, sewing chapbooks, organizing readings and conferences, and/or printing letterpress covers and posters. It was a community based in large part on the collaborative activity of *making*, and I loved it from the start.

An empirical approach to answering this ongoing question of *what has been / is the poetics of the UB Poetics Program?*—which over the years has sometimes led to various tensions among the community—can be found in the rich history of publications produced here by its graduate students. Each of these titles—each made thing—offers its own articulation of a particular poetics, and their sum total demonstrates a wide variety of active traditions (e.g., Objectivism, Black Mountain poetry, New York School, Language poetry, New Narrative, HOW(ever)); a number of emerging aesthetic movements of the 1990s, 2000s, and 2010s (e.g., electronic poetry, post-Language, Flarf, contemporary visual poetry, ecopoetics, Conceptual poetry); and the broad reach of the program as inscribed within a large constellation of overlapping print networks centered in Buffalo and radiating outward. As much as these publications offer in terms of their content and form, they are equally valuable in demonstrating how graduate students in the Poetics Program have been able to participate in the construction of their own literary communities through the activity of publishing themselves, their peers, their teachers, and their colleagues and mentors from around the world. Further extending the ground of poetics made manifest in these publications are the reading, talk, and performance series and the symposia organized over the years by Poetics graduate students. Viewed together these related projects allow one to begin mapping out the particular contributions of the program to the national and international discourses on poetry over the past twenty-five years.

The beginning of this bibliography's historical coverage coincides with the founding of the Poetics Program in the fall of 1991, and the first student publications begin to appear as early as that same semester. Looking through the pages of these chapbooks and magazines, one is continually reminded by their acknowledgements of all the forms of institutional support that made them possible. Certainly there would not have been so many titles without the generosity of those chairs and departments most often thanked, including the David Gray Chair of Poetry and Letters (Charles Bernstein, Steve McCaffery), James H. McNulty Chair (Dennis Tedlock), Samuel P. Capen Chair of Poetry and the Humanities (Robert Creeley, Susan Howe), Graduate Student Association (GSA), the Poetry/Rare Books Collection (now the Poetry Collection of the University Libraries), the English Graduate

Student Association (EGSA), Department of English, the Samuel
Clemens Chair (Leslie Fiedler), the Melodia Jones Chair (Raymond
Federman, Jean-Jacques Thomas), the Poetics Program, and others.

Whatever this bibliography may make visible about the history
of the UB Poetics Program, it does so at the expense of ignoring the
other magazines and presses in Buffalo with which these students and
publications were often in dialogue. To present a more comprehensive
picture then of a larger Buffalo poetics one would need to add at least
the following: other Buffalo magazines (e.g., *Earth's Daughters*, *No Trees*,
Yellow Field); other Buffalo publishers and presses (e.g., BlazeVOX,
Blue Garrote, House Press, Just Buffalo Literary Center, shuffaloff,
Starcherone, sunnyoutside, Weird Sisters, White Pine Press, Writer's
Den); UB undergrad magazines and presses (e.g., *name*, *we the notorious
pronouns*, PressBoardPress); UB faculty publication series (e.g., Buffalo
Broadsides, Buffalo Vortex, Outriders) and magazines (*Intent*, *Becoming
Poetics*); and publications from other schools, colleges, and organizations.

NOTES ON THE BIBLIOGRAPHY

MY PRINCIPLE in selecting materials for these lists has been to identify
those publications produced by students in the Poetics Program (often
difficult to determine, as membership has always been largely the result
of self-identification) and to list only those items that were published in
Buffalo during their time here as students. Presses and magazines that
started elsewhere and/or subsequently moved out of Buffalo to other loca-
tions are marked (*). Notable examples of magazines and presses edited
by Poetics students and published outside of Buffalo (and therefore not
included here) include Roberto Tejada's magazine *Mandorla* and Peter
Gizzi's coedited magazine *O·blék: A Journal of Language Arts* and its cor-
responding O·blék Editions.

Items marked (+) indicate that the archive for that particular
magazine or press is held by the Poetry Collection as one of its manu-
script collections.

CALL FOR CORRECTIONS AND ADDITIONS

DUE TO ITS NATURE this bibliography is undoubtedly guilty of inaccuracies, omissions, and partial information, especially in sections V, Reading, Talk, and Performance Series, and VI, Student-Organized Symposia. For these I apologize in advance, and ask that anyone with any corrections and/or additions to suggest please send them to me at jlm46@buffalo.edu. Also, since this collection was composed almost solely on the basis of the cataloged holdings of the Poetry Collection, anyone with additional materials not listed here is encouraged to donate them to the collection. We are continually looking for chapbooks, magazines, photographs, faculty syllabi, audio/video recordings, reading posters, and other ephemera that document the ongoing history of the Poetics Program.

ACKNOWLEDGMENTS

THANKS TO Edric Mesmer for his enthusiasm in publishing this bibliography as the inaugural chapbook in his *Among the Neighbors* series, Michael Basinski for many years of sharing with me his endless knowledge of the history of poetry in Buffalo, Alison Fraser and Declan Gould for their help in gathering together these publications, everyone who helped provide information and/or donated materials for this publication (far too many to name individually), and the Poetry Collection for its dedication to collecting as completely as possible the publications of students and faculty in the Poetics Program. Two sources that were useful for their bibliographic information regarding publications from the first few years of the program are *Publications from Buffalo, NY* (Buffalo: Poetry/Rare Books Collection, [1994?]) and Kristin Prevallet, "A Selected Bibliography of Buffalo Publications in Poetry and Poetics 1960–1996," *Chloroform: An Aesthetics of Critical Writing* (1997): 272–87.

Finally, I'd like to dedicate this publication—printed in conjunction with a retrospective exhibition titled *Poetry in the Making: The UB*

Poetics Program 1991–2016 in the Poetry Collection coinciding with the conference "Poetics: (The Next) 25 Years" as part of the twenty-fifth anniversary of the program—to all the faculty, staff, and students of the UB Poetics Program past, present, and future. For almost fifteen years now, first as a graduate student and then as curator, I've had the pleasure of seeing these publications assembled, printed, launched, exchanged, discussed, and enjoyed, and I hope (expect!) that the making will continue for many decades more.

—James Maynard

Curator, The Poetry Collection of the University Libraries,
University at Buffalo, The State University of New York
March 28, 2016 (updated December 2016)

I. PRINT SERIALS

apex of the M
Editors: Lew Daly, Alan Gilbert, Kristin Prevallet, and Ram Rehm
Contributing advisers: Susan Howe, David Levi Strauss, John Taggart,
Keith Waldrop, and Rosmarie Waldrop

    1 (Spring 1994)
    2 (Fall 1994)
    3 (Spring 1995)
    4 (Winter 1996)
    5 (Spring 1997)
    6 (Fall 1997)

Broke
Editor: Andrea Strudensky
Layout and illustrations: Joel C Brenden

    [Earlier issues?]
    Vol. 2, no. 1 (Winter 2009)

Celery Flute: The Kenneth Patchen Newsletter
Editor: Douglas Manson
Editorial Board: Michael Basinski, William Howe III, Lisa Phillips, and
Larry Smith

    Vol. 1, no. 1 (June 2006)
    Vol. 1, no. 2 (November 2006)
    Vol. 1, no. 3 (July 2007)
    Vol. 2, no. 1 (May 2009)

Chain (*) (+)
Editors: Jena Osman and Juliana Spahr

    1: Gender and Editing (Summer 1994)
    2: Documentary (Spring 1995)
    3: Hybrid Genres/Mixed Media, Vol. 1 (Spring 1996)
    3: Hybrid Genres/Mixed Media, Vol. 2 (Fall 1996)

Chloroform: An Aesthetics of Critical Writing
Editors: Nick Lawrence and Alisa Messer
Associate Editors: Amy Nestor, Cynthia Kimball, Taylor Brady,
Kristin Prevallet, Martin Spinelli, Ken Sherwood, Michael Stancliff,
Eleni Stecopoulos, and Yunte Huang
    1997

Curricle Patterns: A Magazine of Poetry Manuscripts
Editor: Alicia Cohen
    1 (November 1999)
    2 (July 2000)

Damn the Caesars (*)
Editor: Richard Owens (Punch Press)
    Vol. 1, no. 3 (Autumn 2005)
    Vol. 1, no. 4 (Spring 2006)
    Vol. 2 (2007)
    Vol. 3 (2007)
    Vol. 4 (2008)
    Vol. 5 (2009)
    Vol. N (2010)
    Misc. ephemera

Displace: A Journal of Poetry & Translation
Editor: Yunte Huang
    1 (1997)

Ecopoetics (*)
Editor: Jonathan Skinner (Periplum Editions)
    1 (Winter 2001)
    2 (Fall 2002)
    3 (Winter 2003)

Essex
Editors: Scott Pound and William R. Howe (Essex Studios, Toronto,
and Tailspin Press, Buffalo)
    Vol. 1, no. 1 (Spring 1997)

Vol. 1, no. 2 (Summer/Fall 1997)

Vol. 1, no. 3/4 (Fall 1997–Winter 1998)

Experimental Review: A Channel 500 Newsletter
Editor: Benjamin Friedlander (Channel 500)

Vol. 1, no. 1 (March 2000)

I Am a Child: Poetry after Robert Duncan and Bruce Andrews
Editors: William R. Howe and Benjamin Friedlander (Tailspin Press)

Vol. 1 (April 23, 1994)

Kadar Koli (*)
Editor: David Hadbawnik (Habenicht Press)

4 (Spring 2009)

5 (2010)

6 (2011)

7: On Violence (Summer 2012)

8: Dystranslation (Summer 2013)

9: The Archive (Summer 2014)

Kenning: A Newsletter of Contemporary Poetry Poetics and Nonfiction Writing (*)
Editor: Patrick F. Durgin

9 (Vol. 3, no. 3, Autumn 2000/Winter 20001)

10 (Vol. 4, no. 1, Spring 2001)

11 (Vol. 4, no. 2, July 2001): *Often: A Play* by Barbara Guest
and Kevin Killian

12 (Vol. 4, no. 3, Autumn 2002/Winter 2003): The Audio
Edition (CD)

13 (Vol. 5, no. 1, 2002)

Kiosk: A Journal of Poetry, Poetics, & Experimental Prose (+)
Editors: First published in March 1986 as *The Moral Kiosk* and continuing as
Kiosk: A Magazine of New Writing through 9 volumes into 1996 as a UB English
Department journal, *Kiosk*'s editors over the years included a number of students
from the Poetics Program. In 2002 Gordon Hadfield, Sasha Steensen, and Kyle
Schlesinger restarted the magazine—and associated it more explicitly with the
Poetics Program—as *Kiosk: A Journal of Poetry, Poetics, & Experimental Prose.*

1 (2002)

2 (2003)

3 (2004)

4 (2005)

P-Queue

Editors: Sarah Campbell, Andrew Rippeon, Holly Melgard, Joey Yearous-Algozin, and Amanda Montei

1: Statements of Poetics & Parole (2004)

2: Anomalies (2005)

3: Hybrids (2006)

4: Disobedient/s (2007)

5: Care (2008)

6: Space (2009)

7: Polemic (2010)

8: Document (2011)

9: Volume (2012)

10: Obsolescence (2013)

11: Natality (2014)

12: Fatality (2015)

13: Mourning (2016)

Pilot: A Journal of Contemporary Poetry

Editor: Matt Chambers and Andrea Strudensky

1 (2006)

2 (2007): a box set of chapbooks by sixteen UK poets:
Sean Bonney, Emily Critchley, matt ffytche,
Kai Fierle-Hedrick, Giles Goodland, Jeff Hilson, Piers Hugill,
Frances Kruk, Marianne Morris, Neil Pattison, Reitha Pattison,
Simon Perril, Sophie Robinson, Natalie Scargill, Harriet Tarlo,
and Scott Thurston

Poetic Briefs (*)

Editors: Jefferson Hansen, Elizabeth Burns, Juliana Spahr, Brigham Taylor, Bill C. Tuttle, and Mark Wallace

1 (December 1991)

2 (February 1992)

3 (March 1992)

4 (April 1992)

5 (May/June 1992)

6 (July 1992)

7 (August/September 1992)

8 (October 1992)

9 (December 1992)

10 (February 1993)

11 (April 1993)

12: Interview Issue: Dennis Tedlock, Masani Alexis de Veaux, Robert Creeley, Eric Mottram, Ge(of) Huth, Charles Bernstein, and Rosmarie Waldrop (nd)

President's Choice
Editor: Steven Zultanski

1 (2007)

Rust Talks
Editors: Kristen Gallagher and Tim Shaner

1: Logan Esdale and Graham Foust (June 15, 2000)

2: Eleni Stecopoulos and Jonathan Skinner (September 14, 2000)

3: Roberto Tejada and Richard Deming (October 26, 2000)

4: Kathryn Wichelns and Meghan Sweeney (November 16, 2000)

5: Michael Kelleher and Christopher W. Alexander (February 8, 2001)

6: Laura Penny and Peter Ramos (March 15, 2000)

7: Linda Russo and Greg Kinzer (April 12, 2001)

8: Barbara Cole and Thom Donovan (September 27, 2001)

9: Eun-Gwi Chung, Sandra Guerreiro, Anna Reckin (October 25, 2001)

10: Gregg Biglieri and Nick Lawrence (November 15, 2001)

11: Brandon Stosuy and Patrick F. Durgin (February 14, 2002)

12: Nathan Austin and Elizabeth Finnegan (April 11, 2002)

13: Kristen Gallagher and Tim Shaner (October 3, 2002)

14: ?

15: Martin Corless-Smith and Gordon Hadfield (n.d.)

16: Alicia Cohen and Sasha Steensen (April 17, 2003)
17: James Maynard and Jonathan Stalling (May 7, 2003)
18: ?
19: Thom Donovan and Michael Cross (March 11, 2004)

The Rusty Word
Editor: Joel Kuszai
1 (September 20, 1995)

Satellite Telephone (*)
Editor: Robert Dewhurst
3 (Winter 2010)

Situation (*)
Editor: Mark Wallace
1 (December 1992)
2 (nd)
3 (nd)
4 (nd)
5 (nd)
6 (nd)
7 (nd)

Small Press Collective
Editor: Taylor Brady
1 (April 24, 1997)
2 (November 10, 1997)

Uprising: An Occasional Journal (+)
Editor: Mark Hammer
1 (nd)
2 (nd)

Verdure
Editors: Linda Russo and Christopher W. Alexander
1 (October–November 1999)

2 (March–April 2000)

3–4 (September 2000–Feburary 2001)

5–6 (February 2002)

Wild Orchids

Editors: Sean Reynolds and Robert Dewhurst

1: Melville (2009)

2: Hannah Weiner (2010)

3: William Blake (2011)

Working Papers

Editor: ?

[1] (March 2010)

[2] (May 2010)

II. ONLINE SERIALS

a l y r i c m a i l e r

http://epc.buffalo.edu/ezines/alyric/

Editor: Michael Kelleher

1: Dan Machlin (1998)

2: Garrett Kalleberg (1998)

3: Eléni Sikélianòs (1998)

4: Laird Hunt (1998)

5: Heather Fuller (1998)

6: Stephen Mounkhall (1998)

7: Carrie Ann Tocci (1998)

8: Sheila E. Murphy (1998)

9: Notes from the Place(less Place) (1998)

10 & 11: Anselm Berrigan & Lisa Jarnot (1998)

12: Michael Basinski (1998)

Cartograffiti

URL no longer available

Editor: Taylor Brady and Small Press Collective

Deluxe Rubber Chicken
http://epc.buffalo.edu/ezines/deluxe/
Editor: Mark Peters
>   1 (May 1998)
>   2 (Feb. 1999)
>   3 (May 1999)
>   4 (November 1999)
>   5 (March 2000)
>   6 (May 2000)
>   7 (May 2001)

Lagniappe: Poetry and Poetics in Review
http://www.umit.maine.edu/~ben.friedlander/lagniappe.html
Editors: Graham Foust and Ben Friedlander
>   Vol. 1, no. 1 (Fall 1998)
>   Vol. 1, no. 2 (Winter/Spring 1999)
>   Vol. 1, no. 3 (Summer 1999)
>   Vol. 2, no. 1 (Fall 1999)
>   Vol. 2, no. 2 (Spring/Summer/Millennium/Election 2000)

lume: a journal of electronic writing and art
http://epc.buffalo.edu/ezines/lume/
Editor: Michael Kelleher
>   1 (May 2000)
>   2 (February 2001)

RIF/T: An Electronic Space for Poetry, Prose, and Poetics
http://epc.buffalo.edu/rift/
Editors: Kenneth Sherwood and Loss Pequeño Glazier
>   1.1 (Fall 1993)
>   2.1 (Winter 1994)
>   3.1 (Summer 1994)
>   4.1 (Spring 1995)
>   5.1 (Summer 1995)
>   6.1: Local Effects for Robert Creeley @ 70 (Fall 1997)

III. BOOKS, CHAPBOOKS, BROADSIDES, AND OTHER PUBLICATIONS LISTED BY PUBLISHER

Allerwirklichste Miniatures Press

Editor: ?

> *The World: A Pamphlet Made Especially for the Geoff Ward/Linda Russo Reading @ the Cornershop, Buffalo NY, Friday, 25 September 1998*, 1998

Alyric Press

Editor: Michael Kelleher?

> Michael Kelleher, Jonathan Skinner, and Eleni Stecopoulos, *Three*, 1999

Atticus/Finch (*)

Editor: Michael Cross

> Cynthia Sailers, *Rose Lungs*, 2003
>
> Elizabeth Willis, *Meteoric Flowers*, 2004
>
> Eli Drabman, *The Ground Running*, 2004
>
> Tanya Brolaski, *The Daily Usonian*, 2004
>
> Thom Donovan and Kyle Schlesinger, *Mantle*, 2005
>
> Gregg Biglieri, *I Heart My Zeppelin*, 2005
>
> Myung Mi Kim, *River Antes*, 2006
>
> Lisa Jarnot, *Iliad XXII*, 2006
>
> John Taggart, *Unveiling/Marianne Moore*, 2007
>
> Patrick F. Durgin, *Imitation Poems*, 2007
>
> Taylor Brady and Rob Halpern, *Snow Sensitive Skin*, 2007
>
> C. J. Martin, *Lo, Bittern*, 2008

Bon Aire Projects

Editors: Amanda Montei and Jon Rutzmoser

> Amanda Montei and Jon Rutzmoser, *Dinner Poems*, 2013
>
> Joey Yearous-Algozin, *Holly Melgard's Friends & Family* (introduction by Teresa Carmody, footnotes to introduction by Vanessa Place), 2014
>
> Teresa Carmody and Vanessa Place, *Maison Femme: A Fiction*, 2015

Channel 500

Editor: Benjamin Friedlander

Mark Wallace, *6/20: Poem for O.J.*, 1994?

Richard Roundy, *Inquiring Minds/Inside the White Bronco*, 1994?

Jena Osman, *Victor vs. Nebraska*, 1994?

Cynthia Kimball, *Proof*, 1994?

William R. Howe, *Scream Scream Scream All You Want*, 1994?

Benjamin Friedlander?, *Danger!! Warning!! Bar Your Office Doors and Classrooms!! Anti-Revolutionary Poetics! Anti-Poetic Revolutionaries!*, 1994?

Lucia W. Noi [Luca Crispi?], *Cult u 're tv*, 1994?

Alice Crimmins, *So a Husband Kills a Wife and We All Enter into the Conversation*, 1994?

Abby C. [Coykendall?], *If X Has That Spot*, 1994?

Victoria Lucas, *Social Fantasies*, 1995?

Ted Pearson, *The Fall Classic*, 1995?

Nick Lawrence, *Pensacola Shotgun*, 1995?

Benjamin Friedlander, *Jeff's Hulking Tan Toyota*, 1995?

Robert Creeley, *Help*, 1995?

Carla Billitteri, *Berlusconiana*, Nov. '94, 1995?

Charles Bernstein, *Mao Tse Tung Wore Khakis*, 1995?

Georges Bataille, *The Void* (translated by Victoria Tillotson), 1995?

Kristin Prevallet, *The Princess Is Dead*, 1997?

Benjamin Friedlander, *Crash*, 1997?

William Sylvester?, *Think Big Die*, 1998?

William Sylvester, *(Hesiod's She Who Poem, Eoia, Is in the Loeb Library.)*, 1998?

Mark Peters, *Bill, Bill, Bill*, 1998?

Michael Kelleher, *Immortality, a Jingle*, 1998?

William R. Howe?, *A Ship of the Crime Poplist*, 1998?

Cher Horowitz, *The Survivor Is the Worst Nazi*, 1998?

Photios Giovanis, *Haute Couture Killing*, 1998?

Benjamin Friedlander, *Memories of President Clinton*, 1998?

Benjamin Friedlander, *Ichabod!*, 1998?

Brent Cunningham, *Timely Is a Princess*, 1998?

Cuneiform Press (*)

Editor: Kyle Schlesinger

    Luisa Giugliano, *Chapter in a Day Finch Journal*, 2000

    Luisa Giugliano, *Chapter in a Day Finch Journal*, 2000 (broadside)

    Nick Piombino, *The Boundary of Theory*, 2001

    :prose::acts:, 2001 (limited and regular edition broadsides)

    Michael Magee, *Leave the Light On*, 2002 (with Handwritten Press)

    Patrick F. Durgin, *Color Music*, 2002

    Patrick F. Durgin, *Color Music*, 2002 (broadside)

    Gregg Biglieri, *Los Books*, 2002

    Stacy Szymaszek, *Mummified Arm Indonesian*, 2003

    David Pavelich, *Outlining*, 2003

    Thom Donovan, *Love of Mother a Reason*, 2003

    Gregg Biglieri, *Reading Keats to Sleep*, 2003

    Derek Beaulieu, *With Wax*, 2003

    Derek Beaulieu, *With Wax*, 2003 (deluxe edition)

    Christopher W. Alexander, *Two Poems*, 2003?

    Ron Silliman, *Woundwood*, 2004

    Alan Loney, *Meditatio: The Printer Printed: Manifesto*, 2004

    Andrew Levy, *Scratch Space*, 2004

    Craig Dworkin, *Dure*, 2004

    Robert Creeley, *Oh, Do You Remember*, 2004

    Gill Ott and Christopher Webster (images), *The Amputated Toe*, 2005

    Craig Dworkin, *Andy Warhol's Lost Portraits*, 2005?

    Johanna Drucker, *From Now*, 2005

    Gregg Biglieri, *Sleepy with Democracy*, 2006

    Ulf Stolterfoht, *Lingos VI* (translated by Rosmarie Waldrop), 2007

    I Have Imagined a Center // Wilder Than This Region: A Tribute to Susan Howe, 2007

    Max Jacob and Larry Fagin, *Two Poems*, 2008

Curricle Patterns

Editor: Alicia Cohen?

    Linda Russo, *Secret Silent Plan*, 2000

Dove | Tail

Editor: Victoria Brockmeier

> Laura Mullen, *Turn: Essay*, 2006
>
> Matthew Cooperman, *Still: (to be) Perpetual: Poems*, 2007?

Éditions Hérisson

Editor: ?

> Bob Perelman, *Chaim Soutine*, 1994
>
> Pam Rehm, Nick Lawrence, and Carla Billitteri, *Three Poets*, 1994

Elevator

Editor: Michael Kelleher

> *Sugar in the Raw*, 2000 (anthology)
>
> Ed. Brian Collier, *The Elevator Box*, 2000 (boxed set)
>
> Eds. Michael Kelleher and Isabelle Pelissier, *The Postcard Project*, 2001 (boxed set)
>
> Eds. Michael Kelleher and Isabelle Pelissier, *The Postcard Project*, 2001 (book edition made and designed in collaboration with Handwritten Press)
>
> Ed. Jonathan Skinner, *La Mitad: 11 from Buffalo*, 2001 (anthology)
>
> Ed. Amy Stalling, *The Grid Project*, 2003 (different word grids and book edition)

Essex Publications

Editors: Scott Pound and William R. Howe

> Scott Pound, *How Do You Like Your Blue-Eyed Text Now, Jacques Derrida?*, 1998? (no publisher information listed)

Habenicht Press (*)

Editor: David Hadbawnik

> Micah Robbins, *Crass Songs of Sand & Brine*, 2010
>
> David Hadbawnik, *Sir Gawain and the Green Knight*, 2011
>
> The Rejection Group, *5 Works*, 2011
>
> Sarah Jeanne Peters, *Triptych*, 2011
>
> JodiAnn Stevenson, *Houses Don't Float*, 2011

Richard Owens, *Ballads*, 2012

John Hyland, *The Novice*, 2015

John Hyland, *The Novice*, 2015 (poem card)

David Hadbawnik, *Sports*, 2015

David Hadbawnik, *Sports*, 2015 (poem card)

Handwritten Press (*) (+)

Editor: Kristen Gallagher

Alicia Cohen, *bEAR*, 2000

Michael Magee, *Morning Constitutional*, 2001 (with Spencer Books)

Ikhyun Kim, *Il Jom Oh*, 2001

Aaron Levy, *Tombe: In Conversation with Kristen Gallagher*, 2001

Ed. Kristen Gallagher, *The Form of Our Uncertainty: A Tribute to Gil Ott*, 2001 (with Chax Press)

Michael Magee, *Leave the Light On*, 2002 (with Cuneiform Press)

Dan Featherston, *The Clock Maker's Memoir: 1-12*, 2002

Barbara Cole, *From "Situation Comedies,"* 2002

Nathan Austin, *(glost)*, 2002

Terrence Chiusano, *On Generation and Corruption: Parts I and II*, 2003

Gordon Hadfield and Sasha Steensen, *Correspondence: For La Paz*, 2004

Hostile Books

Editors: Joe Hall, Mike Flatt, Veronica Wong, and Ryan Sheldon

Joe Hall, *No*, 2015

Mike Flatt, *Asbestos*, Vol. 1, 2015

Ryan Sheldon, *Lemon*, 2015

Veronica Wong, *emmenagogue*, 2015

Leave Books

Editors: Kristin Prevallet, Juliana Spahr, Mark Wallace, Bill Tuttle, Elizabeth Burns, Jefferson Hansen, and Brigham Taylor (began as a collective)

Keith Waldrop, *The Balustrade*, 1991

Bill Tuttle, *Private Residence*, 1991

Elizabeth Robinson, *Nearings: Two Poems*, 1991

Ann Pedone, *The Bird Happened*, 1991

Robert Kelly, *Manifesto: For the Next New York School*, 1991

Jefferson Hansen, *Gods to the Elbows*, 1991

Peter Ganick, *As Convenience*, 1991

Elizabeth Burns, *Letters to Elizabeth Bishop*, 1991

Susan Smith Nash, *Grammar of the Margin Road*, 1992 (published by
    Leave Books? no publisher information listed)

Nina Zivancevic, *I Was This War Reporter in Egypt*, 1992

Mark Wallace, *You Bring Your Whole Life to the Material*, 1992

Joseph Torra, *Domino Sessions*, 1992

Juliana Spahr, *Nuclear*, 1992

Cathleen Shattuck, *The Three Queens*, 1992

Rena Rosenwasser, *Unplace . Place*, 1992

Pam Rehm, *Pollux*, 1992

Bin Ramke, *Catalogue Raisonné*, 1992

Nick Piombino, *Two Essays*, 1992

John Perlman, *Imperatives of Address*, 1992

Jena Osman, *Balance*, 1992

Gale Nelson, *Little Brass Pump*, 1992

Joyce Mansour, *Cris/Screams* (translated by Serge Gavronsky), 1992

Le Ann Jacobs, *Varieties of Inflorescence*, 1992

Susan Gevirtz, *Domino: Point of Entry*, 1992

Drew Gardner, *The Cover*, 1992

Tina Darragh, *Adv. Fans—The 1968 Series*, 1992

John Byrum, *Interalia: Among Other Things*, 1992

Dodie Bellamy, *Answer: From "The Letters of Mina Harker,"* 1992

Tom Beckett, *Economies of Pure Expenditure: A Notebook*, 1992

J. Battaglia, *Skin Problems*, 1992

Michael Basinski, *Mooon Bok: Petition, Invocation, & Homage*, 1992

Mark Wallace, *Complications from Standing in a Circle:
    The Dictionary Poems*, 1993

Susan M. Schultz, *Another Childhood*, 1993

Stephen Ratcliffe, *Private*, 1993

Lee Ann Brown, *Crush*, 1993

Julia Blumenreich, *Artificial Memory: 4 Ingathering Texts*, 1993

Bruce Andrews, *Divestiture—E*, 1993

Cole Swensen, *Walk*, 1994

Joe Ross, *Push*, 1994

Eléna Rivera, *Wale; Or, The Corse*, 1994

Joan Retallack, *Icarus Ffffalling*, 1994

Kristin Prevallet, *From "Perturbation, My Sister": (A Study of Max Ernst's "Hundred Headless Woman")*, 1994

Randall Potts, *Recant: (A Revision)*, 1994

Eds. Juliana Spahr, Mark Wallace, Kristin Prevallet, and Pam Rehm, *A Poetics of Criticism*, 1994

Sianne Ngai, *My Novel*, 1994

Kevin Magee, *Tedium Drum, Part II*, 1994

Kimberly Lyons, *Rhyme the Lake*, 1994

Lori Lubeski, *Stamina*, 1994

Cynthia Kimball, *Omen for a Birthday: Unravelled Poems*, 1994

Lisa Houston, *Liquid Amber*, 1994

Barbara Henning, *The Passion of Signs*, 1994

Sally Doyle, *Under the Neath*, 1994

Laynie Browne, *One Constellation*, 1994

Guy R. Beining, *Too Far to Hear*, 1994

Will Alexander, *Arcane Lavender Morals*, 1994

Kim Rosenfield, *Two Poems*, 1995

Mark McMorris, *Figures for a Hypothesis: (Suite)*, 1995

Ira Lightman, *Psychoanalysis of Oedipus*, 1995

Kevin Killian, *Santa*, 1995

C. S. Giscombe, *Two Sections from Giscome Road*, 1995

Marten Clibbens, *Sonet*, 1995

Little Scratch Pad Press/Little Scratch Pad Publications/ Little Scratch Pad Editions/Little Scratch Pad Factory

Editor: Douglas Manson

Douglas Manson, *Edge of Perception: A Poem*, 2000

Douglas Manson, *Or VVV: Sinespoem 1–7*, 2003

Douglas Manson, *The Flatland Adventures of Blip and Ouch: A One-Act Closet Drama*, 2004

Douglas Manson, *A Book of Birthdays*, 2005

Aaron Lowinger, *Autobiography I: Perfect Game*, 2005 (with House Press)

Douglas Manson, *Sections in Four Seasons: From "To Becoming Normal:*
   A Poem of Limit," 2006 (Bird in the Tree Edition)

Tom Yorty, *Words in Season: Poems*, 2007 (Little Scratch Pad Editions 6)

Nick Traenkner, *Accidental Thrust*, 2007 (Buff & Rust 2)

Kristianne Meal, *TwentyTwo: First Pallet*, 2007 (Buff & Rust 2)

Kristianne Meal, *TwentyTwo: First Pallet*, 2007 (Little
   Scratch Pad Editions 1)

Douglas Manson, *At Any Point: From "To Becoming Normal:*
   A Poem of Limits," 2007 (Buff & Rust 4)

L. A. Howe, *NTR PIC E ST R*, 2007
   (Little Scratch Pad Editions Chapbook 5)

Michael Basinski, *Of Venus 93*, 2007
   (Little Scratch Pad Editions Chapbook 3)

Overherd at the River's Hip: 15 Buffalo Poets: Poems in Conversation, 2008
   (Little Scratch Pad Editions number 2.3)

Jaye Bartell, *Ever After Never Under: 20 Choruses*, 2008
   (Little Scratch Pad Editions second series 2)

Jonathan Skinner, *With Naked Foot*, 2009
   (Little Scratch Pad Editions second series 4)

Geof Huth and Tom Beckett, *Interpenetrations: Buffalo*, 2009

Low Frequency
Editor: Michael Flatt
   Please Welcome: Intros 14–15, 2015
   a rawlings and Chris Turnbull, *The Great Canadian*, 2015
   Nathaniel Mackey, *From "Blue Fasa,"* 2016

M Press
Editors: Alan Gilbert, Kristin Prevallet, Ram Rehm, and Lew Daly
   Lew Daly, *Swallowing the Scroll: Late in a Prophetic Tradition with*
      the Poetry of Susan Howe and John Taggart, 1994
      (*apex of the M* supplement #1)

Meow Press (+)

Editor: Joel Kuszai

Bill Tuttle, *Epistolary: First Series*, 1993

Elizabeth Robinson, *Iemanje*, 1993 (2nd printing March 1996)

Joel Kuszai?, *Brooklyn Yards*, 1993 (published by Meow Press? no author
or publisher information listed)

Benjamin Friedlander, *Anterior Future*, 1993

Michael Basinski, *Cnyttan*, 1993 (2 states)

Misko Suvakovic, *Pas Tout: Fragments on Art, Culture, Politics, Poetics
and Art Theory, 1994–1974*, 1994

Leslie Scalapino, *The Line*, 1994

Pierre Joris, *Winnetou Old*, 1994

Robert Fitterman, *Metropolis (1–3)*, 1994

George Albon, *King*, 1994

Juliana Spahr, *Testimony*, 1995

James Sherry, *Four For*, 1995

Mark Johnson, *Three Bad Wishes*, 1995

Loss Pequeño Glazier, *The Parts*, 1995

Peter Gizzi, *New Picnic Time*, 1995

Benjamin Friedlander, *A Knot Is Not a Tangle*, 1995

Dubravka Djuric, *Cosmopolitan Alphabet*, 1995

Charles Bernstein, *The Subject*, 1995

Rachel Tzvia Back, *Litany*, 1995

Bruce Andrews, Charles Bernstein, and James Sherry, *Technology/Art:
20 Brief Proposals for Seminars on Art & Technology*, 1995
(no publisher information listed)

Gary Sullivan, *Dead Man*, 1996

Ron Silliman, *Xing*, 1996

Kenneth Sherwood, *That Risk*, 1996

Lisa Samuels, *Letters*, 1996

Lisa Robertson, *The Descent: A Light Comedy in Three Parts*, 1996

Meredith Quartermain, *Terms of Sale*, 1996

Kristin Prevallet, *28 for the Road*, 1996
(Meow Press Ephemera Series #6)

Jena Osman, *Jury*, 1996

Hank Lazer, *Early Days of the Lang Dynasty*, 1996

Wendy Kramer, *Patinas*, 1996

Cynthia Kimball, *Riven*, 1996 (Meow Press Ephemera Series #4)

Jorge Guitart, *Film Blanc*, 1996

Deanna Ferguson, *Rough Bush*, 1996

Robert Duncan, *Copy Book Entries* (transcribed by Robert J. Bertholf), 1996

Robert Creeley, *The Dogs of Auckland*, 1996

Natalee Caple, *The Price of Acorn*, 1996

Jonathan Brannen, *The Glass Man Left Waltzing*, 1996

Taylor Brady, *Is Placed Leaves*, 1996

Dodie Bellamy and Bob Harrison, *Broken English*, 1996

Natalie Basinski, *How the Cat Got Her Fur*, 1996
   (Meow Press Ephemera Series #12)

Michael Basinski, *Barstokai*, 1996 (Meow Press Ephemera Series #5)

Michael Basinski, *Heebie-Jeebies*, 1996

Cynthia Kimball, *Annotations for Eliza*, 1997

Kevin Killian, *Argento Series*, 1997

William R. Howe, *A #'s: Onus*, 1997

Dodie Bellamy, *Hallucinations*, 1997

Charles Alexander, *Four Ninety Eight to Seven*, 1997

Susan M. Schultz, *Addenda*, 1998

Denise Newman, *Of Later Things Yet to Happen*, 1998

Noemie Maxwell, *Thrum*, 1998

Andrew Levy, *Elephant Surveillance to Thought*, 1998

Joel Kuszai, *Castle of Fun*, 1998 (Meow Press Ephemera Series #22)

Daniel Kanyandekwe, *One Plus One Is Three at Least: Selected Writings of
   Daniel Kanyandekwe* (edited by Julie Husband and Jim O'Loughlin),
   1998

Benjamin Friedlander, *Selected Poems*, 1998

Stephen Cope, *Two Versions*, 1998 (Meow Press Ephemera Series #23)

Don Cheney, *The Qualms of Catallus & K-mart*, 1998

Graham Foust, *3 from Scissors*, 1998

Nickel City

Editor: Christopher W. Alexander

Christopher W. Alexander, *Admonitions*, 2000

Nominative Press Collective (*)

Editor: Christopher W. Alexander

 Judy Roitman, *Diamond Notebooks 2*, 1998

 Keston Sutherland, *Scratchcard Sally-Ann*, 1999

 Matthias Regan, *The Most of It*, 1999

 Christopher W. Alexander, *History Lesson*, 1999

Otamolloy

Editor: Michael Kelleher?

 Michael Kelleher, *The Necessary Elephant*, 1998

Phylum Press (*)

Editors: Richard Deming and Nancy Kuhl

 Richard Deming and Nancy Kuhl, *Winter 2000*, 2000

 Roberto Tejada, *Amulet Anatomy*, 2001

 Graham Foust, *6*, 2001

 Joel Bettridge, *Shores*, 2001

Poetic Briefs

Editors: Jefferson Hansen, Elizabeth Burns, Juliana Spahr, Brigham Taylor,
Bill C. Tuttle, and Mark Wallace?

 Sterling D. Plumpp, *Blues for My Friend's Longings*, 1993
  (Poetic Briefs Broadside #1)

Poetics Program

 Ed. Jena Osman, *Lab Book*, 1992

 Charles Bernstein, *What's Art Got to Do with It?: The Status of the Subject
  of the Humanities in the Age of Cultural Studies*, 1992

 Brandon Boudreault, Allison Cardon, George Life, Claire Nashar, Sean
  Pears, Jacob Reber, and Corey Zielinski, *Launched in Context: Seven
  Essays on the Archive*, 2016 (published by Spring 2016 graduate stu-
  dent reading group on archives supervised by James Maynard)

Porci Con Le Ali (*)

Editor: Benjamin Friedlander

 Benjamin Friedlander, *Mininotes*, 1996

Heiner Müller, *ABC*, 1996 (translated by Benjamin Friedlander)

Benjamin Friedlander, *Period Piece*, 1998

Benjamin Friedlander, *Partial Objects*, 1999

P-Queue/Queue Books

Editor: Andrew Rippeon

Richard Taransky and Michelle Taransky, *The Plans Caution*, 2007

Eds. Michael Cross and Andrew Rippeon, *Building Is a Process, Light Is an Element: Essays and Excursions for Myung Mi Kim*, 2008

Erica Lewis (poems) and Mark Stephen Finein (artwork), *The Precipice of Jupiter*, 2009

José Felipe Alvergue, *Us Look Up/There Red Dwells*, 2008

Geof Huth, *Eyechart Poems*, 2009

Jimbo Blachly and Lytle Shaw, *Pre-Chewed Tapas*, 2010

Simone de Beauvoir and Vanessa Place, *The Father & Childhood*, 2011

Punch Press (*)

Editor: Richard Owens

Richard Owens, *From "Bel & the Dragon,"* 2007

Brian Mornar, *Repatterning*, 2007

Bill Griffiths, *And the Life (The Motion) Is Always There*, 2007

Dale Smith, *Susquehanna: Speculative Historical Commentary and Lyric*, 2008

Rave On: Punch Press, Damn the Caesars, 2008

Richard Owens, *Two Ballads*, 2008

Ben Lyle Bedard, *Implicit Lyrics*, 2008

Sotère Torregian, *Envoy*, 2009

Richard Owens, *Punch Press*, 2009?

Thomas Meyer, *Kintsugi*, 2009

Natalie Knight, *Archipelagos*, 2009

Carrie Etter, *Divinations*, 2010

Richard Owens, *Cecilia Anne at One*, 2010

Quinella Press

Editor: Nicholas Laudadio

Michael Kelleher, *Three Poems*, 1998

Graham Foust, *Three Poems*, 1998

Taylor Brady, *Three Poems*, 1998

Joel Bettridge, *Three Poems*, 1998

RIF/T

Editors: Kenneth Sherwood and Loss Pequeño Glazier?

Loss Pequeño Glazier, *Electronic Projection Poetries*/Kenneth Sherwood,
Hard [HRt] Return, 1995

Rubba Ducky (*)

Editors: Christopher W. Alexander and Matthias Regan

William Fuller, *Avoid Activity*, 2003

Henry Card, *People's History Pop-Up: For the People by the People*, 2003?
(published by Rubba Ducky? no publisher information listed)

Henry Card, *Freedom Fighter Portraits*, 2003?
(published by Rubba Ducky? no publisher information listed)

Tailspin Press

Editor: William R. Howe

Mark Wallace, *The Sponge Has Holes: A Bibliophilic Event*, 1994
(Tailspin Press Chapbook 002)

William R. Howe, *Tripflea: (Book)*, 1994

Eds. Raymond Federman and William R. Howe, *Sam Changed Tense*,
1995 (with Weird Sisters Press)

Michael Basinski, *SleVep: A Performance*, 1995
(Tailspin Press Chapbook 003)

Michael Basinski and William R. Howe, *Place Your Text Here*, 1995

Nils Ya, *Chastisement Rewarded: A Poetics of the Fragment*, 1996

William R. Howe, *Pollywannahydral: A Shape*, 1996
(Tailspin Press Chapbook 006)

Kenneth Sherwood, *Text Squared: A Word-Sculpture*, 1997?
(Tailspin Press Chapbook 004)

Peter Jaeger, *Stretch Conflates: An Exquisite Corpse*, 1997
(Tailspin Press Chapbook 007)

William R. Howe, *A*, 1997

Trifecta Press
Editor: Nicholas Laudadio
  Graham Foust, *Endless Surgery*, 1997

Troll Thread (*)
Editors: Joey Yearous-Algozin, Holly Melgard, Chris Sylvester, and Divya Victor
  Joseph Yearous-Algozin, *The Lazarus Project: Alien vs. Predator*, 2010
  Chris Sylvester, *The Republic*, 2010
  Chris Sylvester, *Grid*, 2010?
  Chris Sylvester, *Biography: There Past*, 2010?
  Joseph Yearous-Algozin, *Buried*, 2011
  Divya Victor, *Partial Dictionary of the Unnamable*, 2011
  Divya Victor, *Partial Directory of the Unnamable*, 2011
  Chris Sylvester, *Total Walkthrough*, 2011
  Holly Melgard, *Colors for Baby*, 2011 (Poems for Baby Trilogy 1)
  Holly Melgard, *Foods for Baby*, 2011(Poems for Baby Trilogy 2)
  Holly Melgard, *Shapes for Baby*, 2011 (Poems for Baby Trilogy 3)
  Shiv Kotecha, *Paint the Rock*, 2011
  Joey Yearous-Algozin, *The Lazarus Project: Night and Fog*, 2012
  Joey Yearous-Algozin, *The Lazarus Project: Faces of Death*, 2012
  Joey Yearous-Algozin, *The Lazarus Project: Heaven*, 2012
  Joey Yearous-Algozin, *911 9/11 Calls in 911 Pt. Font: Part 1*, 2012
  Joey Yearous-Algozin, *9/11 911 Calls in 911 Pt. Font: Part 2*, 2012
  Joey Yearous-Algozin, *The Lazarus Project: Nine Eleven*, 2012
  Divya Victor, *Partial Derivative of the Unnamable*, 2012
  Chris Sylvester, *Junk Rooms*, 2012
  Chris Sylvester, *Still Life with Every Panda Express Food Item
    Three Times: For Chris Alexander's "Panda,"* 2012
  Maker, *Poems for Money*, 2012
  Holly Melgard, *The Making of the Americans*, 2012
  Trisha Low, *Purge Vol. 1: The Last Will & Testament of Trisha Low*, 2012
  Isaac Linder, *The Moviegoer*, 2012
  Shiv Kotecha, *Outfits*, 2012
  Josef Kaplan, *1–100*, 2012 (16 vols.)
  Sarah Dowling, *Birds & Bees*, 2012

Jeremiah Rush Bowen, *Nazi (Argument on the Internet (5/31/11–8/31/11)*
vol. 1), 2012

Jeremiah Rush Bowen, *Faggot (Argument on the Internet (5/31/11–8/31/11)*
vol. 2), 2012

Uprising Press (+)

Editor: Mark Hammer?

Barbara Tedlock, *From "The Beautiful and the Dangerous"/*
Michael Basinski, *Egyptian Gods 6*, 1991 (Uprising 1)

Elizabeth Willis, *From "Songs for (A)"/*Stephen Ratcliffe, *Nostalgia*, 1991
(Uprising 2)

Susan Howe, *From "Melville's Marginalia,"* 1991
(published by Uprising Press? no publisher information listed)

Rachel Blau DuPlessis, *From "Draft 2: She,"/*Michael Boughn,
Stone Work V 1991 (Uprising 3)

Michael Basinski, *Her Roses*, 1992 (Uprising 9)

Edward Dorn, *The Denver Landing: 11 Aug 1993*, 1993

Vigilance Society (*)

Editor: Anonymous

Eli Drabman, *From "Daylight on the Wires,"* 2006?

Eli Drabman, *Daylight on the Wires*, 2007?

Wild Horses of Fire Press

Editor: Thom Donovan

Thom Donovan (with images by Abby Walton), *Tears Are These Veils*, 2004

IV. BOOKS, CHAPBOOKS, BROADSIDES, AND OTHER PUBLICATIONS PRINTED WITHOUT A PUBLISHER (ORGANIZED CHRONOLOGICALLY)

Ed. Mark Hammer, *The Image of Language, The Language of Image: UB Poetic
Voices: 1992*, 1992 (publisher unknown)

Jonathan Fernandez, *Ah! Thel Is Like a Watry Bow*, 1993? (published by the author)

William R. Howe, *Projective Verse: A Preformance Script with/out Type Writer in 5 Parts*, 1994 (published by the author)

Alan Gilbert and Kristin Prevallet, *A Selective Bibliography of French Poetry in Translation Published in American Small Press Poetry Journals from 1980–1992*, 1995 (publisher unknown)

Joel Kuszai, *Filmic 10: Salt Series*, 1995 (published by the author)

Cynthia Kimball, *Song for a Handfasting: (For Two Voices)*, 1995 (publisher unknown)

Benjamin Friedlander, *The Missing Occasion of Saying Yes*, 1996 (published by the author)

Kristin Prevallet, *The Rhyme of the Ancient Mariner: An Interpretation of the Poem by S. T. Coleridge*, 1997 (VHS recording)

William R. Howe, *Notions of Nationalistic Feverish Paradigmatic Coronal*, 1998 (published by the author)

Christopher W. Alexander, *Eschatology: A Reader*, 1999 (published by the author)

Terrence Chiusano, Ikhyun Kim, and Brandon Stosuy, *Last Friday, May 12, 2000*, 2000 (publisher unknown)

Sandra Guerreiro, *Finger Print: Impressão Digital*, 2001 (published by the author)

Terry Cuddy and Mirela Ivanciu, *Transient Views of Western New York*, 2001 (VHS recording)

A Degraded Textual Affair, 2002 (edited by William R. Howe?)

Linda Russo, *Solvency*, 2005 (publisher unknown?)

Susan Howe, *Loving Friends and Kindred*, 2006 (printed by Sarah Campbell?)

Steve McCaffery, *Appelle's Cut*, 2007 (printed by Matt Chambers, Michael Cross, and Richard Owens?)

Michael Cross, *Foresting*, 2007 (printed by Andrew Rippeon?)

George Oppen, *The Poem*, 2008 (printed by Andrew Rippeon?)

Susan Howe, *I heard myself as if you*, 2008 (printed by Richard Owens and Andrew Rippeon)

Michael Sikkema, David Hadbawnik, and Nava Fader, *Sideways*, 2009? (printed by David Hadbawnik)

Scrap Paper: A Small Press Portfolio, 2009

Richard Owens, *Archer Disowns*, 2010 (printed by Andrew Rippeon?)

Andrew Rippeon, *The hill I am off*/Julia Bloch, *The Selfist*, 2010? (printed by Andrew Rippeon)

Andrew Rippeon, *5 from "Flights,"* 2010? (printed by Andrew Rippeon?)

Divya Victor, *From "Sutures 3.11.10,"* 2010? (printed by Andrew Rippeon?)

V. READING, TALK, AND PERFORMANCE SERIES

These student-organized series have been in addition to the Poetics Program's departmental series Wednesdays at 4 Plus (Fall 1990–Fall 2004) and Poetics Plus (Spring 2005–present)

Another Reading Series
Organizers: Barbara Cole, Gordon Hadfield, and Sasha Steensen
Early 2000s

BYOB
Organizer: ?
2011

(co)ludere
Organizer: Divya Victor
2008

Cornershop
Organizer: Anya Lewin
1998

Deluxe Rubber Reading Series
Organizer: Mark Peters
1999

Dove | Tail
Organizer: Victoria Brockmeier
2014

Emergency Poetry Reading
Organizer: ?
Dates?

Exchange Rate
Organizer: ?
2004?

Last Friday
Organizers: Linda Russo and Christopher W. Alexander
1999

**ñ (enye), Poesía y Crítica en la SUNY-Búfalo:
A Non-Unilingual Reading Series of Poetry, Criticism
and Translation**
Organizers: Rosa Alcala and Kristin Dykstra
2000–2002

Opening Night
Organizers: ?
Fall 2008–present

Poetics Plus Plus
Oganizers: Graduate Poetics Group
2015

Poets Theater
Organizer: David Hadbawnik
2009–2012

Portable Lecture Series/Portable Talk
Organizer: ?
Dates?

Red Flannel (+)
Organizer: Mark Hammer
1988–1995

Refer
Organizer: Divya Victor
2009, 2011

Rust Talks
Organizers: Kristen Gallagher and Tim Shaner
2000–2004

Saloon Conversation Series
Organizer: ?
2006

Scratch and Dent
Organizers: Cornershop and Small Press Collective
Dates?

Small Press in the Archive
Organizers: Margaret Konkol (founder), Nicholas Morris, and
Ronan Crowley
2007–2014

Steel Bar
Organizer: Jonathan Skinner
2001

VI. STUDENT-ORGANIZED SYMPOSIA

**Writing from the New Coast: First Festival of New Poetry
at SUNY Buffalo**
Organizers: Juliana Spahr and Peter Gizzi
March 31–April 3, 1993

Place(less Place): A Gathering of Poets
Organizers: Small Press Collective
June 19–20, 1998

**Eye, Ear & Mind: A Conference on the Poetry of
Ronald Johnson**
Organizer: Joel Bettridge
March 15–18, 2000

Prose Acts
Organizers: Christopher W. Alexander and Brandon Stosuy?
October 18–21, 2001

A Degraded Textual Affair
Organizer: William R. Howe?
June 6, 2002

Rereading Louis Zukofsky's *Bottom: On Shakespeare*:
A Symposium for Students, Poets & Scholars
Organizers: Kyle Schlesinger and Thom Donovan?
October 31–November 1, 2003

(Re:)Working the Ground:
A Conference on the Late Writings of Robert Duncan
Organizers: James Maynard, Robert J. Bertholf, and Michael Basinski
April 20–22, 2006

Contemporary British Poets
Organizer: Matthew Chambers
April 12, 2007

George Oppen: A Centenary Conversation
Organizers: Andrew Rippeon and ?
April 23–25, 2008

A Symposium on *Dura*
Organizer: Andrew Rippeon
November 21, 2008

Poet-publishers: A Small Press Symposium
Organizers: Richard Owens and Andrew Rippeon?
April 19–20, 2009

Modes of Love and Reason: A Bernadette Mayer Symposium
Organizer: Robert Dewhurst?
April 1, 2011

Clairvoyant Codes: A Symposium on the Work of Hannah Weiner
Organizers: Robert Dewhurst and Sean Reynolds?
October 19, 2012

VII. RADIO SHOWS

T-n-T Broadcasts
Edited by Martin Spinelli
1995

LINEbreak (+)
Hosted by Charles Bernstein
Coproduced by Charles Bernstein and Martin Spinelli
Recorded 1996–1996 in Buffalo and elsewhere

Inks Audible (WHLD 1270 AM, Buffalo)
Hosted and produced by Doug Manson
Broadcast ca. 2005

Spoken Arts (WBFO 88.7 FM, Buffalo)
Hosted by Sarah Campbell
Broadcast ca. 2006

Schedule for the Robert Creeley Lecture and Celebration of Poetry, April 7–10, 2016

Robert Creeley and France: International Innovative Poetry

Thursday, April 7, 2016

Buffalo Marriott Niagara Hotel

3:30 Vincent Broqua, "Echoes and Repercussions of the Poetics Program in France"

4:15 Abigail Lang, "Creeley's Reception in France"

5:00–6:30 Jean Daive and Norma Cole, translation dialogue

6:45–8:00 Welcome Reception

Robert Creeley Lecture and Celebration of Poetry

Friday April 8, 2016

Albright-Knox Art Gallery

2:00 Welcome by Satish Tripathi, President of the University at Buffalo, SUNY and Penelope Creeley

2:15 *Willy's Reading*, a film by Diane Christian and Bruce Jackson

2:45 Reading by the winner and honorable mentions of the UB English Department and Poetics/riverrun Poetry in the Community contest

3:15 The Inaugural Robert Creeley Lecture in Poetry and Poetics: Nathaniel Mackey, "Breath and Precarity"

4:30 Open invitation to read a favorite Creeley poem

5:00 Reception in Muse Café

8:00 Community poetry reading, Westminster Presbyterian Church, 724 Delaware Avenue

"Poetics: (The Next) 25 Years" Conference

April 9–10, 2016

UB North Campus

Saturday, 9 April

9:00–10:45 Conference seminars (see seminar schedule, Appendix 3)

11:00 Opening Remarks, Myung Mi Kim and Judith Goldman

11:15–12:30 Panel 1: Landscapes, Mappings, Networks: Digital/Material Crossings

> *Moderator: Ming Qian Ma*
>
> Stephen Voyce and Adalaide Morris, "Poetic Cartographies: Maps, Poems, & Plans for Action"
>
> Jennifer Scappettone, "Copper Lyres and Aeolian Harping of the House: Materiality of Poetry in the Age of Digital Reproduction and Ecoprecarity"
>
> Heriberto Yépez, "The Opening of the (Transnational Battle) Field: Poetics in North America in the Now-Future"
>
> Mark Wallace, "Landscape as Activity in *The End of America* Poems"

1:30–2:45 Panel 2: Biopolitical, Post-Sovereignty, Post-Recognition Poetics

> *Moderator: Judith Goldman*
>
> Sarah Dowling, "Materials Toward a Theory of the Supine Body"
>
> Shannon Maguire, "Abandoning Recognition: Some Poetic Stakes"
>
> Cassandra Troyan, "Post-Sovereign Poetics: The Politics of Resistance in Traumatic Violence"
>
> Rick Snyder, "Biopoetics: Exploring the Intersections of Biopolitics and Poetry"

3:00–4:15 Panel 3: Language, Composition, Reading.

> *Moderator: Steve McCaffery*
>
> Andrew Joron, "Radical as Nature Itself: Materialism, Poetics, and the Origin of Language"
>
> Bob Perelman, "If Words Don't Exist, Then . . ."
>
> Carla Billitteri, " 'Dissipative Structures' and Aggregative Transactions: Notes toward a Poetics of Reading"

4:30–5:30 Readings/Reflections: Charles Bernstein and Elizabeth Willis

5:30–6:30 Reception and exhibit, "Poetry in the Making: The UB Poetics Program 1991–2016," Poetry Collection, UB Libraries

7:15 Buffet/reception, Trinity Church

8:00 Poetics Conference Reading, Trinity Church

Sunday, 10 April

9:00–10:15 Panel 4: Constructive Alterities in Feminist Ecological Poetics

Moderator: Cristanne Miller

Joan Retallack, "Constructive Alterities, The Experimental Feminine"

Angela Hume, "Writing 'true history': Audre Lorde's Feminist Surplus Poetics"

Brenda Hillman, "Nexting and Driving: Ecology, Ego-Abatement, Empathy, Energy, and Ethics Experiments in Women's Poetry"

Evelyn Reilly, "Camille Henrot's *Grosse Fatigue* and Feminist Eco-W(e)aryness"

10:30–11:45 Panel 5: Grief, Endings, and Post-Endings.

Moderator: Myung Mi Kim

Jocelyn Saidenberg, "Rituals of Language in M. NourbeSe Philip's *Zong!*"

Benjamin Friedlander, "Three Theses and a Few Observations"

Julie Joosten, "The duration of ending: contemporary poetry and states of dissolve"

11:45–12:30 Panel 6: A Poetics of Invisibility.

Moderator: James Maynard

Susan Vanderborg, " 'The World Ends at Your Doorstep': A Poetics of Invisibility in Andrew Plotkin's *Shade*"

Christian Bök, "The Xenotext: Phage Phi-X174"

Ming Qian Ma, "From Blind to Blinding: Saturated Phenomena and the Speculative Lyric of the Invisible in Andrew Joron's Poetry"

Joseph Donahue, "Acousmatic Orphism: Sounding Out Susan Howe"

João Paulo Guimarães, "The Life of the Void: Life and the Negation of Sense in Chris Vitiello's *Nouns Swarm a Verb*"

12:30–1:30 Buffet lunch and closing discussion.

Cosponsored by UB Poetics Program and Department of
English, David Gray Chair Steve McCaffery, Melodia Jones Chair
Jean-Jacques Thomas, riverrun Foundation, UB Humanities Institute,
Albright-Knox Art Gallery, Just Buffalo Literary Center, UB Libraries
Poetry Collection, UB College of Arts and Sciences Development,
UB Department of Comparative Literature, Westminster
Presbyterian Church, Trinity Church, and the Buffalo News

"Poetics: (The Next) 25 Years" Conference, Seminar Topics and Participants, April 9–10, 2016

Post-Crisis Militant Word

Conveners, Brian Ang and Jeff Derksen

Nicholas Komodore, "Amphoterics: Collective militant poetics and the destruction of dialectics: the case of the anarchist project Mayakov+sky Platform"

David Lau, "Art of the Commune"

Jeanine Webb, "Border Poetics, Mourning and the Politics of the Disappeared"

Brenda Iijima, "The Writing Modes of the Nigerian Biopolitical Activist, Ken Saro-Wiwa"

Thomas Marshall, "If Then Is to Be Change: Working Beyond the Aesthetic"

alex cruse, "Weaponizing Sickness: Gendered Representation, Theory, and Capital"

Ryan Sheldon, "Hope in a Loveless Place? Nihilism, Erotics, and Resistance in Militant Lyric"

Ian Davidson, "Eileen Myles and Mobilities of Form"

Fred Wah, "Treaty Talk"

Andrew McEwan, "Toward a Poetics of Stuckness: Poetry, Depression, and Crisis"

Helen Dimos, "The Question of Revenge in Six UK Poets"

Auditor: Christine Stewart

Poetic Interventions in Past and Future Contingents

Convener: Joan Retallack

Rachel Zolf, "A language No one speaks: Witnessing the Dangerous Perhaps in Twenty-First-Century Poetics"

Davy Knittle, "Urgent Locality: Levitsky and Willis/Neighborhood and Nation"

Julia Bloch, "Conceptive Risk and Reproductive Precarity in Contemporary Poetry"

NourbeSe Philip, "Finding Space in the Word"

Simone White, "Criteria of Black Intellectual Art Crisis"

Linda Russo and Marthe Reed, "No Safe Distance: Paradigms of Place in the Ecopoetics of Planetary Crisis"

Amy Catanzano, "Quantum Poetics: Spacetime, Language, and Matter"

George Life " 'Chang'an's Like a Chessboard': A Reading of Du Fu's Late Poems through the Subway Drawings of William Anastasi"

Johanna E. Skibsrud, "Infinite Address: Lyric Encounters at the End of the World"

erica kaufman, "DYKE FUTURE(S): Building a Poet(h)ics for Dire Times"

Faith Barrett, "Becoming Animal in the Work of Leslie Scalapino"

Kaia Sand, "Serei Poesia: On Prophetic Inquiry"

Heather Milne, "Post/National Feminist Poetics: Rachel Zolf's *Janey's Arcadia* and Jena Osman's *Corporate Relations*"

Tonya M. Foster, "Afrodisian Encounters on a Revolutionary Commons"

Auditors: A. J. Carruthers, Elizabeth Willis, Jocelyn Saidenberg, and Sonja Greckol

New Poetic Ecologies

Convener: Stephen Collis

Adam Dickinson, "Anatomic: Metabolic Poetics in the Anthropocene"

Mandy Bloomfield, "Ecopoetic Futures: Reworking the Open Field"

Oana Avasilichioaei, "Bordering Poem to Phonotope: A Techno-Polyglot Poetics"

James Sherry, "Against One Model Alone"

Joshua Schuster, "Earth Art Poetics"

Jonathan Skinner, "Poetics in the Breach: Peter Culley's Hammertown Trilogy"

Marty Cain, "Steve Roggenbuck: Poetic Disembodiment and Internet Post-Ecologies"

David James Miller, "Attending the Sonic Commons: Acoustic Ecology and Poetics"

Dale Enggass, "Ecopoetics of the Desert"

Ada Smailbegovic, "Soft Architectures: Non-Monumental Temporalities of Change in Human and Non-Human Material Worlds"

Sam Truitt, "Quantum Dumb: The Poetics of Nothing Doing"

Artists Who Write Objects

Convener: Patrick Durgin

Jamal Russell, "Literatures of Interfacial Life: Speculations on Ubiquitous Computing and the Near-Future of Digital Poetics"

Dani Spinosa, "Subsequent Screenings: The Legacy of bpNichol in Canadian Digital Poetry & Elit"

Ella O' Keefe, "Reams & Reels: Fabricating the Film Poem"

Nicholas Knouf and Claudia Pederson, "Poetic Engagement with Contemporary Surveillance"

Jennifer Gradecki and Derek Curry, "Qualculative Poetics"

Julietta Cheung, "Between the Binary: Yasuko Yokoshi's Performance Work, ZERO ONE (2015)"

Francesco Levato, "Semi-Peripheral 3D"

John Melillo, "Sonic Emblems: Reference and Reinscription in Field Recordings and Frolic Architecture"

Devin King, " 'Two gees in eggs, one gee in fogs': Text and Musical Objects"

Rachael Michelle Wilson, "Shannon Ebner's Long Poems"

Tim Anderson, "The Lines of Robert Lax"

Michael Flatt, "Unknown Materiality"

Rachel Valinsky, "Guy de Cointet: Encoder"

Luke Heister, "Marianne Moore's Poetry as Treatment of Objects and as an Object Treated"

Caitlin Murray, "Carl Andre: Mapping Poetry onto the Visual Arts"

Translingual Poetics and the Network

Conveners: Ariel Resnikoff and Orchid Tierney

Adam Mitts, "The Virus as a Model for Poetic Production"

Michael Nardone, "The Media of Poetics"

Jonathan Stalling, "Transgraphonic Poetry and Poetics"

Caleb Beckwith, "Smash that Like Button, Smash that Buy Button? Measuring the Efficacy of Social Media Activism"

Kristen Gallagher and Christopher Alexander, "Collective Translation at LaGuardia Community College: Building Community with a New Model for Teaching Poetry"

Stephen Ross, "Mikhl Likht's *Processions* and Modernist Diasporic Networks"

Lynne DeSilva-Johnson, "The Community of the Act: Rhizomatic Roadmaps Toward Translingual Creative Connectivity"

Don Wellman, "Transcultural poetics and a return to the proprioceptive"

Aaron Beasley, " 'red tides of nonpoint source': Significant Departures in Caroline Bergvall's *Drift*"

Linda Kinahan, "Caroline Bergvall and Visual Technologies"

Wanda O'Connor, "Performing interregnum and the new automatic"

Active States: Transnational, Post-Nation, and New Relationships Between the Global and the Local

Convener: Matthew Hall

Matthew Hall, "Active Poetics: Transculturation and Transformation of Voice in the Work of Lionel Fogarty and Ouyang Yu"

Edric Mesmer, "Yellow Field and the International Local"

Ann Vickery, "Anthologies Upping the Ante: Motion-Capture or Mobile Constitutions of Feminist Poetry"

David Herd, "Unwritten State: Language in the Age of Deportation"

Janet Neigh, "Disrupting Memories of Assimilation in Indigenous Women's Performance Poetry"

Dale Smith, "Black Style in Modern and Contemporary Poetry and Poetics"

JoNelle Toriseva, "Mapping Worlds: The Role of Self-Creation, Self-Governance, and Civic Engagement in the Transnational Poetic Landscape"

Sean Manzano, "Against Balikatan/Against EDCA: Inspiring a Poetic Counter-Narrative to American Military Resurgence in the Philippines"

Eun-Gwi Chung, "Nanjing Massacre Poems, Post-Nation, and Witness"

John Wrighton, "Denise Levertov: A Trans-National Pilgrimage"

Auditor: Katy Bohinc

Poetics and Pragmatics or, Bahktin for Tomorrow!

Conveners: Donato Mancini and Louis Cabri

Nicole Markotic, "DIS-FIXINGS: word roots in some recent poetry"

Scott Inniss, "I Don't Have Any Scare Quotes so Shut Up: Bruce Andrews, Irony, and the Use-Mention Distinction"

Scott Pound, "From Notation to Capture: Pushing Print"

Simina Banu, "Speech genres in contemporary poetry"

Joelle Mann, "A Word from the Dead: Rukeyser, Graham and the Politics of Pragmatics"

Roger Farr, "Discourse of the Barbarians"

New Narrative: Why New Narrative Now?

Conveners: Rob Halpern and Robin Tremblay-McGaw

Rob Halpern, " 'Where No Meaning Is' ": Appropriation and Scandal in the Writing of Robert Glück"

Thom Donovan, "Teaching New Narrative"

Kaplan Harris, "Poetry with Feelings"

Cathy Wagner, "Naming Names in the Fabulous Real: A Letter to the New Narrator"

Kathy Lou Schultz, "Gossip and Literary Communities in Dodie Bellamy's Academonia"

Eric Sneathen, "Describing It: Twenty-First-Century Fag Poetics"

Robert Dewhurst, "A Superficial Estimation: John Wieners & New Narrative"

Joel Farris, " 'A Promise of Things to Come': On Bruce Boone and Community"

Magdalena Zurawski, "Some Notes Towards an Ethics of the Poet in the University"

Jane Malcolm, "New Narrative and New Feminism(s): Gail Scott and Nathanaël Negotiating the 'I' "

Contemporary Renovations in Lyric

Conveners: John Beer and Megan Kaminski

Sarah Arkebauer, " 'Machine-like but Utterly Sincere': Lyric and Lyrics in Sarah Dowling's *Down*"

Chad Bennet, "The Obsolete Lyric"

Maureen Gallagher, "The Possibility of Ethical Encounter in Claudia Rankine's American Lyric Collections"

Danielle LaFrance, "On the Abolition of All Subjects: The Lyric 'I' in Post-Language Feminist Literature"

Jacob Schepers, " 'Correction of Disfigurements': Rhetoric, Lyric, and the Rewriting of History in Susan Howe's *Singularities* and Geraldine Monk's *Interregnum*"

Jeanne Heuving, "Love, Lyric Poetry, and the Medium of Language"

Adam Katz, "Shifting Groundwork"

David W. Pritchard, " 'Read My Poems': Political Commitment and Lyric Immediacy"

Elizabeth Savage, "The Late Allusion"

Sean Pears, "Confessional Writing and the Suicidal (sui-Seidel)"

Toby Altman, " 'To not be and to be': Anticipatory Plagiarism as Literary Method"

Alan Golding, "Rachael Blau DuPlessis's *Drafts* as New Lyric Studies"

Lisa Fishman, "A Reading of a Translation"

Ed Luker, "Contemporary Lyric Poetry and Concealment"

Claire Nashar, "Form's Future and Stacy Doris's *Paramour*"

Conceptualism/Post-Conceptualism

Convener: Michael Leong

Eric Rettberg, "Being Serious, 'Being Dumb,' and the Affective Economies of Conceptualism"

Lauren Neefe, "Being Serious, 'Being Dumb,' and the Affective Economies of Conceptualism"

Rod Smith, "Zultanski, Inc."

Louis Bury, "Conceptual Poetry and the Craft of Criticism"

Jessica Hallock, " 'The Make of a System that Listens': Prescriptive Procedures in Dworkin's DEF"

Michael Gossett, "Dark Swell: Conceptualizing the Riddle and Riddling the Conceptual in Five Hurricanes"

Keegan Cook Finberg, "Conceptual Writing's Theory of Reading"

Anca Bucur, "The violence of language and the politics of appropriation"

Anthony Reed, "Poetics, Black Life, and the Matter of Mourning"

Jared Wells, "Kieran Daly's Null Modeling and the Suspension of Conceptual Sufficiency"

Jake Reber, "Complicit Poetics & Slacker Aesthetics: A Series of Thoughts on Conceptual Writing and Violence"

Lee Ann Brown, "Why Birth Control Won't Work on Conceptual Poetry: 25 Years of Tender Buttons Press"

Joey Yearous-Algozin, "Poetry and the University or, What We Talk about When We Talk about Conceptualism"

Auditor: Adalaide (Dee) Morris

Somatics/Illness/Disability

Conveners: Petra Kuppers and Stephanie Heit

Andrew Giles, "The antipsychiatric aesthetic"

Sarah Nance, " 'Sick' Spaces: Chronic Illness, Poetry, & the Environment"

Jay Besmer, "The Body at the Crossroads: Toward a Queer Poetics of Radical Re-Abling"

Jesse Miller, "Bibliotherapy as Curative Performance"

Amy Hilhorst, "Re-Reading Psychosis in Francis Webb's 'Ward Two' Sequence: The Implications for Future Poetics"

Christina Vega-Westhoff, "SOLELY SOULY: On Practice, Awareness, Embodiment, between, with, in, and out of poetry, dance, circus"

Declan Gould, "Vulnerability, Disability, and Somatics in the Poems of Rankine, Kapil, and CAConrad"

Auditors: Stefanie Cohen, Michelle Naka Pierce, Corey Gearhart

CONTRIBUTORS

VINCENT BROQUA is a writer, translator, and professor of North American arts and literature at the University of Paris 8 Vincennes Saint-Denis. His research focuses on questions related to experimentalism (poetry, music, arts), translation studies (heterodox translation, the performance of translation), and creative criticism. Recently, he has published on the infinitesimal and the literal (*A partir de rien: esthétique, poétique et politique de l'infime*, 2012). Among the poets he has translated are David Antin, Caroline Bergvall, Thalia Field, and Anne Waldman. His *Récupérer* (Petits Matins, 2015) is currently being translated by Cole Swensen. He is the cofounder and cocurator of the Double Change collective (www.doublechange.org).

SARAH DOWLING is assistant professor at the University of Washington Bothell, teaching creative writing and literary and cultural studies. She is the author of two books of poetry, *DOWN* (Coach House, 2014) and *Security Posture* (Snare, 2009), and two chapbooks, *Entering Sappho* (above/ground, 2017) and *Birds and Bees* (TrollThread, 2012). She has published numerous critical articles in journals such as *American Quarterly*, *Canadian Literature*, *GLQ*, and *Signs: Journal of Women in Culture and Society*. Dowling is the recipient of the American Comparative Literature Association's Helen Tartar First Book Subvention Award (2016) and the Robert Kroetsch Award for Innovative Poetry (2009).

MYUNG MI KIM is James H. McNulty Chair of English and director of the Poetics Program at the University at Buffalo, SUNY. Kim is the author of *Penury*, *Commons*, *DURA*, *The Bounty*, and *Under Flag*, winner of the Multicultural Publisher's Exchange Award of Merit. Her fellowships and honors include awards from the Fund for Poetry, the Djerassi Resident Artists Program, Gertrude Stein Awards in Innovative North American Poetry, and the SUNY Chancellor's Award for Excellence in Scholarship and Creative Activity.

NATHANIEL MACKEY is the Reynolds Price Professor of English at Duke University and author of six books of poetry, the most recent of which is *Blue Fasa* (New Directions, 2015); an ongoing prose work, *From a Broken Bottle Traces of Perfume Still Emanate*, whose fifth and most recent volume is *Late Arcade* (New Directions, 2017); and two books of criticism, the most recent of which is *Paracritical Hinge: Essays, Talks, Notes, Interviews* (University of Wisconsin Press, 2005). *Strick: Song of the Andoumboulou 16–25*, a compact disc recording of poems read with musical accompaniment (Royal Hartigan, percussion; Hafez Modirzadeh, reeds and flutes), was released in 1995 by Spoken Engine Company. He is the editor of the literary magazine *Hambone* and coeditor, with Art Lange, of the anthology *Moment's Notice: Jazz in Poetry and Prose* (Coffee House Press, 1993). His awards and honors include the National Book Award for poetry, the Stephen Henderson Award from the African American Literature and Culture Society, a Guggenheim Fellowship, the Ruth Lilly Poetry Prize from the Poetry Foundation, and the Bollingen Prize for American Poetry.

JAMES MAYNARD is a graduate of the UB Poetics Program and Curator of the Poetry Collection of the University Libraries, University at Buffalo, SUNY. He has published widely on and edited a number of collections relating to the poet Robert Duncan, including *Ground Work: Before the War/In the Dark* (New Directions, 2006), *(Re:)Working the Ground: Essays on the Late Writings of Robert Duncan* (Palgrave Macmillan, 2011), and *Robert Duncan: Collected Essays and Other Prose* (University of California Press, 2014), which received the Poetry Foundation's 2014 Pegasus Award for Poetry Criticism. *Robert Duncan and the Pragmatist Sublime* is forthcoming from the University of New Mexico Press (2018), and he is editing a volume of Duncan's uncollected prose.

CRISTANNE MILLER is SUNY Distinguished Professor and Edward H. Butler Professor of Literature at the University at Buffalo, SUNY. She has published extensively on nineteenth- and twentieth-century poetry, most recently a new edition of Dickinson's poems, *Emily Dickinson's Poems: As She Preserved Them* (Harvard University Press, 2016; co-winner of the MLA Scholarly Edition Prize, 2015-16), and she directs the *Marianne Moore Digital Archive*, which will publish all 122 of Moore's working notebooks as manuscript images with facing-page annotated transcriptions, along with a variety of supporting materials by or about Moore (https://moorearchive.org/).

ADALAIDE MORRIS, Professor emerita at the University of Iowa, writes on modern and contemporary poetics, including information art, counter-mapping, documentary, and the digital. Her books include *How to Live / What to Do: H.D.'s Cultural Poetics* and edited and coedited collections of essays: *Sound States: Innovative Poetics and Acoustical Technologies*, and *New Media Poetics: Contexts, Technotexts, and Theories*. Recent and forthcoming essays include "Minding Machines/Machining Minds: Writing (at) the Human-Machine Interface," in *The Oxford Handbook of Modern and Contemporary Poetry*, and "Hellocasting the Holocaust," in *The Fate of Difficulty in Contemporary Poetry*. With Alan Golding and Lynn Keller, she edits the University of Iowa Contemporary North American Poetry Series.

M. NOURBESE PHILIP is an unembedded poet, essayist, novelist, playwright, and former lawyer who lives in the space-time of the City of Toronto. She is a Fellow of the Guggenheim, and Rockefeller (Bellagio) Foundations and the MacDowell Colony. She is the recipient of many awards, including the Casa de las Americas prize (Cuba). Among her best known published works are: *She Tries Her Tongue, Her Silence Softly Breaks*; *Looking for Livingstone: An Odyssey of Silence*; and *Harriet's Daughter*, a young adult novel. Philip's most recent work is *Zong!*, a genre-breaking poem, which engages with ideas of the law, history, and memory as they relate to the transatlantic slave trade.

JOAN RETALLACK is a poet and essayist, author of *The Poethical Wager* and *Procedural Elegies/Western Civ Cont'd/*. Her most recent book, *The Supposium: Thought Experiments & Poethical Play in Difficult Times*, is published by Litmus Press. She is John D. and Catherine T. MacArthur Professor Emerita of Humanities at Bard College.

JENNIFER SCAPPETTONE is associate professor of English, creative writing, and Romance languages and literatures, and faculty affiliate of the Center for the Study of Gender and Sexuality at the University of Chicago. She is the author of *Killing the Moonlight: Modernism in Venice* (Columbia University Press, 2014) and of two hybrid-genre verse books: *From Dame Quickly* (Litmus, 2009) and *The Republic of Exit 43: Outtakes & Scores from an Archaeology and Pop-Up Opera of the Corporate Dump* (Atelos Press, 2016). Her translation from the Italian, *Locomotrix: Selected Poetry and Prose of Amelia Rosselli*, won the Academy of

American Poets' biennial Raiziss/De Palchi Book Prize. In 2016, she shared a Mellon Fellowship with Caroline Bergvall and Judd Morrissey to work on a project called *The Data That We Breathe* at the Gray Center for Arts and Inquiry.

STEPHEN VOYCE is associate professor of English at the University of Iowa, where he also holds appointments in the Digital Studio for the Public Arts and Humanities and the Center for the Book. He is the author of *Poetic Community: Avant-Garde Activism and Cold War Culture* (University of Toronto Press, 2013), the editor of *a book of variations: love – zygal – art facts* (Coach House Books, 2013), and the director of the Fluxus Digital Collection. His work appears in journals such as *Modernism/modernity*, *Criticism*, *Postmodern Culture*, and *Open Letter*. Voyce is now working on a book about twenty-first-century culture, surveillance, and foreign policy.

ELIZABETH WILLIS joined the faculty of the Iowa Writers' Workshop in 2015. Her most recent book, *Alive: New and Selected Poems* (New York Review Books, 2015), was a finalist for the Pulitzer Prize. Other books include *Address* (Wesleyan, 2011); *Meteoric Flowers* (Wesleyan, 2006); *Turneresque* (Burning Deck, 2003); and *The Human Abstract* (Penguin, 1995). Her essays on poetry, politics, gender, and labor have appeared in *Transatlantica*, *Evening Will Come*, *Contemporary Literature*, *Arizona Quarterly*, *Textual Practice*, *Boundary 2*, and the anthology *Active Romanticism*. She is also the editor of *Radical Vernacular: Lorine Niedecker and the Poetics of Place* (Iowa, 2008).

HERIBERTO YÉPEZ is the author of more than a dozen books in Spanish. In English his *Babellebab (Non-Poetry on the End of Translation)* was published by Duration Press (2003); *Wars. Threesomes. Drafts. & Mothers* by Factory School (2008); *Transnational Battle Field* by Commune Editions (2017); and he coedited *Eye of Witness: A Jerome Rothenberg Reader* (Black Widow, 2013). He currently lives between Tijuana, México and the Bay Area, in the United States, where he is currently finishing a PhD at the University of California, Berkeley. He defines himself as a post-Mexican writer.

INDEX

Made in the USA
Middletown, DE
25 February 2020